DEFINING MOMENTS

MAPLE LEAFS EDITION

DEFINING MOMENTS

MAPLE LEAFS EDITION

MIKE LEONETTI

Red Deer Press

Published in Canada by Red Deer Press
195 Allstate Parkway, Markham, ON, L3R 4T8
www.reddeerpress.com
Published in the United States by Red Deer Press
311 Washington Street, Brighton, Massachusetts, 02135
Text design by Kerry Plumley
Cover design by Daniel Choi
Cover image courtesy of Graig Abel
We acknowledge with thanks the Canada Council for the Arts, and the Ontario Arts Council for their support of our publishing program. We acknowledge the financial support of the Government of Canada through the Canada Book Fund for our publishing activities.

Library and Archives Canada Cataloguing in Publication
ISBN 978-0-88995-508-0
Data available on file

Publisher Cataloging-in-Publication Data (U.S)
ISBN 978-0-88995-508-0
Data available on file

Printed and bound in Canada
5 4 3 2 1

These stories are dedicated to all the players
who have worn the fabled Toronto Maple Leaf sweater
from 1927 to 2014.

CONTENTS

ACKNOWLEDGMENTS

The author would like to thank long time hockey writer John Laboni for his invaluable assistance in creating the outline for this book and for suggestion on players to be profiled.

Thank you as well for all the staff at Red Deer Press who helped to create this book with special acknowledgments to Richard Dionne and Daniel Choi.

The writer would also like to thank his wife, Maria, and his son, David, for their usual support and understanding.

GARY ROBERTS

 MOLSON
CANADIAN.
RIVALRY NIGHT

SAT OCT 9, 2010

PUCK DROP 7PM

V E R S U S

SECTION	ROW	SEAT	PRICE
324	11	7	$95.00 INCL $8.40 TAX

Enter Through Nearest Gate

 MOLSON
CANADIAN.
PROUD SEASON SPONSOR

764412680127

INTRODUCTION

The Toronto Maple Leafs have been a special hockey team ever since they first put on sweaters with the national symbol of Canada on the front of their jersey in 1927. Win, lose or draw, the Maple Leafs have garnered attention from all hockey fans from coast to coast in Canada and many people remember great moments in the history of the Toronto-based club as much as they do special times in their own lives. In the first 40 years of their existence, the success of the team Conn Smythe built helped to grow the game across the country, inspiring generations to dream about playing on the brightest hockey stage in the history of the game. Hockey Night in Canada, which brought the game to the Canadian audience via television, was the domain of the Maple Leafs for so many years and was (along with the great success of the Montreal Canadiens) the biggest reason why National Hockey League teams now exist in Vancouver, Edmonton, Calgary, Winnipeg and Ottawa. Once the Maple Leafs moved into the hockey palace known as Maple Leaf Gardens (in 1931) and their games were broadcast on radio by the legendary voice of Foster Hewitt all across an emerging country, the Canadian sports landscape was forever changed.

In this book a tribute is paid to the many great players who have worn a Maple Leafs uniform over the history of the team. The supporters of the team have a special bond with many performers past and present who have left an indelible mark on Maple Leafs history. Toronto fans are incredibly loyal (some will say too much so) and hold steadfast to their love of the blue and white. Anyone who has grown up or lived in Toronto knows that the fortunes of the fabled Maple Leafs are what holds the attention of everyone in the vibrant metropolis made up of people from all parts of the world. The love of the Maple Leafs may have been built on past glories but it still lives on today even as the franchise (one of two founding NHL teams in 1917-18—Montreal being the other) approaches its 100th anniversary. Putting on the Leafs sweater makes you an instant hockey hero and the player can rest assured that someone will recall that he put on one of the truly classic uniforms in sports history. One appearance as a Maple Leaf will not only make a player part of the alumni but it will also put him in the hearts and minds of every member in what has now become known as "Leaf Nation."

It is of course a well-known fact that the Maple Leafs have not experienced the ultimate success of winning a Stanley Cup since 1967 and that the Montreal Canadiens have been champions 10 more times since the two teams met in the '67 finals. The reality is that the Maple Leafs have only made the final four teams competing for the league championship, a grand total of five times since George Armstrong took the Cup from NHL president Clarence Campbell on the night of May 2, 1967. In fact, they have too often even missed competing in the playoffs! However the memories and moments ranging from great to the very bad still bind the fiercely devoted fans together. No true Maple Leaf fan will ever deny the very uneven history of the club, nor will they ever give up the hope that the team may one day return to glory and capture a title.

This writer has chronicled much of Leaf history in many books (such as Maple Leaf Legends and Maple Leafs Top 100: Toronto's Greatest Players of All Time) and takes another look at more Toronto hockey history in this work. Since the previously mentioned books covered the entire history of the team, this volume of Leaf history looks mostly at players who played in 1960 and beyond. Legendary players from the 1930s (such as King Clancy, Hap Day, Charlie Conacher, Red Horner and Joe Primeau) are not specifically listed in this volume of Leaf history but their names may appear at appropriate points in other profiles. However we have still included many of the most popular and best remembered Maple Leafs of all time including the likes of Syl Apps, Ted Kennedy, Bill Barilko and Turk Broda from the triumphant 1940s and early 1950s. Frank Mahovlich, Dave Keon, Johnny Bower and Tim Horton are profiled from the glorious '60s era while Darryl Sittler, Rick Vaive, Wendel Clark, Doug Gilmour, Curtis Joseph and Mats Sundin are highlighted from 1970 onward.

This work also profiles many players who did not appear in previous books and tells their stories as well. These players include the likes of Les Costello, Gerry Ehman, Brian Conacher, Peter Stemkowski, George Ferguson, Rick Kehoe, Inge Hammarstrom, Dan Daoust, Bruce Boudreau, Joel Quenneville, Randy Carlyle, Dave Reid, Peter Zezel, Mike Foligno, Bob McGill, Bill Berg, Alyn McCauley and Carlo Colaiacovo, to mention just a few who at one point excelled in their time as a Maple Leaf. Also included are current Leaf stars like Dion Phaneuf, Joffrey Lupul, James Reimer, Jake Gardiner, Cody Franson, Colton Orr and Phil Kessel (all of whom helped the Leafs get back into the playoffs in 2013 after a long absence from the postseason) to give the reader more than 100 players with a noteworthy moment as a Maple Leaf.

This book has been organized into chapters which are particular to the Maple Leafs. Many players listed in one chapter could just as easily be listed in another but it is our hope that we have slotted players in the right spot. However if Leaf fans want to discuss where each player best fits in their view, then let the debate begin! There is no doubt the members of "Leaf Nation" have the ultimate say and we welcome the feedback.

Defining Moments: Maple Leafs Edition will serve as a season ticket to a history of unforgettable moments for all Maple Leaf fans who love a special team that has dominated a great city for so many years. We hope you enjoy reliving some of the best of times brought to hockey fans right across Canada by one of the game's most legendary teams—the Toronto Maple Leafs!

Mike Leonetti

Tim Horton (left) and Allan Stanley celebrate the 1963 Stanley Cup victory.

COMEBACKS

Tim Horton • Inge Hammarstrom • Walt McKechnie • Todd Gill
Mike Foligno • Yanic Perreault • Alyn McCauley • Curtis Joseph
Joffrey Lupul • James van Riemsdyk

THE WORD COMEBACK IS often overused when it comes to sports and this is especially true in the case of hockey. However, there are occasions when "comeback" just seems to be the best way to describe a special situation. In many instances it involves a player coming back to play after a potentially career-ending injury. The team and the fans are all anxious to see if the player is able to return and still make a strong contribution. There are also other types of comebacks such as the player who is re-acquired in a transaction or the player who has endured some off-ice situation that he must overcome and show that it does not bother him anymore. Whatever dilemma sparks the comeback, it can be said for sure that the story can be both engaging and compelling. The following Leaf players all had such comebacks at some point in their careers with Toronto.

Tim Horton

Tim Horton

Leaf Record:
109 Goals,
349 Assists,
458 Points

Maple Leaf Moment: April 22, 1962

When the Toronto Maple Leafs recruited Tim Horton and assigned him to their junior development team at St. Michael's College, they had great expectations for the sturdy defenseman. Powerfully built at five foot ten and 185 pounds, Horton was one the strongest recruits the Leafs had under their control. Toronto was looking to rebuild their team in the early fifties after the great years they had in the Forties. After a two-year stint at St. Mike's, Horton was sent to the Leafs main farm team in Pittsburgh to learn the pro game. He played three full seasons for the Hornets and was finally promoted to the Leafs for good starting in the 1952–53 season. He quickly established himself as a hard-hitting defenseman who was not afraid to carry the puck. Horton also had a low, hard shot that he unleashed from the point with the hard-rock defender also showing a fine ability to set up goals from his position on the blue line. After his second season, Horton was named to the National Hockey League's second All-Star team in 1954. He and the other young Leaf recruits, such as George Armstrong, Hugh Bolton, Larry Cahan, Rudy Migay, Eric Nesterenko, and Ron Stewart, seemed poised to get Toronto back into championship contention—

but there would be obstacles to overcome.

Late in the 1954–55 season, Horton suffered very serious injuries that nearly ended his career. During a game against the New York Rangers on March 12, 1955, the Leaf defender was nailed with a devastating bodycheck from Bill Gadsby. The Ranger blueliner caught Horton with his head down as he was carrying the puck up the ice at full speed. It was by all accounts a clean check (as film of the hit proved), but Horton's leg buckled underneath him, snapping the limb right above his ankle—a sound that was heard all through Maple Leaf Gardens. Horton also hit his face right against Gadsby's body and the impact broke his jaw. Horton was in hospital for an entire month with his jaw wired shut. His leg was in a full cast until July and when it came off, Horton's leg looked terrible. Despite Horton's determination to return, even he had doubts he could make it *all* the way back. But soon he was working to get his leg into proper condition (it took two years to make a complete recovery) and incredibly, he was able to play half the 1955–56 season.

Tim Horton wore glasses off the ice and until he started using contact lenses, he had to rely on his excellent hockey instincts to compensate for his bad eyesight during games. He was inducted into the Hockey Hall of Fame in 1977.

Interestingly, the Leafs management cut Horton's salary while he recuperated and they nearly traded him away during that period (Montreal and Boston were reportedly interested in acquiring Horton).

The Leafs were not a very good team in the mid- to late fifties as their rebuilding plan sputtered. Four different coaches were tried, but they had little success. Horton was not the favourite of one coach, Billy Reay, who tried to curtail Horton's puck-rushing style. But when George "Punch" Imlach became the Leafs bench boss early in the 1958–59 season, one of the first things he did was tell Horton to play *his* game. "I like to carry the puck, have a good look before I pass it. Imlach instructed me to do so. Now I am looking forward to every shift on the ice instead of worrying about the possibility of making mistakes."

The Leafs made a remarkable run to a playoff spot to end the 1958–59 season (secured by winning the last game of the season) and the Leafs became a contender for the next ten years. Toronto made it to the Stanley Cup finals in '59 and '60 but lost both times. Their next chance at the championship came after the 1961–62 season and Horton was determined to make sure the Leafs were going to win their first Cup since 1951.

Toronto got past a pesky New York Ranger club in six games during the '62 semi-finals and then faced defending champions the Chicago Black Hawks in the final. The Leafs took the first 2 games at home but the Black Hawks quickly evened the series in Chicago. Horton then took over the fifth game of the series as he set up 3 Leaf goals, helping Toronto storm back to win the contest 8–4. The Leafs were now one game away from the Cup.

It was a raucous crowd that greeted the Leafs at Chicago Stadium the night of April 22, 1962, but it remained a 0–0 game until the third period. Toronto outplayed the home team by a good margin, but could not score. Then Bobby Hull intercepted an errant Leaf pass and put one past goalie Don Simmons to give the Hawks a 1–0 lead. The crowd went wild and littered the ice with all sorts of debris; however, this break gave the Leafs a chance to recover. Toronto quickly tied the score and then Chicago took a minor penalty. Horton took the puck up the ice and made two passes before Dick Duff scored the winning goal. It was Horton's sixteenth point (3 goals, 13 assists) of the playoffs—a remarkable total for a defenseman of that era. The Leafs held onto to a 2–1 win and Horton's eleven-year wait for a championship was finally over.

Horton would go on to win three more Stanley Cups with the Leafs—an amazing record for a player who came back from near career-ending injuries to become one of the best defensemen of all time.

INGE HAMMARSTROM L.WING

Inge Hammarstrom

Leaf Record:
85 Goals,
87 Assists,
167 Points

Maple Leaf Moment: December 21, 1974

The Maple Leafs signed two Swedish-born free agents in the off-season prior to the 1973–74 season hoping these two would help revive a slumping Toronto squad who missed the playoffs the year before. Defenseman Borje Salming was one of the two recruited by the Leafs and the other was smallish (listed at six feet, 180 pounds) but skilled left-winger Inge Hammarstrom. Good at handling the puck in close, Hammarstrom scored 21 goals in 1973–74 as an NHL rookie, helping push the Leafs back into the playoffs. However, when the start of the 1974–5 season went badly for Toronto, Hammarstrom's rather soft style on the wing came into question. Not surprisingly, the person who took the greatest shot at Hammarstrom was owner Harold Ballard, who claimed the skilled Swede could skate into any rink corner with six eggs in his pocket and not break one!

It would be difficult for any player to keep his composure when publicly humiliated by a coach, let alone an owner—after all, he is the one that signs the checks. Hammarstrom managed to keep his dignity (unlike the bombastic Ballard) and was ready to play when called upon by Leafs coach Red Kelly. The Leafs bench boss, though, did not play him as often as he had a year earlier. And it did not look like Hammarstrom would get to see much ice against the Boston Bruins when they came to Toronto on December 21, 1974.

The Bruins had already registered 19 wins on the season and the 1974 Stanley Cup finalists still had Bobby Orr and Phil Esposito (who would score three versus the Leafs) on their club. Plus they had a new coach, Don Cherry, who would pace behind the Bruins bench for the next five seasons. The Leafs, on the other hand, were hoping the return of star center Darryl Sittler would give them a spark. He had missed the previous 7 games and his absence was greatly felt. (The Leafs were injury riddled all season long in 1974–75, winning only 31 games and recording just 76 points.)

In the ultimate irony, Inge Hammarstrom became a scout for the Philadelphia Flyers after he retired from hockey. It was on his recommendation that the Flyers selected Peter Forsberg in the 1991 NHL Entry Draft.

Nevertheless, Hammarstrom was put on a line with Sittler on this night with great results. The slick winger opened the scoring at 8:34 into the contest with the assist going to Sittler. The second period featured a total of 9 goals: 5 by the Leafs and two of those off the stick of Hammarstrom. Toronto scored 2 more in the third to skate off with a surprising 8–4 win. The first star of the game also added an assist (on a goal by Sittler) for a tremendous 4-point night. If Ballard was not so impressed with his team, the Bruins coach certainly thought the Leafs were better than their record. "When the Leafs play like that, I can't understand why they are so low in the standings," Cherry said after the game. "They tied us at home in the only other game we've played them this year. In this game they completely outplayed us."

As for his role in the lopsided victory, Hammarstrom was hardly gloating. "Defeating Boston [for the Leafs tenth win of the season] is a very big thing for our team. The forwards played very well but the most important thing was how our defense moved the puck up to us very quickly. And [Leaf netminder] Dunc Wilson was very good in goal," said Hammarstrom. While he refused to address Ballard's comments directly, he did make the point that in Sweden the forwards were not used to heavy or consistent body contact. The larger European rinks where he was trained did not often require strong work along the boards either. As for his riding the bench over many games, Hammarstrom made the point that he was still able to learn a great deal by just observing. "I picked things up that I have to do to play well in the NHL."

Throughout his stay as a Maple Leaf, Hammarstrom was a consistent 20-goal man who would record 40 or more points every season. He was not a large or physical player, but his soft hands should have made him a more prized player in Toronto. The NHL of the 1970s, however, valued toughness, size, and fighting (mostly due to the success of the brawling Philadelphia Flyers) and Hammarstrom's role was often reduced, especially in the playoffs. As long as Kelly was coaching the Leafs, there was something of a role for Hammarstrom to play on the team. However, when Roger Neilson took over, Hammarstrom's days became numbered and he was soon dispatched to St. Louis for grinding winger Jerry Butler in 1977.

While Hammarstom's contribution to the team was limited, his ability to come back in the face of some of the harshest criticism ever aimed at a Toronto player should always be remembered as something truly courageous.

WALT McKECHNIE

Walt McKechnie

Leaf Record:
32 Goals,
72 Assists,
104 Points

Maple Leaf Moment: April 10, 1979

Center Walt McKechnie was selected in the first round (sixth overall) by the Maple Leafs during the first-ever Amateur Draft in 1963. The Leafs liked the lanky pivot (six foot two, 195 pounds) after watching him play Junior B hockey in his hometown of London, Ontario. By the time he was ready for pro hockey as a twenty-year-old in 1967, the Leafs had no room for McKechnie. Instead, they dealt him to Phoenix of the Western Hockey League (WHL). His good play with the Roadrunners (54 points in 67 games in 1967–68) got him noticed by the expansion Minnesota North Stars who acquired his NHL rights in 1968. Thus began McKechnie's long journey all over North America before his comeback to Toronto over a decade later in 1978.

Even though McKechnie had wandered through many NHL teams before finally donning a Leafs sweater, he had played in just nine career playoff games (with Minnesota in 1968, recording 5 points). No wonder then that he was happy to be back in the post-season now with the Leafs. The game was against the Atlanta Flames in the best-of-three preliminary round series, and the 1978–79 Leafs were supposed to be a team on the rise after they had beaten a pretty good New York Islander team in seven games the previous spring. McKechnie actually provided good secondary scoring at center (behind captain Darryl Sittler) with 25 goals and 61 points in 1978–79; however, the team failed to improve. The Leafs became a slow, grinding club, worn down by trying to play a close-checking game night after night under coach Roger Neilson. The Leafs bench boss expected his club to play 1–0 or 2–1 contests throughout the year and it was a strategy that led them to a very average 34–33–13 regular-season record. Neilson's style of game was perhaps better suited to playoff hockey, but it was unknown how the team would react in the '79 post-season.

The series against the Flames was scheduled to start on the night of April 10, 1979, in Atlanta. The Flames had a large team (shaped by general manager Cliff Fletcher) and featured goal scorers such as Jean Pronovost, Eric Vail, Guy Chouinard, Bobby MacMillan, and Tom Lysiak. Atlanta won 41 games during the season and accumulated 90 points making the Flames a clear favorite over the Toronto club; however, many of the Leafs were battle-tested from their run to the semi-finals in 1978 and really had nothing to lose in this series.

Walt McKechnie played for nine different NHL teams spanning 955 regular-season games. He recorded 606 points (214 games, 392 assists). McKecknie played in only 15 career playoff games, but recorded 12 post-season points (7 goals, 5 assists).

It turned out to be one of the roughest games in NHL history with both teams accounting for 222 total penalty minutes in the contest that saw the Leafs prevail by 2–1 margin. A wild brawl broke out near the end of the second period (featuring Tiger Williams, Dave Hutchison and Dave Burrows of the Leafs and Brad Marsh, Willie Plett, Ken Houston, Dave Shand and Darcy Rota of the Flames) marring the game but somehow galvanizing the Leafs to play some inspired hockey. McKechnie scored both Leaf goals (one of them short-handed) in the second period as he celebrated his return to the playoffs in memorable fashion. The Flames took 12 shots at the Leaf net in the third period (the Leafs only had 4) but a tight defensive effort saw Toronto leave Atlanta with a win.

"When we went out for the third period, the spirit was unbelievable," McKechnie said. "You know how this team likes that kind of stuff. It's going to take me quite a bit of time to get my feet back on the ground. We just got one big effort from every guy on this club to win that one," he continued. Linemate Dan Maloney assisted on both goals while defenseman Borje Salming and goalie Mike Palmateer were simply outstanding. Toronto also had to play the final period without stars Sittler and defenseman Ian Turnbull who were tossed out of the game because of their participation in the second stanza fight.

The Leafs returned home and gave the Flames a severe 7–4 beating to win the series in two straight games. Toronto set a playoff record at the Gardens that night by scoring 3 goals in twenty-three seconds in the first period. The series win over Atlanta gave the Leafs some small measure of satisfaction, but Montreal quickly ended the year by wiping the Leafs out in four consecutive games in the next round. The elimination by the Habs brought about many changes to the Leafs team, their coaching staff, and upper management.

And McKecknie soon found himself back on the road, quickly gone from the team early in the following year. It ended a nice but brief return to the Leaf organization for McKechnie but at least he had the chance to play for the blue and white once in his career.

Todd Gill

Leaf Record:
59 Goals,
210 Assists,
269 Points

Maple Leaf Moment: February 14, 1993

Defenseman Todd Gill was prepared for the NHL by his junior coach Wayne Maxner who had played some big-league hockey years earlier. The Maple Leafs liked what they saw from the Windsor Spitfires captain and selected the six-foot, 180-pound Gill in the second round (twenty-fifth overall) of the NHL Entry Draft in 1984. It took time before Gill became a full-time member of the Leaf's lineup but he did so by the 1986–87 campaign. Gill always played his hardest but would get into trouble when he over-handled the puck, especially in his own end. One night in Chicago, Gill lost the puck to Troy Murray of the Blackhawks who went in to score a goal and knock the Leafs out of the playoffs on the final night of the regular season. From that moment on Gill had to fight that horrible memory throughout his tenure with the Leafs. Determined and mentally strong, Gill came back to play some very good hockey for Toronto when they became a contending team.

The 1992–93 season was not only a year of redemption for Gill, it was also the year the Maple Leaf team was reborn. The season began slowly for the Leafs under new coach Pat Burns but as the year rolled along, the Leafs quickly became a force to be reckoned with as new players mixed in well with seasoned veterans. Gill was one of the few Leaf players (along with Wendel Clark) who had survived a strong purge implemented by general manager Cliff Fletcher starting in 1991. Suddenly, the Leafs actually believed they could win on any given night. Victories over old rivals, such as Boston, Detroit, and Montreal, during the season gave the Leafs hope that they could put the past behind them and start a new winning tradition.

Gill thrived when he was paired with the very talented but somewhat understated Dave Ellett on defense. And they both chipped in offensively when the opportunity arose. Ellett scored a goal when Leaf center Doug Gilmour recorded a 6-assist evening on February 13, 1993 as the Leafs beat Minnesota 6–1 at the Gardens. The North Stars could not wait to get back at the Leafs the very next night on home ice to complete the weekend series. It would be a night for the other half of the Leafs defensive duo to show what he could do on the attack.

> Todd Gill went on to play for Detroit, San Jose, St. Louis, Phoenix, Colorado, and Chicago, before completing his 1,007-game NHL career. He recorded 354 career points and was captain of the Sharks for two seasons.

It certainly looked like the North Stars were going to exact their measure of revenge when they jumped all over the Leafs with a 4–1 lead before the game was even half over. Backup netminder Daren Puppa was between the pipes for the Leafs and it looked like he was not going to make any saves nor was his defense providing any support. However this was a different group of Maple Leafs—and they were not going to roll over anymore.

Before the second was over the Leafs managed to get the score to 5–3 for the Stars with Gill scoring 1 goal on a power-play opportunity. Gill's marker gave the Leafs some new life, and in the third it was the Leafs who stormed out with 2 goals to tie the game. The equalizer came from the stick of the red-hot Gilmour who re-directed a Gill blast from the blue line at 15:02 of the final frame.

It looked like the game was headed for overtime when Toronto decided to swarm the Minnesota net with Gill sneaking in from the point to swipe a puck past North Star netminder Jon Casey for the winner. There were just forty seconds to play. It was a hard-earned goal with players such as Mark Osborne, Peter Zezel, and Bill Berg creating havoc in front of the net. The Leafs had roared back with 40 shots on goal by the end of the night securing a 6–5 road victory. "Mike McPhee had been watching me all the time Peter [Zezel] was hounding the puck but he pulled off just when Peter got it clear," Gill explained about how the win developed. "I went to the net, the puck was there and it was an easy shot."

Burns was less than thrilled with his team's performance in the early portion of the game, even benching a few players who were underperforming. "We had to dig ourselves out of a hole we should not have been in," the coach said. There was no need for Burns to be so concerned—the Leafs had turned a corner and a game like this one against the North Stars was one of the highlights of the year.

Gill would record 43 points (including 11 goals) in 1992–93, the best total of his NHL career. He was thrilling Leaf fans, coming back from a time when it looked like he would only be remembered for his mistakes. Gill's character carried him through the tough times so he could see some measure of glory as a Maple Leaf.

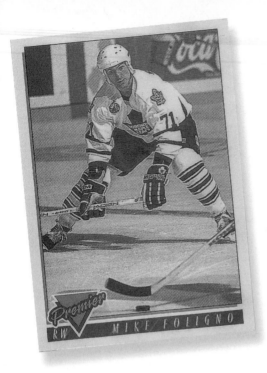

Mike Foligno

Leaf Record:
27 Goals,
20 Assists,
47 Points

Maple Leaf Moment: April 27, 1993

When Mike Foligno cut across the middle of the ice at Maple Leaf Gardens and locked legs with Winning Jet player Luciano Borsato, the result was more than jarring. Foligno lay sprawled out with a badly broken leg while the Leafs team doctor was summoned to the ice to administer to the big right-winger. Foligno's 1991–92 season was over after 33 games (he had recorded 14 points) and, perhaps his career had just come to an end as well; however, the six-foot-two, 195-pound player worked extremely hard to recover from the serious leg injury, and was eventually able to return to the Leaf lineup during the 1992–93 season.

Foligno was in and out of that Leafs lineup but did get into 55 games managing a respectable 13 goals, 2 of which were game winners. Even though the Leafs had put together a very good regular season (44 wins), it was unclear how they would fare in the opening round of the playoffs against a very talented Detroit club that featured the likes of Steve Yzerman, Sergei Fedorov, and Nicklas Lidstrom. It was expected that the multi-talented Red Wings would eventually subdue the Leafs. After winning the first two games (6–3 and 6–2) rather easily on home ice, a Toronto recovery seemed a long shot., The Leafs, however, had become a tougher and resilient team under new coach Pat Burns, and they played hard and scrappy to even the series with a pair of close wins (4–2 and 3–2) on home ice. The Leafs now knew they had to win at least once in Detroit and on the night of April 27, 1993, they had a chance to get that precious road victory.

Despite the Leafs high hopes, the Red Wings made a concerted effort to regain the upper hand and had their opponents down 4–1 midway through the contest. The Leafs had taken a rather unimpressive 6 shots on goal and looked to be more concerned about winning the next game back in Toronto. But then some Maple Leaf magic came into play and the Toronto comeback hit full gear. Burns decided to stop trying to match lines, which seemed to loosen up his team. Toronto defenseman Dave Ellett scored twice before the second period was over, putting the Leafs down by just 1 at 4–3. More importantly, the Toronto club had regained the momentum.

The Maple Leafs acquired Mike Foligno from the Sabres when they sent Brian Curran and Lou Franceschetti to Buffalo on December 17, 1990.

Leaf captain Wendel Clark tied the game in the third when the puck took a lucky bounce into the net while there was a large group in front of the Detroit crease. The Leafs had only taken 19 shots on goal but were tied 4–4 with the game going into overtime. But the Toronto players were very confident going into the extra session and soon enough the puck landed on Foligno's stick (after some good work by Clark). Foligno was right in the slot in the Detroit end just 2:05 into the first overtime period. He quickly let a shot go that beat goalie Tim Cheveldae for the winner. Foligno performed his patented post-goal leap while his teammates jumped all over him, delirious that they had won the game 5–4. "It's the biggest goal of my career," said the thirty-four-year-old Foligno, the oldest Leaf on the team. "I got in the slot, got the puck and tried to put it on net. One of the big pluses with this club has been its ability to play well right up to the end of every game. You saw it tonight." It seemed only fitting that the player who had worked so hard to come back would score the winner on the night the team made its best rally of the playoffs.

The Leafs beat Detroit in 7 games to close out the first round of the playoffs and then eliminated St. Louis in another 7-game series. A loss to the Los Angeles Kings in the next round ended the Leafs march to the Stanley Cup final. It was also the last chance Foligno had to play for a championship team. He played 39 games for the Florida Panthers in 1993–94 to complete his 1,018-game NHL career during which he earned 727 points.

Yanic Perreault

Leaf Record:
54 Goals,
69 Assists,
123 Points

Maple Leaf Moment: April 30, 1999

The Maple Leafs had traded away their first- and second-round draft choices for the 1991 Entry Draft, but made their first choice (forty-seventh overall) count for something when they selected high-scoring star center Yanic Perreault from the Quebec Major Junior Hockey League. Never fleet of foot on his skates, Perreault was a naturally gifted goal scorer (191 markers in 200 junior games) and that caught the Maple Leafs' attention. Even though the team needed scoring at the big-league level, they mostly kept Perreault in the minors despite the fact he scored 132 and totaled 276 points in 203 American Hockey League contests. In fact, he played just 13 games for the Leafs in 1993–94 before being traded away to the Los Angeles Kings in 1994 for a fourth-round draft choice!

When the Leafs announced they had re-acquired Perreault in March 1999, Toronto fans were not sure why a player who they had given away five and half years earlier was suddenly back on the team. Sure, a season-ending injury to Alyn McCauley created a need for a second-line center, but bringing back the slow-footed Perreault seemed a rather odd choice. There were still those in Leaf management, however, who recalled what a good goal scorer Perreault had been with the St. John's Maple Leafs. In the end, bringing Perreault back proved a wise choice, considering that the team was preparing to face the Philadelphia Flyers in the first round of the 1999 playoffs.

The 1998–99 Maple Leafs had experienced a strong resurgence under new coach Pat Quinn who implemented an offensive attack style of game, a departure from the rather dull and ineffective methods employed by coach Mike Murphy the previous two years. Perreault seemed to fit right into the lineup and had the benefit of playing alongside high-scoring winger Sergei Berezin and veteran Gary Valk. The Leaf center had 15 points (7 were goals) in 12 games to close out the regular season, but the 7-game series against the Flyers presented a serious challenge to the largely inexperienced Maple Leafs. However, the Leafs had two things going in their favor: goalie Curtis Joseph was better than Philadelphia's John Vanbiesbrouck; and the Flyers best player, Eric Lindros, was out with an injury.

The Maple Leafs let Yanic Perreault walk away as a free agent in 2001, but re-acquired him in February ·2007 in a trade with Phoenix. He registered 516 points in 859 career games with six NHL teams.

The Flyers opened the series with a 3–0 win at the Air Canada Centre, but the Leafs staged a late rally to win the next game 2–1. The teams split the next two games to even the series and returned to Toronto on the night of April 30 to see who would get the upper hand. The teams scored a goal each in the first period and the game stayed that way right to the end of regulation time. At the 11:51 in the first overtime, Valk let a shot go that came right back to Perreault. The sharp-shooting Leaf then put a precise backhand shot past Vanbiesbrouck from a bad angle for the game-winning tally. It was Perreault's first shot of the game (both teams took 34 shots on goal) and his first point of the series.

"We knew this series would be very close, with not many scoring chances so every goal is important," Perreault stated. "We're just trying to get the puck on the net when we can." Coach Pat Quinn was happy to see the Perreault line finally get going. "They've been standing and watching," said Quinn of the line he set up late in the year. "But tonight was [Perreault's] best outing. For a few games, he was not as good as we've seen him play but tonight he was *good*." All Leaf fans were glad Perreault (who finished the playoffs with 9 points in 17 games) had come back to his original team after all.

The win gave the Leafs a 3–2 series lead which they ended in Philadelphia with a 1–0 victory in the sixth game. The series win over the Flyers was the first time Toronto had defeated Philadelphia in a post-season series and still remains the only time the Leafs bested the Flyers during the playoffs in six attempts.

Alyn McCauley

Leaf Record:
33 Goals,
49 Assists,
82 Points

Maple Leaf Moment: May 8, 2002

When the Maple Leafs acquired the rights to center Alyn McCauley, his junior coach Brian Kilrea assured everyone in Toronto that the very smart pivot was indeed going to play in the NHL. McCauley came to the Leafs from the New Jersey Devils in a trade that saw Doug Gilmour leave Toronto in 1997. McCauley recorded 284 points in 208 career games for the Ottawa 67's of the Ontario Hockey League, so it is no wonder Kilrea gave him a complete endorsement. McCauley joined the Leafs for the 1997–98 season and the rookie recorded 16 points in 60 games for a very average team. McCauley had 24 points in 39 games the following season, but suffered a concussion when his head was thrown into the boards by Sheldon Souray of the New Jersey Devils. McCauley did not recover until the 2001–02 season when the Leafs were a strong contender.

When Mats Sundin was injured early in the first round of the 2002 playoffs, it was thought that the Maple Leafs would be in deep trouble. With no one else to turn to, Leaf coach Pat Quinn took McCauley from his usual fourth-line position and put him in the middle of the first line (in 82 games played during the 2001–02 season, the twenty-four-year-old center had scored only 6 goals and totaled 16 points). Although it was a tough, ugly 7-game series versus the New York Islanders, the Leafs eventually prevailed only to face a healthy Ottawa Senators club in the next round.

The Senators beat the Leafs 5–0 in the first game, a contest the Toronto club was never in from the opening face-off; however, the injury-riddled Leafs bounced back to tie the series with a 3–2 double-overtime win. Ottawa regained the lead on home ice with a 3–2 victory, which made the fourth game all the more important for the team in blue and white. The Ottawa crowd sensed that the Leafs were on the ropes, but it was not to be for the Senators on this night.

After a scoreless first period, Ottawa drew first blood when Senators defenseman Wade Redden scored on the power play early in the second. The Leafs did not fold, and then got 2 consecutive goals from McCauley to grab a 2–1 lead. Both goals came off rebounds as McCauley drove to the net to put home shots taken by line mates Gary Roberts and Jonas Hogland. The second of the two markers came late in the second period giving the Leafs the impetus to hold on to the lead. Ottawa outshot the Leafs 11–5 in the third; however, Leaf goalie Curtis Joseph turned all shots away to maintain Toronto's slim lead and tie the series once again.

The Maple Leafs traded Alyn McCauley to the San Jose Sharks in the deal that brought Owen Nolan to Toronto. McCauley had his best NHL season with San Jose in 2003–04 when he had 20 goals and 47 points in 82 games.

Named first star of the game, McCauley thought his team played the game perfectly. "It was just the kind of game we needed to play," he said. "We were smart-aggressive, not too aggressive. We were patient … and that's what led to my two goals." He might have added the Leafs never panicked and relied on their star netminder when they had to. The Leafs lost a controversial contest back home, but rebounded to take the next two games and win the series 4–3.

The entire 2002 playoffs proved that McCauley could perform in pressure situations and contribute to the attack as well (5 goals and 15 points in 20 post-season games); however, Quinn never had much faith in McCauley because he did not play a physical game. But the talented youngster had undoubtedly proved to his coach that he had successfully bounced back from a serious injury. Trying to fill Sundin's spot was pretty much an impossible task, but McCauley did it beautifully and nearly helped the Leafs to the Stanley Cup finals for the first time since 1967. The dream ending was stopped by the Carolina Hurricanes in the Eastern Conference final.

CURTIS JOSEPH
Goaltender / Maple Leafs®

Curtis Joseph

Leaf Record:
138 Wins,
97 Losses,
28 Ties,
17 Shutouts

Maple Leaf Moment: March 24, 2009

Goaltender Curtis Joseph was very good at surprising Maple Leaf fans. As a free agent in 1998, he shocked the hockey world by signing with the Maple Leafs when everyone was expecting him to sign with a contending team (like Philadelphia). Joseph's stay with the Leafs between 1998 and 2002 represented some of the best seasons the team has experienced in recent times (including two trips to the Eastern Conference final). However, "Cujo" refused to re-sign with Toronto before the start of the 2002–03 season and went to the Detroit Red Wings instead. His departure upset many Leaf fans, but his stay in Detroit did not go as well as he would have hoped. After two seasons in Phoenix and one in Calgary, the acrobatic netminder was once again a free agent in 2008. The Leafs decided to see if Joseph had a little more magic left when they signed him for the 2008–09 campaign. He would win just 5 games for the Leafs during his comeback year, but one of the wins was noteworthy.

It was one of the strangest ways for a goaltender to earn the first star of the game. Joseph was on the end of the Leaf bench as the backup goalie for more than fifty-nine minutes of the game against the Washington Capitals on March 24, 2009. But when Leafs starter Martin

Gerber shot the puck toward referee Mike Leggo to protest a late-game tying goal by Washington, Gerber was immediately tossed from the game. So Joseph had to go in cold—and then face overtime! Before the extra session started, the forty-one-year-old netminder had to make a good save on Capital's star Alex Ovechkin (who had already scored his fifty-first of the season earlier in the game) on a one-timer as regulation time was winding down. Two defensemen had scored for the Leafs on this night: Pavel Kubina got 1 goal while the other came from the stick of rookie Phil Oreskovic (who scored his first NHL goal). All said, though, at the end of this rather strange evening, it was the cool Joseph who saved the game.

> Curtis Joseph ended his career with 454 career wins—the fourth best career total of any goaltender to play in the NHL.

The five-minute overtime passed without a goal and the two teams lined up for a shoot-out. The Leafs got the only goal from Jeff Hamilton (who played a total of 15 career games for the Leafs) while Joseph stopped the first two Washington shooters (Nicklas Backstrom and Alexander Semin—both good snipers). However, Joseph had to face Ovechkin who represented the Capitals third shooter. The Toronto crowd of 19,362 chanted "Cujo, Cujo," as they had done so many times before, trying to inspire the veteran after coming into the game so late in the contest. There was a large cheer when Joseph stopped Ovechkin with a low-pad save stopping the Russian winger from lifting the puck into the net, preserving a 3–2 Leafs victory over the favored Capitals.

Joseph was selected first star of the game. He played a grand total of 5:57 but made a total of 9 saves. After the game, he commented that he had faced great players such as Wayne Gretzky and Mario Lemieux during his long career and that experience prepared him to face hockey's newest superstar. "Ovechkin is the greatest player in the game right now [but] I've played long enough," Joseph stated. "I'm never amazed in this game, but you can use that word if you like it. Certainly there's a lot of fresh faces that are wide-eyed and bushy-tailed, which is exciting too and to look down the bench and see the big grins. It's good, it's fun. I'm enjoying that."

Washington netminder Jose Theodore was also impressed by Joseph's performance. "You don't know how hard it is just to step in when you're not playing and then in the last minute when it's a tie game like that … It just showed the character and experience [of Joseph]," the former NHL most valuable player said. Joseph would win one more game as a Maple Leaf to bring his 2008–09 season record to 5–9–1 in the 21 games he appeared in that year. He would never play in the NHL again, but Toronto fans got to enjoy one last campaign for one of their all-time favorite goalies. It had been well worth it for Joseph to sign and come back for one final whirl as a Maple Leaf.

Joffrey Lupul

Leaf Record:
67 Goals,
80 Assists,
147 Points

Maple Leaf Moment: November 2, 2011

Joffrey Lupul has gone through a great deal in his NHL career and despite all the moving and dealing with injuries, he has found a way to be one of the best wingers in hockey. The six-foot-one, 200-pound left-winger was once a first-round draft choice (seventh overall) of the Anaheim Ducks in 2002, but only played a couple of seasons there (including one 28-goal year) before moving to the Edmonton Oilers in the trade that saw stalwart defenseman Chris Pronger go to the Ducks. Lupul missed out on the Ducks' Stanley Cup run in 2007 and he had a mediocre season with the Oilers in 2006–07, scoring just 13 times. He was then traded to Philadelphia in July '07 but had a difficult time as a Flyer even though he scored 20 goals his first year there and then 25 in the second. The Flyers then wanted Pronger in a trade so Lupul found himself back in Anaheim to start the 2009–10 season!

Ducks coach Randy Carlyle told Lupul he would never make it as a consistent left-winger in the NHL (he is a right-handed shot), but that was the least of his worries when a herniated disk (diagnosed in early December 2009) nearly ended his career. The native of Fort Saskatchewan, Alberta, faced a long and uncertain recovery period that worsened when an infection set in, which puzzled his doctors. Eventually he regained his health, but struggled to play his style of game; however, he did manage 14 points in just 23 games played in 2009–10. As Lupul looked forward to a healthier year in 2010–11, another trade was in the offing and he was on the move again—this time to Toronto.

The Ducks wanted defenseman Francois Beauchemin back, a player they had signed as a free agent. So they worked out a deal where the Leafs would get prospect defenseman Jake Gardiner on the condition that Toronto take over Lupul's contract. The Leafs insisted they were happy to acquire Lupul even though others said his back injury and lack of production made his contract one the Ducks were pleased to move out. Lupul had 18 points (9 goals, 9 assists) to finish the 2010–11 campaign, offering the Leafs hope that his injury woes were indeed behind him.

The 2011–12 season proved that Lupul could indeed bounce back and play some very effective hockey, working alongside winger Phil Kessel and center Tyler Bozak. A late season injury limited Lupul to 66 games but in that time he scored 25 goals and added 42 assists. He was in the top ten of all NHL scorers

Just as the 2012–13 season began (shorted due to a lockout), Joffrey Lupul signed a new five-year deal to stay with the Maple Leafs (valued at more than $26 million). Although Lupul suffered a fractured arm in the third game of the year and missed considerable time, he still earned 18 points in 16 games played and is considered a cornerstone of a resurging Maple Leaf team.

the entire season prior to his injury and had one of his best nights on November 2, 2011, when the Leafs faced goaltender Martin Brodeur and the New Jersey Devils. The visiting Leafs had got off to a good season start (7–3–1) but the Devils were always a very tough team to play, especially in their arena.

The Leafs were up 2–1 after one period, but New Jersey tied it up on a power play early in the middle frame. Then Lupul went to work getting the Leafs back on top 3–2 with his first goal of the night. He was able to put home a rebound off a shot from the point by Mike Komisarek. After New Jersey tied the score again, Lupul put a drive past

Brodeur that may have hit a Devil stick on the way in. He then added another off a scramble in front of the goal to make it 5–3 for the Leafs. The third goal not only marked a hat trick for Lupul but it was all done in less than seven minutes—and it was also the first time a Leaf had recorded 3 goals in one period since Hall of Famer Darryl Sittler pulled off the same feat 1980!

Lupul was naturally pleased to score the 3 goals especially against a great goalie like Brodeur. "I played a ton against this guy [Brodeur] when I was in Philadelphia and he always seemed to have my number. It's pretty cool to do it against him." Lupul noted the Devils netminder had been off for some time (recovering from an injury) and that the Leafs wanted to take advantage of any rustiness. "We talked about it," he said. "Anyone who is off for three weeks—you want to test that guy." The Leafs hung on to the 5–3 lead and posted their eighth win of the young season.

Lupul was an outstanding performer the entire time he played in 2011–12 proving beyond a doubt that he had come all the way back to be a star winger in the National Hockey League.

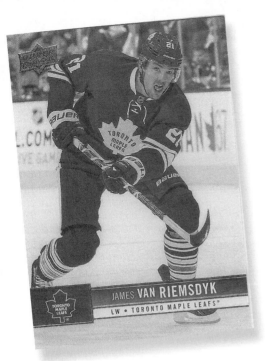

James van Riemsdyk

Leaf Record:
48 Goals,
45 Assists,
93 Points

Maple Leaf Moment: January 23 and February 5, 2013

When the Maple Leafs drafted defenseman Luke Schenn fifth overall in 2008, it was anticipated that the bruising blueliner would be in Toronto for a long time. It was even speculated that one day he might be considered for the team captaincy. But a funny thing happened to Schenn on the road to stardom in Toronto—he got traded after four uneven seasons as a Maple Leaf. It was a surprising deal considering his untapped potential, but the Leafs had other young defensemen in their system who could cover for the loss of the physical but low-scoring blueliner.

The main reason the Maple Leafs got rid of Schenn was that the Philadelphia Flyers offered the six-foot-three, 200-pound left-winger, James van Riemsdyk, in return. "JVR" as he is known, was selected second overall by the Flyers in 2007 and had a couple of good seasons in the "City of Brotherly Love." Blessed with soft hands, van Riemsdyk scored at a good pace for a young player with 15 goals in his rookie season and 21 in 2010–11. He was especially good in the playoffs with 10 goals in 32 post-season games during his first two years. He was also with the Flyers when they made it to the 2010 Stanley Cup final.

Nevertheless, van Riemsdyk had a terrible season in 2011–12 mostly due to a foot injury that saw him play in just 43 games (although he did record 24 points). Rumors about the Schenn deal circulated as early as the 2011–12 season, but it wasn't realized until June 2012. Most hockey experts looked at the deal as an exchange of "problems," but each team was hoping to get the best out of a player who once had great expectations. For the Leafs it was a matter of trying to add a quality young forward who had a knack for scoring goals. Toronto management cautioned that van Riemsdyk was not the prototypical power forward all NHL teams covet. The native of Middletown, New Jersey, is more of a thoroughbred, not a roughneck, but the Leafs certainly were hopeful the twenty-three-year-old would develop more of a physical presence as he matured.

James van Riemsdyk recorded his one hundredth career point when he scored his first goal as a Maple Leaf in the game against the Pittsburgh Penguins on January 23, 2013. He had 7 points (2 goals, 5 assists) in 7 playoff games in the 2013 post-season.

When the 2012–13 season finally got going in January, van Riemsdyk did little in his first 2 games and Leaf fans were wondering why such a large man was virtually invisible. But when the Leafs went to Pittsburgh for the third game of the year on January 23, van Riemsdyk started to show what all the fuss was about. He scored twice and added 1 assist, helping the Leafs to a 5–2 victory. The Penguins opened the scoring, but the Leafs tied it early in the second period. Then van Riemsdyk scored his first as a Maple Leaf to give his team a 2–1 lead. Even though Sidney Crosby tied it soon after, the speedy van Riemsdyk took advantage of a miscue by Evgeni Malkin to score his second of the night with a quick wrist shot from the face-off circle that got past Penguins netminder Marc-Andre Fleury. The Leafs never looked back, spoiling the Penguins home opener. After the game van Riemsdyk was rather modest when he said of his 2 goals, "I really didn't have to do much."

On February 5, the Maple Leafs traveled to Washington to play the Capitals who were seeking revenge after the Leafs had edged them in Toronto a few days earlier. Two first-period goals by van Riemsdyk got the Leafs off to a good start on their way to the 3–2 victory. His first goal came when he stole the puck from Washington defender Tom Poti and put it into an empty net when the Caps netminder Michal Neuvirth was out wandering behind his net. The second came as van Riemsdyk knocked in a loose puck around the Washington crease. "I'm getting a great opportunity to play some key minutes [on the Leafs top line replacing the injured Joffrey Lupul]. In the past when I got that opportunity [in Philadelphia], I put up good numbers," van Riemsdyk reminded reporters after the contest. When the Flyers came to the Air Canada Centre one week later, van Riemsdyk scored a pretty goal using his speed to get around Schenn before depositing a shot into the Flyers net during a 5–2 Leafs victory. It was some sweet revenge for the lanky winger.

Time will tell who won the trade between Toronto and Philadelphia but the early returns for the Maple Leafs are promising. It also appears likely that JVR has put his inconsistent play behind him and is coming back to play to the level expected of someone drafted second overall. In 2013-14 he scored 30 times for the Maple Leafs— the second best total on the team next to Phil Kessel who had 37.

Borje Salming wore #21 for the Maple Leafs during his Hall of Fame career.

EUROPEANS

Borje Salming • Miroslav Frycer • Peter Ihnacak
Nikolai Borschevsky • Alexander Karpovtsev • Fred Modin
Sergei Berezin • Nik Antropov • Mikhail Grabovski
Nikolai Kulemin

IN 1973 THE Maple Leafs signed free-agent defenseman Borje Salming, a Swedish-born blueliner who had never played in North America. Salming soon proved that European-born players could compete in the National Hockey League, something that led to many more European players being signed (and later drafted) by National Hockey League teams. Before Salming's success with the Leafs, only a few players born and trained in Europe had ever tried to play in North America, with little success. When the World Hockey Association began playing in 1972, quite a few Europeans players appeared in the new league, especially with the Winnipeg Jets. Both the NHL and the WHA were expanding in the 1970s and new sources of players were needed to ensure that the leagues could survive. The Maple Leafs organization was ahead of the curve when they signed Salming who turned out to be a Hall of Famer. While many other European-born players have played with the Leafs since Salming, few have been as successful as Toronto's first "Euro." One who achieved as much success as Salming was fellow Swede Mats Sundin, who the Leafs acquired in a trade in 1994. In fact, Sundin became the first European-born player to ever captain the Maple Leafs.

In this chapter we'll look at some of the better-known European-born players who had defining moments as Toronto Maple Leafs.

BORJE SALMING

★ 1st TEAM ALL★STAR

Borje Salming

Leaf Record:
148 Goals,
620 Assists,
768 Points

Maple Leaf Moment: April 17, 1976

Defenseman Borje Salming would likely have been perfectly content to play hockey in his native Sweden, even if it meant he was only going to be a part-time professional player (and there was little money to be made). He was good enough to play on the top teams in Sweden by the time he turned twenty and could make the national team without much difficulty. However, the National Hockey League seemed so far away that the odds of him even trying to play in North America were very remote. His brother, Stig, had been considered a good player in Sweden, but he would never get the chance to play in the NHL. The most famous Swede to play in the big league, Ulf Sterner, had returned home unable to adjust to the style of play used in Canada and the United States. Yet there was no doubt Salming was a very talented and gifted athlete. Eventually he caught the eye of the Toronto Maple Leafs who were initially not even aware of him.

Toronto scout Gerry McNamara was in Sweden wanting to look at a goalie when he saw Salming's team play a squad from Barrie, Ontario, in 1972. McNamara was quickly struck by Salming's play and made note that the six-foot-one, 193-pound defenseman would not back down against the aggressive Barrie Flyers. In fact, Salming was even tossed out of the game at one point and, while he was in the dressing room, McNamara went in and handed him a business card. He also asked, "Would you like to come over to Canada and play for the Toronto Maple Leafs?" Not knowing what else to say, Salming replied with a simple, "Yes." The Leafs then put Salming's name on the negotiation list and by September 1973, he was in Toronto for training camp. Salming's initial two-year contract with the Leafs had him making more money than he could ever dream about in Sweden.

Seventies' hockey was pretty rough, with one team, the Philadelphia Flyers, implementing a brawling approach to the game. "The Flyers were feared and renowned throughout the NHL," Salming wrote years later. "They didn't have just a couple of ruffians, they had twenty! They played a violent style, fighting at the drop of an insult and they were successful. No team was tougher or more intimidating. The Flyers were the undisputed heavyweight champions of the NHL and they didn't take kindly to rookies from Sweden." Salming and his fellow countryman Inge Hammarstrom prepared for the show by getting into top physical condition before arriving in Toronto. And the lean defenseman refused to be intimidated by anything on or off the ice. Salming's first physical encounter was against noted fighter Dave Schultz of the Flyers and although he did not exactly win, he showed he was ready to take on all challenges. It was important for Salming to stand up to the physical abuse because Swedish players had developed a reputation for using their sticks and not fighting. It would have been easy for Salming to return home and forget about the NHL, but that was not in his nature.

Borje Salming holds the Leafs record for most points by a Toronto defenseman (768) and most assists (620). He was inducted into the Hall of Fame in 1992.

In his rookie year, Salming recorded 39 points (in 76 games with a team best, plus 38 during the 1973–74 campaign) and he never looked back or wondered if he belonged in the league. Soon he was a league All-Star (a total of six times over his career) and a resilient force on the blue line over his entire Maple Leaf career.

Perhaps Salming's greatest challenge came on his twenty-fifth birthday, April 17, 1976, when the Leafs were in the middle of a best-of-seven playoff series against the Flyers. The Leafs dropped the first two games but won the first game on home ice to get back into the series. During the Leafs 5–4 win, Salming got into a fight with Mel Bridgeman and took a truly savage beating. Salming's face absorbed the brunt of punches thrown by the unrelenting Bridgeman.

Leaf fans had seen Salming take some hard punishment before and hoped he could bounce back as he had so many times before. In typical fashion, Salming responded with some great play. The fourth game of the series turned on a goal Salming scored when he took a pass from captain Darryl Sittler. He then cut straight through the middle of the ice to go in all alone on Flyers goalie Bernie Parent. "I know Parent always stands up as much as he can, so all I did was shoot up high. It went in on his glove side, up under the crossbar," Salming recounted. The Gardens crowd erupted in cheers for a man who had been so destroyed just a game ago. "I don't think I am a hero. But when it [the crowd reaction to the goal] happens in the game, you just can't think about anything else. It just feels real nice." The Leafs won the game 4–3 and pulled even with the Flyers in the series. Injuries and an extra home game for Philadelphia eventually cost the Leafs the series in seven hard-fought games

Although the Leafs were a good team through the early years of Salming's NHL career, they were not able to get very far in the playoffs. Salming's consistent play, however, made him a Toronto favorite and his successful stay in the NHL opened the doors for many other Swedes and European players. Salming had beaten the odds to become an NHL star. He did it with skill, finesse, and determination.

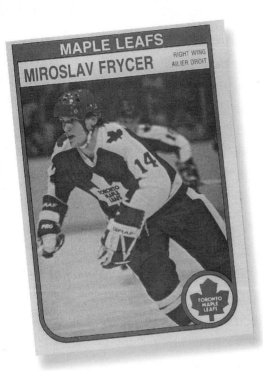

MAPLE LEAFS
MIROSLAV FRYCER
RIGHT WING
AILIER DROIT

Miroslav Frycer

Leaf Record:
115 Goals,
153 Assists,
268 Points

Maple Leaf Moment: January 8, 1986

When the Maple Leafs traded star right-winger (and future Hall of Famer) Lanny McDonald to the Colorado Rockies in 1979, the main player coming back to Toronto was Wilf Paiement. A big, tough winger, it was expected that Paiement (drafted second overall in 1974) was going to be a Maple Leaf for a long time. But in 1982 he was abruptly dealt to the Quebec Nordiques for the virtually unknown and thus unheralded Miroslav Frycer. (Frycer was originally signed by the Nordiques as a free agent without ever being drafted.) A swift, darting skater with great moves, the Czechoslovakian-born left-winger was all about scoring goals. Frycer, who clearly played a European style of game, first impressed the Maple Leafs by scoring a hat trick against them in November 1981. And he was four years younger than Paiement.

After he arrived in Toronto, Frycer hoped he could combine with fellow countryman Peter Ihnacak to give the Maple Leafs a successful Czech duo much like the Stastny brothers (Peter and Anton) in Quebec City. When Frycer faced the Nordiques for the first time as a Maple Leaf all he did was score 3 goals (including the game winner) in a 6–3 Toronto victory at Maple Leaf Gardens!

Frycer scored 25 goals in his first full year as a Leaf (in just 67 games) in 1982–83 and hit the same number of goals two years later in 1984–85. He had a breakout year in the 1985–86 campaign when he netted 32 goals—the most in the club—for a Leaf team filled with young players. The 1985–86 team could not play defense at all allowing 386 goals against but with 311 goals for over the regular season, they were certainly exciting to watch.

One particular night stood out this season: January 8, 1986, when Wayne Gretzky's high-flying Edmonton Oilers came into town. Before it was over, the two teams combined for a total of 20 goals (1 short of the NHL record)—and Frycer had 4 all on his own!

Miroslav Frycer was traded to the Detroit Red Wings on June 10, 1988, in exchange for defenseman Darren Veitch, a rearguard who had once been drafted fifth overall by the Washington Capitals in 1980. Frycer also played for the Edmonton Oilers for 14 games during the 1988–89 season.

The Leafs jumped out to a 5–1 lead in the first period on 2 goals from Russ Courtnall while singles went to Steve Thomas, Brad Smith, and Frycer. Gretzky had the lone Edmonton marker in the first, but he had 2 goals and an assist in the second as the Oilers climbed back into the game to make the score 7–6 for the Leafs. Edmonton scored the first 2 goals of the final frame to take the lead, but then Frycer went to work and scored twice to get the lead back for Toronto. Glenn Anderson responded for Edmonton, but then Frycer scored the go-ahead goal to make it 10–9 when he beat Grant Fuhr in the Oilers net. Another Toronto goal made it 11–9 with just over a minute to play. The Leafs managed to kill off the remaining time to escape with the victory. Interestingly, the Leafs were missing Rick Vaive from their lineup while Mark Messier was sitting out for the Oilers. If those two sharp shooters had played there is no telling how many goals might have been scored!

"I've scored four goals back in Czechoslovakia but that's forgotten. This is a new life," Frycer said. "It's great to beat them. Ninety per cent of the Oilers are superstars. We usually try to play a tight game against them." Obviously that did not go according to plan. Nevertheless,

Toronto coach Dan Maloney was just happy to escape with a victory. "Of course you're happy to take the two points, which we needed, and run out of the building... but scoring 11 goals was a big lift." The game was obviously important to Frycer's point total and by the end of the season he had recorded a career-best 75.

Frycer was never as good for the Leafs and he had significant trouble (on and off the ice) when John Brophy took over as the Toronto coach after Maloney was allowed to get away to Winnipeg. Frycer's point total of 268 in just 328 games as a Maple Leaf is impressive; however, the talented winger never quite lived up to those hockey expectations that grew out of the Paiement trade in 1982.

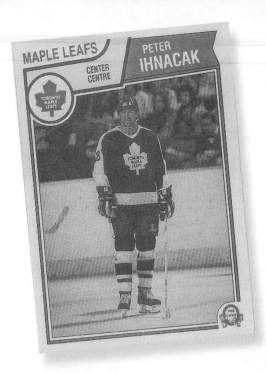

Peter Ihnacak

Leaf Record:
102 Goals,
165 Assists,
267 Points

Maple Leaf Moment: April 10, 1986

When the Maple Leafs had no choice but to trade team captain Darryl Sittler in 1981, they received two players (Rich Costello and Ken Strong) from Philadelphia who did virtually nothing for Toronto. However, they also obtained a second-round draft choice in the deal and used it to select center Peter Ihnacak twenty-fifth overall in the 1982 Entry Draft. Considering Sittler was one of the great players in Maple Leafs history, it was far too little in return from the Flyers. But at least the selection of Ihnacak gave them something to hope for in the immediate future. The Leafs got Ihnacak under contract only after he defected from his native Czechoslovakia (where he had played all his developmental hockey) during the 1982 World Hockey Championship in Finland.

Ihnacak was already twenty-five years old when he joined the Leafs for the start of the 1982–83 season. He scored 25 times while setting a club record for rookies with 66 points. The following year saw Ihnacak play in only 47 games (recording 23 points), but he was back with 22 tallies the next season. The problem was the Leafs were so bad during those years that Ihnacak's performance was overlooked much of the time; however, by the 1985–86 season (a year that saw Ihnacak score

18 times and total 45 points), the Leafs had a team full of youngsters who would improve over the course of the season. They made the playoffs with just 25 victories in the weak Norris Division, but faced the Chicago Blackhawks in the first round of the post-season, a team that had finished with 29 more points. However the youthful Toronto club had a nasty surprise for the Blackhawks in their best-of-five playoff round.

The Leafs won the opening game in Chicago by a 5–3 score which made the second game, played on April 10, 1986, all the more important for the Blackhawks. However the Leafs opened the scoring on a goal by Dan Daoust just after the four-minute mark of the first period. Chicago superstar Denis Savard then scored twice to give his team a 2–2 tie at the end of one. Savard scored 2 more in the second to give him 4 on the night and more importantly, a 4–2 lead for Chicago. But Wendel Clark scored before the second stanza ended to get the Leafs back to within 1.

Peter Ihnacak would record 267 points in 417 games as a Maple Leaf. He is listed as a European scout for the team in the 2012–13 media guide.

At this point nobody would have been surprised if the young Leafs just folded, happy to go home with their one victory. But it did not happen that way. With less than six minutes to play and still down a goal, Ihnacak scored the key marker of the series. Defenseman Bill Root sent a pass Ihnacak's way and he roofed it over the shoulder of Chicago netminder Bob Sauvé to tie the game. If that was not enough, Ihnacak put a perfect pass on the stick of Walt Poddubny who promptly put it home with just fifty-six seconds to play. An empty-net goal by Steve Thomas made it 6–4 for the Leafs and gave them a 2–0 lead in games.

It was only natural that Savard's 4-goal night was the focus after the game, but that did not seem to bother the Leafs one bit. "I am the happiest I have been," said Ihnacak, expressing the general sentiment in the Leaf dressing room. Leaf coach Dan Maloney complimented the Czechoslovakian-born center. "Peter made a great effort on the winning goal—keeping it in and feeding Poddubny for the winner." The Leafs knew they had the Blackhawks on the ropes and then finished them off with a 7–2 win on home ice two nights later—making Leaf fans happy for the first time in a long while. Ihnacak's performance was some sweet vindication for the Leafs who finally knew that they had received something of value for Sittler—even if they had to go all the way to Europe to find it!

Peter's brother Miro was also signed by the Maple Leafs, but after some considerable fanfare when he joined the team in 1985–86, the younger Ihnacak proved a complete bust scoring just eight times in 55 games for Toronto. Peter would only play in the NHL with Toronto and their farm team in Newmarket, Ontario. He returned to Europe to play in Germany and Switzerland between 1990 and 1997 before retiring as a player.

NIKOLAI BORSCHEVSKY • RW

Nikolai Borschevsky

Leaf Record:
48 Goals,
65 Assists,
113 Points

Maple Leaf Moment: May 1, 1993

The Maple Leafs drafted twenty-eight-year-old Nikolai Borschevsky in the fourth round of the 1992 Entry Draft with the hope he could help the team right away. The smallish (generously listed at five-foot-nine, and 180-pound left-winger had played all his hockey in his native Soviet Union and was not an especially prolific goal scorer, but in 1991–92 he scored 25 times in just 40 games for Spartak Moscow, and that gave the Leafs some impetus to select him in the fourth round, seventy-seventh overall. He came to training camp ready to play and impressed new coach Pat Burns enough to stick with the revamped Toronto club for the 1992–93 season. It turned out to be a good move since Borschevsky added some much needed scoring to a team looking for some punch on the wing.

The final year of the Norris Division (1992–93) saw the Leafs finish in third place with 99 points and 44 wins in the regular season—one of the best years in the club's history. Despite their strong showing, the Leafs were considered an underdog going into the first round of the playoffs against the Detroit Red Wings. The Red Wings, who had won 47 games and recorded 103 points, were generally considered a much more talented and deeper team. The underdog status probably suited the Toronto side better under Burns, who had made his team a much grittier club in his first year behind the bench. Toronto had not qualified for the playoffs the year before, so any playoff games this year were considered a bonus. It is speculation to say the Red Wings underestimated the Leafs, but the Doug Gilmour–led club was ready to do something special in the playoffs.

The first two games saw Detroit pretty much wipe the Leafs out with 6–2 and 6–3 wins at Joe Louis Arena. To top it off, Borschevsky was injured in the first contest, and likely out for the rest of the series, with what was initially determined an eye injury. The Leafs drew even with a pair of hard-fought wins on home ice and took the lead back in Detroit with an overtime goal by Mike Foligno. Detroit roared back to take the sixth game in Toronto to set up a game-seven showdown on May 1, 1993. Much to everyone's surprise Borschevsky was now ready to play and Burns inserted the slight winger into the lineup.

> Nikolai Borschevsky scored 31 goals for Toronto in 1992–93 (and had 9 points in 16 playoff games), but would only play one more full season before being moved to Calgary during the shortened 1994–95 season. He finished with 122 points in 162 games played in the NHL with injuries playing a significant role in shortening his career.

The Leafs struck first on a goal by Glenn Anderson, one of the best clutch players in hockey history. Detroit took a 2–1 lead early in the second period, but Leafs defenseman Bob Rouse tied it again. Detroit got the go-ahead goal when Dallas Drake put a shot past Toronto netminder Felix Potvin before the second period ended. It stayed 3–2 for the Red Wings until the 17:17 mark of the third when Gilmour scored to tie the game once more with help from Wendel Clark and Dave Ellett. Gilmour's tally (his third of 4 points on the night) forced the game into overtime and put the pressure squarely on the hometown Red Wings who were supposed to win the series.

After an early chance by Nicklas Lidstrom was turned away, the Leafs went on the attack. Rouse shot the puck back into the Detroit end and Clark picked it off the boards. The puck went to Gilmour who passed it over to Rouse at the point. The Leafs defender let a shot go that was perfectly redirected past Detroit netminder Tim Cheveldae by Borschevsky (who was well placed right in front of the Red Wings net) for the series winner. It was quite the comeback for Borschevsky who was not expected to return to play in the tough series.

"Good play by Rouse," Borschevsky later said. "Great pass. Very good. I score. Big goal. Big for team. Happy." His English may have been broken but his sentiments were clear. The Leafs were thrilled with their exciting overtime victory and felt they could now move on to win the next series against the St. Louis Blues (which they did in 7 games).

"I think we've gained some respect," Gilmour said.

"I love this," chimed in coach Burns. "We had to put Nicky in there because we needed another threat of some kind." On this night all the moves worked out as the smallest player became a big star with the most important goal of his career and one of the most memorable in Maple Leaf history.

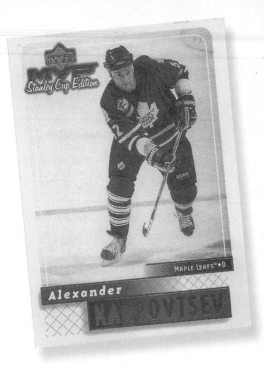

Alexander Karpovtsev

Leaf Record:
5 Goals,
39 Assists,
44 Points

Maple Leaf Moment: 1998–99 Season

The trade the Maple Leafs made to acquire defenseman Alexander Karpovtsev made perfect sense. The team did not want to keep blueliner Mathieu Schneider and the veteran had no real interest staying in Toronto. The problem was to find a good fit and make a deal and that finally happened early in the 1998–99 season. The New York Rangers were interested in bringing in name players and Schneider had developed a reputation as a talented but somewhat enigmatic defenseman over his career with the Canadiens, Islanders, and Maple Leafs. When the Rangers offered Karpovtsev, a 1994 Stanley Cup champion, the Leafs jumped at the deal. And they would be happy with the result for at least a couple years.

Karpovtsev was a year younger than Schneider and cost about $1 million less. He also had attributes that made him a very attractive player. "Karpovtsev is a little bigger and more of a physical presence [at six foot three, 221 pounds] and I think we need that," said Ken Dryden who was managing the Toronto team at the time. "From a power-play perspective he offers the best shot we have from the point." The big blueliner was not a goal producer in his career to date, but he was good at setting up plays (29 assists in 1996–97, his career-best total). The Leafs were hoping he would be a steadying influence on young defensemen such as Tomas Kaberle and Dany Markov, but he would have to avoid the injury bug to do so.

Karpovtsev joined the Leafs in late October and would go on to play in 57 games for the team in 1998–99. He would score just 2 goals but would post a very respectable 25 assists on the year. One of his 2 markers was a game-winning tally that came on the night of April 3, 1999, in Calgary as the Leafs toured western Canada late in the regular season. The Flames opened the scoring, but goalie Curtis Joseph shut them out the rest of the way while the Leafs poured 5 goals past former Toronto netminder Ken Wregget.

Alexander Karpovtsev was an assistant coach for Lokomotiv Yorosavl in his native Russia when, in October 2011, the team plane crashed. He died along with many other former NHL players, including fellow Russian Igor Korolev who was a Leaf in 1998–99. Karpovtsev was originally drafted 158th overall by Quebec in 1990.

Mats Sundin tied the score for the Leafs early in the second and then Karpovtsev scored his goal at 15:09 of the same period to give the Leafs a lead they would not give up. A shot from the point by Karpovtsev deflected off the skate of Calgary defenseman Steve Smith and it went past Wregget for the go-ahead goal. Sundin added another goal before the middle frame was over and then two more from Sergei Berezin made it a 5–1 final for Toronto.

The victory in Calgary brought their record against the three western Canadian teams to a strong 8–1–0. While the Leafs were glad to beat up on the Flames, Oilers, and Canucks, Toronto coach Pat Quinn acknowledged those teams were having some difficulties. "We caught a couple of teams that were very, very tense. It didn't seem like anything was going for them at all and we got a lot of good bounces and some good saves." The Leafs finished with 45 wins for the 1998–99 season and made their way back to the playoffs after being out for a couple of years.

Karpovtsev was so good for the Leafs that he recorded a league-high plus 39 and was good in 14 playoff games that saw him score 1 power-play goal and total 4 points. His defensive play slipped, however, and his excellent plus/minus ranking dropped to minus 7 during the post-season. He was a Maple Leaf for just one more year (playing in 69 games during 1999–2000), but excessive contract demands eventually had Karpovtsev moving on once again, this time to Chicago.

Dealing Karpovtsev to the Blackhawks turned out to be another good trade for the Leafs who received defenseman Bryan McCabe (83 goals and 297 points in 523 games as a Leaf) in return. McCabe was named as a second team league All-Star in 2003–04 while Karpovtsev would play in just 24 games for the Hawks before moving on to the Islanders and the Panthers before his 596-game career came to an end in 2006.

FREDRIK MODIN • LEFT WING

10/19/96 MODIN TAKES IT TO THE
STARS IN AN EARLY-SEASON TILT.

Fred Modin

Leaf Record:
38 Goals,
38 Assists,
76 Points

Maple Leaf Moment: 1998–99 Season

Toronto general manager Cliff Fletcher made a big trade to obtain Swedish-born Mats Sundin just prior to the 1994 Entry Draft. He also made a move during the second day of the draft that got the Leafs another big Swede (six foot four, 220 pounds) by the name of Fredrick Modin. Sensing that the Dallas Stars were about to make a move in the third round to take Modin, Fletcher sent a second-round draft choice in 1995 to the New York Islanders for the right to make the sixty-fourth selection in 1994, and used it to take the large left-winger. To say the least it was one of Fletcher's better deals as Leaf general manager.

Modin had never played in North America and had not put up overwhelming numbers in his native Sweden; however, scouts saw some real potential and thought he could be an effective NHL player. He first joined the Leafs for the 1996–97 season without ever playing in the minors. He scored 6 times and made 7 assists for 13 points in 76 games as rookie. While he showed some flashes of good play, it was not until his second season when he scored 16 times and totaled 32 points that the Leafs thought they might have something special in Modin. The Leafs were not very good during his first two seasons but became contenders during the 1998–98 campaign.

Modin was more noticeable during the 1998–99 campaign and had some notable games, the first coming on November 25, 1998, when the Leafs hosted the Vancouver Canucks at the Air Canada Centre. The Leafs were up 3–1 by the end of the second period, mostly behind the great netminding of Curtis Joseph. In the third, Modin salted the game away with 2 goals as the Leafs cruised to a 5–1 victory. Modin stole the puck off Vancouver defenseman Mattias Ohlund on his first goal and broke in alone before snapping a wrist shot past goalie Garth Snow. The Vancouver netminder did not even move on the shot as it went in off both goal posts and into the net. "I think I've been playing all right for the past couple of games," Modin said. Playing with Sundin certainly helped and he had 6 goals in just 22 games to that point in the season.

> Fred Modin's shot was registered at 100.7 miles per hour during the Leafs skills competition in the 1996–97 season. He would go on to score 232 career goals.

"He has terrific physical skills," Leaf coach Pat Quinn said of Modin. "He skates and he's strong. He likes the heavy work. One reason he's getting a chance with Sundin is that he digs some pucks out of the boards." He should have also noted that Modin had a blistering shot that he did not use nearly enough.

Sundin and Modin combined their efforts for the game-winning goal when Anaheim visited on December 30, 1998. With the Leafs up 1–0, Sundin fed a perfect pass to Modin who redirected the shot past Mighty Ducks goaltender Guy Herbert. It turned out to be the winner in the Leafs 4–1 victory. Modin registered 5 shots on net and got first star of the game. He would score 16 times during the regular season and total 31 points, but would have a difficult time getting untracked in the playoffs. He was a healthy scratch on more than one occasion in the playoffs (playing in just 8 games and not recording a single point) and was replaced by the Lonny Bohonos, a regular minor leaguer.

The large Swede was not given any chance at redemption by the Maple Leafs who suddenly dealt him to Tampa Bay for defenseman

Cory Cross right before the start of the 1999–2000 season. It was too bad Quinn didn't remember his earlier praise of Modin now that he was general manager! Had the Leafs shown more patience they might not have spent so much time looking for a winger to play alongside captain Sundin.

Modin would score a career-best 32 goals for the Tampa Bay Lightning in the 2001–02 season and would score 29 times for the Florida-based club in 2003–04 year that saw them win the Stanley Cup (Modin had 19 points in 23 playoff games in the 2004 post-season.) He also helped Sweden capture an Olympic gold medal in 2006.

Sergei Berezin

Leaf Record:
126 Goals,
94 Assists,
220 Points

Maple Leaf Moment: May 2, 1999

When a player is selected in the tenth round of the Entry Draft, not much is expected of him. This is how the Maple Leafs saw it when they selected Sergei Berezin 256th overall in 1994. However, because the twenty-year-old, five-foot-ten, 200-pound winger was based in Russia, not tested in North America and therefore a bit of a wildcard, there was always a chance. Sure enough, three years after the draft, Berezin came to North America and joined the Leafs for the 1996–97 season. He proved he could play by scoring 25 times as a rookie, but his all-round game left plenty to be desired.

Berezin was on the Maple Leaf roster because of his goal-scoring ability, but in his first two seasons with the team he had not scored any goals of significance. Although he had scored a total of 41 goals over the first couple of years, the 1998–99 season was really the first time Berezin did something important in a Leaf uniform. Comfortable in his second-line role, Berezin scored 37 times that year and helped the Leafs get back into the playoffs under new coach Pat Quinn. A big reason why Quinn was given the head coaching job by the Maple Leafs was to get more out of players like Berezin who had been languishing under previous coach

Mike Murphy. In fact, Berezin was often listed as a healthy scratch the previous season. But the Leafs were now placing more emphasis on the attack—and that suited Berezin just fine. He posted his best goal-and-point total (59) of his career in 1998–99. At this point, the Leafs were not so sure about advancing in the playoffs when they drew Philadelphia in the first round of post-season. The Flyers were always a playoffs nemesis having beaten the Toronto side in all three post-season meetings to date. Would this year be any different?

The Flyers were without superstar Eric Lindros and that only helped the Leafs' cause, but they did play some good hockey mainly supported by Curtis Joseph's goaltending. An overtime win in the fifth game at the Air Canada Centre gave the Leafs a 3–2 series lead, but they had to go back to Philadelphia for the sixth contest. Most Toronto fans probably felt that their club would not go the distance, but the Leafs had a surprise in store for their supporters, waiting until the last minute of the game to do it!

Sergei Berezin finished the 1999 playoffs with 8 points (4 goals, 4 assists) in 12 games for the Maple Leafs. He would go on to play for Phoenix, Montreal, Chicago, and Washington before ending his 502-game NHL career. He had a 26-goal season for the Leafs in 1999–2000 and notched 22 in 2000–01, his last year with Toronto. Berezin registered the 10,000th goal in the Montreal Canadiens' history.

The low-scoring series (the teams combined for a total of just 20 goals over the 6 games) continued at the same pace with no goals for nearly three periods. Joseph was simply not going to let the Flyers score despite 26 shots on goal. Joseph's teammates, however, could only muster 19 shots on Philadelphia netminder John Vanbiesbrouck. A late penalty (at 17:06 of the third) to John LeClair gave the Leafs a power-play chance as regulation time wound down. The Leafs managed to keep the puck alive in the Flyers end and defenseman Bryan Berard let a shot go. The rebound came right out to Berezin who drove a shot cleanly past Vanbiesbrouck for the game winner with exactly one minute to play. It was Toronto's ninth goal of the series and Berezin was the right man in the right spot. They managed to kill the clock for the final sixty seconds, but every Leaf remained concerned until the final buzzer sounded.

After the game, the first star of the night commented on his happy season with the Leafs. "This is a great feeling, but it's just the first stage," Berezin said about the Leafs chances to move further along in the '99 playoffs. "I tried to shoot low as I usually do, going for the five hole. As soon as I got the puck, I didn't even think, I just shot it," adding that "It was the biggest goal I've ever scored in the NHL." Actually, it was fortunate for the Leafs that Berezin was even in the Leaf lineup because it was feared he had suffered a broken jaw in a late-season game against Montreal. But he persevered and even took off a bothersome face guard that had been designed for him.

Most of all Berezin was pleased to put the past behind him and do something positive for the Maple Leafs. And it was a great night on which to do it: May 2, a very special date in Toronto hockey history, as it marks the last time the Leafs won the Stanley Cup in the twentieth century!

Nik Antropov

Leaf Record:
125 Goals,
166 Assists,
291 Points

Maple Leaf Moment: December 20, 1999 and December 6, 2007

More than a few NHL teams were interested in drafting Nik Antropov (who would eventually grow to be six foot six and 245-pounds) when the 1998 Entry Draft was held. It seemed every team drafting after the top five had the big center from the USSR on their list. Teams such as Detroit and Edmonton were very interested in Antropov, as was Pittsburgh. Many believed the lanky center had flown under the radar, almost totally undetected. However, Mike Smith, in his role as associate general manager of the Maple Leafs at the time, was usually very knowledgeable about all non–North American prospects, and especially informed about Russian players.

Antropov had not played in many games, but his goal-scoring total had been impressive when he was seventeen years old and playing in his native Kazakhstan. The Leafs were scheduled to select eighth overall, but knew Chicago wanted to draft Mark Bell in that slot. So they sent that pick to the Blackhawks for the tenth choice and another draft pick. The New York Islanders followed by selecting Michael Rupp in the ninth position and then the Leafs had the floor. Pens flipped into the air and groans were heard throughout the Buffalo arena as the Leafs announced they wanted Antropov.

Although he was not a gifted skater by any means (in fact his skating was quite laborious), Antropov tantalized with his great size and ability to handle the puck. He joined the Leafs during the 1999–2000 season and scored 12 times as a rookie. His big night in his first season came on December 20, 1999 when the Leafs visited the Florida Panthers. Leaf defenseman Bryan Berard set up Antropov for the first goal of the game when he one-timed a pass into the Panthers net. The Leafs went up 2–0 before the end of the first on a goal by Mats Sundin, but Florida tied it up with 2 goals in the second. It was a wild third period that first saw the Leafs fall behind 4–2 before evening the score with a couple of markers of their own. Then Antropov scored twice more to give him his first-ever career hat trick and the Leafs a 6–4 win. On both of his goals in the third, Antropov stole the puck, slapping a shot home on the first steal and then applying a deke on the goalie for the second. "My first NHL hat trick," Antropov said. "I'm too happy." Antropov would finish the 1999–2000 season with 30 points in 66 games.

Nik Antropov returned to play in Canada when the Thrashers moved to Winnipeg for 2011–12. The thirty-one-year-old had more than 20 assists for the Jets and the club competed for a playoff spot for most of the season.

Antropov battled some serious injuries over the next few years as a Maple Leaf, never scoring more than 18 goals. But in 2007–08 he broke through with a 26-goal effort. The highlight of the season for him was his second career hat trick when the Leafs were in New York on December 6, 2007. Once again the Leafs were outshot by a good margin, 25–16, but Antropov put 2 behind Rangers goalie Henrik Lundqvist to help the Leafs win 6–2. The game was tied 2–2 when Antropov scored a pair in the second stanza including one on the power play and the other on a tip-in of an Ian White shot. The Rangers switched to goalie Steve Valiquette for the third, but Antropov got his stick on a shot from Pavel Kubina to make the score 5–2.

When Antropov had games such as these, the Leafs would think the large pivot was finally reaching expectations. Even though he was not fast on his blades, Antropov was usually a plus player and he was up to 56 points by the end of the 2007–08 season. He was doing rather well the following season with 21 goals when the Leafs decided to give up on their great experiment and shipped Antropov to the Rangers for a second-round draft choice. One year later as an Atlanta Thrasher, Antropov recorded 67 points—his best season to date in the league. The Leafs, however, did not have a plan to replace one of their top centers.

Toronto selected winger Kenny Ryan with the 2009 draft choice obtained in the Antropov trade, but as of the 2012–13 season the youngster still had not played a game as a Maple Leaf. Ryan spent the year establishing himself on the Marlies' roster in the American Hockey League.

MIKHAIL GRABOVSKI
toronto maple leafs
c • 84

Mikhail Grabovski

Leaf Record:
91 Goals,
117 Assists,
208 Points

Maple Leaf Moment: October 22, 2011

In 2007–08 when Cliff Fletcher returned to the Maple Leafs as general manager for the second time, he knew he was filling an interim position. Despite Fletcher's temporary status, he didn't hesitate to make trades when he thought he could improve the team. Such was the case when the Montreal Canadiens wanted to move center Mikhail Grabovski. The five-foot-eleven, 183-pound player had limited NHL experience (only 27 games and 9 points with Montreal), but he was only twenty-four and the Leafs were looking to rebuild with younger players.

Grabovski was born in the former East Germany but moved as a young child to the Belarus, which was once a part of the former Soviet Union. He played his junior hockey in Russia and the Canadiens selected him 150th overall in the 2004 Entry Draft. He was sent to the Habs farm team in Hamilton and helped the Bulldogs win the Calder Cup in 2007. Grabovski was unhappy with his lack of ice time with the big-league team and let his displeasure be known. He was a restricted free agent and the Habs were not really interested in bringing him back. Fletcher said the Leafs had been looking at Grabovski for some time and liked his skill set.

"He has loads of talent and plenty of dash and flash," Fletcher said upon the completion of the July 3, 2008, trade. "He has that experience with the championship team in Hamilton and he will play for us."

Grabovski scored 20 goals for the Leafs in his first full NHL season in 2008–09 but only had 35 points in 59 games the following year after an injury held him out of more than 20 games. The swift-skating Grabovski bounced back in 2010–11 with 29 goals and 58 points in 81 games—almost perfect numbers for a second-line center. The Leafs were hoping for more of the same as the 2011–12 season began. The Leafs were 4–1–1 after the first 6 games of the new season before they traveled to Montreal for a Saturday night match on October 22, 2011. Naturally, Grabovksi was pumped to play against the team that traded him away.

The teams exchanged goals in the first period but the Leafs lost starting goaltender James Reimer to an injury after he took a hit to the head. Montreal were ahead 2–1, but goals by Phil Kessel and Dion Phaneuf gave Toronto a 3–2 lead after two. Montreal then scored twice in the third to take the lead but Phaneuf and Grabovski set up winger Nikolai Kulemin to even the score once more. The game went into overtime when Grabovski worked some magic in the Montreal end to beat goalie Carey Price with a nice move to end the game 5–4. Kessel and John-Michael Liles helped Grabovski on the game winner just 1:23 into overtime allowing netminder Jonas Gustavsson to claim a victory for the first time since January 6 of the previous season.

"We have to stop thinking and just score goals," said Grabovski.

In exchange for the rights to Mikhail Grabovski, the Maple Leafs sent defensive prospect Greg Pateryn and a second-round 2010 draft choice (which Boston eventually used to select Jared Knight). The trade between Toronto and Montreal was the first between the two long-time rivals since the Leafs acquired Doug Gilmour from the Canadiens for a sixth-round draft choice in 2003. Grabovski had a mediocre 2012–13 regular season (only 9 goals) and playoff (no goals in 7 games), which did not make him a favorite of Toronto coach Randy Carlyle. The Leafs bought out his contract in July 2013, but he will go down as one of the most colorful European players to wear the Toronto sweater.

"It's a little bit special to score in Montreal. I know a lot of people here. I know my friends from Montreal were happy tonight." Grabovski was one of two Leaf players (defenseman Mike Komisarek was the other) booed all night by the Montreal fans, but the Toronto center was not bothered by it at all. Toronto captain Phaneuf commented that the Grabovski line was finally moving in the third period. "That line made the difference after a not-so-good first 50 minutes."

The hard shooting Grabovski (he has a wicked wrist shot) finished the 2011–12 season with 23 goals and 51 points, a good but not great season from someone who needed to produce at least 60 points. Still, the Leafs rewarded Grabovski with a new five-year contract that will pay him more than $5 million a season. Time will tell if the deal was a good one, but there is no question Grabovski is one of the most-talented European players ever to play in Toronto. After one year with Washington in 2013-14, Grabovski signed a new long-term deal with the New York Islanders.

Nikolai Kulemin

Leaf Record:
84 Goals,
111 Assists,
195 Points

Maple Leaf Moments: March 9, 2010 and March 24, 2011

Left-winger Nikolai Kulemin is a fairly robust six-foot-one, 225-pound forward who has much to offer. Yet he does not show it often enough for Maple Leafs. Drafted forty-fourth overall in 2006, the native of Magnitogorsk, Russia comes from a region renowned for producing some very good hockey players, including Evgeni Malkin of the Pittsburgh Penguins. In fact, the two were teammates for a while (they also played together in the World Junior Tournament and at the World Championships). Malkin, though, was obviously rated higher in the eyes of scouts. However, former NHL coach Dave King, who was in Russia for some time, noted that Kulemin had the potential to be a good player in North America. The Maple Leafs must have agreed seeing that they took the youngster so high in the draft.

Kulemin did not come to Toronto until he was twenty-two. He made the team out of training camp for the start of the 2008–09 season. New coach Ron Wilson was willing to give some new players a chance since the 2008–09 Leafs were not expected to make the playoffs and their star player, Mats Sundin, had decided not to return to Toronto. Kulemin played 73 games as a rookie and scored 15 times while adding

16 assists on a team that earned 81 points in the regular season. One of the main highlights for Kulemin was opening night in Detroit against the defending Stanley Cup champions. He scored the game-winning goal in the third period of a 3–2 Leafs victory when he beat Red Wings netminder Chris Osgood at the 7:25 mark of the third frame. It was Kulemin's lone game winner of the season.

The following season saw the Maple Leafs earn just 76 points, but Kulemin scored 16 times and raised his point total to 36. One of his most memorable nights came on March 9, 2010, when the Maple Leafs hosted the Boston Bruins. Kulemin excited all the Leaf fans in attendance with an overtime marker to give Toronto a 4–3 win. Kulemin took a pass from teammate Mikhail Grabovski and then waited patiently as Boston goalie Tim Thomas got all tangled up with back-checking forward Michael Ryder.

The most penalty minutes Nikolai Kulemin recorded in one season was 26 when he was with the Maple Leafs in 2010–11.

Kulemin then deposited a high drive over the pair to give the Leafs the victory. The Leafs winger was named the first star of the game and said afterward, "I was just waiting. I saw the puck [come to me] and put it in." Kulemin has never been one to give long explanations!

Kulemin's first two seasons were average in terms of points, but he could be counted on to give a solid effort on most nights., The 2010–11 season, however, proved to be something entirely different as the skills of the Russian-born Kulemin started to shine on an almost nightly basis. He would finish the year with 30 goals and 57 points while playing in all 82 games. One of his best games came late in the year when he scored twice against the Colorado Avalanche to help the road team win 4–3. Kulemin notched his twenty-seventh and twenty-eighth goals of the year in the first period of the game as he beat Avalanche netminder Brian Elliott on both occasions. The win helped the Leafs fading playoff hopes as they earned their seventy-eighth point and trailed eighth place (in the overall Eastern Conference standings) Buffalo by just 3 points but with 7 games to play.

The first goal of the night for Kulemin came after the Avalanche opened the scoring when he wacked a puck through Elliott's pads at 10:32 of the first. Then just before the end of the opening period, Kulemin grabbed a loose puck from a scramble behind the Colorado net and knocked one past Elliott to give the Leafs a 2–1 lead. His 2-goal effort earned Kulemin the first star of the game and only Phil Kessel would score more goals (32) than the swift winger by the end of the season.

It is not surprising that Kulemin's name comes up in trade rumors since many teams covet a player with his talents. Kulemin is deceptively strong for a player who is not especially physical and very hard to knock off the puck when he is determined. His superior skating skills are not displayed enough because he stresses strong positional play, but he does have an excellent wrist shot and that allows him to score some goals. Kulemin struggled mightily in 2011–12 (only 7 goals and just 28 points in 70 games played), but found his good two-way game (to some extent) again in 2012–13 with 23 points in 48 regular season games. If Kulemin reaches the level of play shown in the past, he will join the group of elite European-born players to wear the Leaf uniform. However, in the summer of 2014 Kulemin decided to sign with the New York Islanders as a free agent, bringing an end to his career in Toronto.

The Maple Leafs first signed Johnny Bower when he was 33 years old.

FAN FAVORITES

Dick Duff • Eddie Shack • Johnny Bower • Ron Ellis
Brad Smith • Brad Marsh • Guy Larose • Gary Roberts
Darcy Tucker • Tie Domi

A BIG PART OF being a Maple Leaf fan is cheering for particular players who have for some reason or other worked their way into the hearts and minds of those who follow the Toronto club. This situation is by no means particular to Leafs fans and many a great or average player has earned the respect of Toronto's huge following. Some of these players are gritty, some are tough, some are very talented, and all play with great heart. There is one point they all have in common: they have given their all while wearing the Leaf sweater game after game. These players have stirred the fans' emotions and will always be well remembered—even when they leave the team or retire—because they have tried so hard to make the Leafs a winner. Their faults as players are often overlooked and the cheers that rain down from the stands for them are sometimes all too generous, but that is what being a fan favorite is all about. There is no doubt a special relationship that exists between the performer and the fans. The following players found such favor among the Toronto fans while they played for the Maple Leafs.

12   Dick Duff

Dick Duff

Leaf Record:
174 Goals,
165 Assists,
339 Points

Maple Leaf Moment: March 22, 1959

Dick Duff's best year as a Maple Leaf was the 1958–59 season when he scored a career-high 29 times. Dickie Moore of Montreal and Alex Delvecchio of Detroit would earn the end of season All-Star selections on left wing, but Duff's 53 points in 69 games were also worthy of recognition. Toronto, though, had been a lowly team for at least the first half of the year and perhaps that kept the spotlight off Duff's achievements. A late-season charge, however, had the Leafs within a point of a playoff position on the last night of the season. The Leafs would have to get help from the Montreal Canadiens who were playing the team Toronto was chasing, the New York Rangers. While the Habs invaded Broadway, the Maple Leafs headed to Detroit on March 22, 1959. It would prove to be one of the most interesting nights in Maple Leaf history.

The Rangers-Canadiens game started earlier than the Toronto-Detroit contest, so the final result would be known and posted while the Leafs would try their best to ensure they had a chance to clinch a spot. Things got off to a bad start in "Motor City" as the Red Wings took a 2–0 lead on goals by Norm Ullman and Marcel Pronovost. Toronto got back into the game early in the second on goals by Larry Regan (his first of 2 on the night) and Bobby Baun. The two teams then exchanged goals to make the score 4–4 by the end of the second. Then word came that the Canadiens had done the Leafs a huge favor by knocking off New York by a 4–2 score (the Rangers sixth defeat in their last 7 games). It was all up to the Leafs now as the third period began. Their fate was going to be decided with one last period of hockey in the 1958–59 regular season.

Duff was out for a face-off in the Leaf end when Regan came up to him and said, "You're going to get the winner, just be there." Sure enough the Leafs took the puck down the ice and Regan got a pass over to Duff who made no mistake by beating Terry Sawchuk in the Detroit net. Billy Harris (with his twenty-second of the year) added one more for Toronto to make it a 6–4 final and the Leafs miracle finish had become a reality. The 11,646 fans in attendance at the Detroit Olympia were mostly cheering for the Leafs on this night sensing that something special was happening right in front of their eyes.

Dick Duff scored the Stanley Cup–winning goal in 1962 when the Leafs defeated the Chicago Black Hawks in 6 games. In 2006, Duff was inducted into the Hockey Hall of Fame, well-deserved recognition for the six-time Stanley Cup winner (two with Toronto and four with Montreal).

As great as that moment was for Duff and his teammates, there was one more glorious evening left and it came in the 1959 Stanley Cup final. After defeating Boston in 7 games in the semi-final, the Leafs met the mighty Montreal Canadiens for the Cup. Montreal took the first 2 games at home, but the Leafs were back at Maple Leaf Gardens for the third game on April 14, 1959. The game went into overtime tied 2–2 when Duff let a shot go just as he crossed the Montreal blue line and it got past Canadiens goalie Jacques Plante. It was the Leafs only win of the final but it was still a memorable moment for the young Leafs.

"It hit [Tom] Johnson's skate and changed direction just enough to fool Plante," Duff explained. "I was actually sick from the heat of the building and the pace of the game when I went out for that shift. That was my last spurt and I had to make it good." Duff was named the first star of the game and his performance in the season and playoffs showed he was going to be a clutch hockey player for the rest of his career. It was one of the main reasons he was one of the most popular Leafs of all time.

Eddie Shack

Leaf Record:
99 Goals,
96 Assists,
195 Points

Maple Leaf Moment: April 18, 1963

Rough-and-tumble Eddie Shack was pretty miserable playing under New York Rangers coach Phil Watson. The Ranger bench boss disliked the large (six-foot-one, 200-pound) free-wheeling left-winger so much that after just two seasons in New York, Shack had to be moved out. The Maple Leafs saw potential in his raw skills and sent two players (Johnny Wilson and Pat Hannigan) to the Blueshirts to acquire the hard-skating Shack who quickly became known as "the Entertainer" in Toronto. Between 1960 and 1967, Shack gave the Maple Leafs exactly what they needed with some toughness and, on occasion, some timely goal scoring.

Even Shack's most ardent fans did not expect their favorite player to be out on the ice with the Stanley Cup on the line. Leaf fans were known to chant, "We want Shack!" whenever a Toronto home game got too dull or the team needed some life, but on the night of April 18, 1963, the Maple Leafs had a chance to win their second straight championship on home ice and nobody was chanting that now. However, with the game tied 1–1 late in the third, Shack was, in fact, out with a face-off in the Detroit end. Shack's line mates were center Bob Pulford and right-winger Bob Nevin.

The Leafs opened the scoring when Dave Keon scored a short-handed goal to give Toronto the lead late in the first period. Detroit tied the game early in the second on a goal by Alex Delvecchio and it remained that way until past the thirteen-minute mark of the final period. The Leafs were up 3–1 in the Stanley Cup final series and wanted to wrap it up in front of the 14,403 fans at Maple Leaf Gardens. Pulford moved in for the face-off and got the puck back to defenseman Kent Douglas at the point. The Leaf rearguard could really fire a puck and let a shot go toward Terry Sawchuk in the Red Wings net. It struck a Detroit player before hitting Shack and ending up in the net. The Leafs had their lead! A few tense minutes later, which included some very strong shifts by Shack, the issue was settled when Keon golfed a drive into the empty net to make it 3–1, clinching the Cup for the Leafs. It was another goal for Keon with the Leafs down a man (establishing a playoff record in the process—most short-handed goals in one game) and there were only five seconds left to play.

Eddie Shack played with seven different teams over the course of his NHL career, but won an incredible four Stanley Cups as a Maple Leaf. He also had his best goal-scoring season in blue and white when he notched 26 in 1965–66. He was so popular in Toronto that a song written about him titled "Clear the Track, Here Comes Shack" made it to the top of the local charts in the mid-sixties.

In the dressing room after the game, Shack insisted he had no intention of touching the puck. "I was trying to get out of the way," he said. "It hit my stick and went in." He then added a little more about the wining tally. "I was cruising near the goal and the puck hit [my] stick on the handle. I never even saw it." Douglas also claimed he did not know exactly what happened. "The puck grazed a couple of guys. I think [Doug] Barkley [a Red Wing defenseman] was one of them. The next thing I knew it was in. I don't know how and I don't care," said the twenty-seven-year old rookie defenseman who was filling in after an arm injury took blueliner Carl Brewer out of the game.

The goal was Shack's only one in the final series though he did have 1 assist. It was a great ending to the year for Shack who had scored a career best (to that moment) 16 times in the regular season.

Leaf coach Punch Imlach shook the hand of the man who had scored the winning goal on the ice after the game was over. Shack was the Leaf player who got to take the Cup back to the dressing room and the fans applauded as he went through the crowd to get the silver trophy loaded with champagne. The Toronto crowd called for Keon to come out and say a few words to the fans and was able to do so before the *Hockey Night in Canada* television broadcast ended. Shack was also called back by the fans, but he could not wade through the crowd around the Leafs dressing room to make it out in time.

Many great players have been credited with scoring the Stanley Cup–clinching goal including Hall of Famers Maurice Richard, Jean Beliveau, Gordie Howe, Bobby Orr, Jacques Lemaire, Wayne Gretzky, Mike Bossy, and Mark Messier. Shack's name is forever among this group and, while he may not have been as talented as many of those on the prestigious list, nobody was more popular than Shack during his greatest days as a Maple Leaf.

GOALTENDER

Johnny Bower

Leaf Record:
220 Wins,
161 Losses,
79 Ties,
32 Shutouts

Maple Leaf Moment: 1964 Stanley Cup Playoffs

Goaltender Johnny Bower was already thirty-three years old when the Toronto Maple Leafs decided they wanted him for their rebuilding team. Leafs' scout Bob Davidson was watching the netminder closely during the 1957–58 season when Bower was once again starring for the Cleveland Barons of the American Hockey League. Bower had already played in the NHL for the New York Rangers in the early and mid-fifties, but they sent him down to the minors despite a fine performance in the 1953–54 season. Bower had played in all 70 games for the New York club that season, winning 29 games and recording 5 shutouts. However, the Rangers decided to replace him with Lorne "Gump" Worsley, relegating Bower to the minors. Bower made the most of his situation playing for Providence, Cleveland, and Vancouver (of the Western Hockey League). He won championships and a plethora of individual awards that made the NHL seem like a distant memory. It's easy to understand why Bower didn't want to leave a secure job in Cleveland, but Toronto drafted his rights in June 1958 and told the netminder he had no choice but to go back to the big leagues. Bower, who was earning a $10 bonus for every shutout he earned as a Baron, asked the Maple Leafs for $10,000 a year.

Toronto agreed and offered Bower a two-year deal.

The Leafs really wanted Bower for just a couple of years to give the young team a veteran presence in net. The idea appealed to Bower who decided to give it one more try, but he made it clear that if he did not make the Leafs, he would be heading back to Cleveland. He would share the netminding duties with Ed Chadwick to start the 1958–59 season but soon found himself the number-one goalie. The Toronto club had many young players on the rise and made the playoffs with a miracle finish to end the 1958–59 campaign. The Leafs made it all the way to the 1959 and 1960 finals, although they lost the Stanley Cup both times to the mighty Montreal Canadiens. But by that time, Bower had established himself not only as the Leafs top netminder but as one of the best in the entire NHL. In April 1962 the Leafs won the first of three straight Stanley Cups and Bower finally fulfilled his boyhood dream of lifting the fabled trophy.

Johnny Bower recorded his thirty-seventh and final NHL shutout during the 1968–69 season when he was forty-four years old. It came in Philadelphia on December 12, 1968, during a 1–0 victory on a goal by Ron Ellis. Bower made 27 saves. Bower retired after appearing in one game during the 1969–70 season.

In the '62 finals against Chicago, Bower injured himself stretching to make a save in the fourth game of the series and subsequently missed the last 2 games. Don Simmons filled in capably and was in net the night the Leafs clinched their first Cup in eleven years. In the 1963 playoffs, the Leafs were such a strong team that they only needed 10 games to take the Cup for the second year in a row. But in the 1964 playoffs, the Leafs needed the forty-year-old Bower to be better than ever if they were going to beat Montreal and Detroit.

The first-place Canadiens, led by snipers such as Jean Beliveau, Bernie Geoffrion, Bobby Rousseau, and Gilles Tremblay, were a formidable opponent. The Habs took a 3–2 series lead and many were blaming Bower for the losses. Bower responded with a 3–0 shutout in the sixth game forcing the teams back to Montreal for a seventh. It took a magnificent effort from Bower and a hat trick from Keon to turn the

Habs back 3–1. Montreal did not score their only goal until the third period and pressed for the equalizer throughout the final stanza, but Bower turned back all their drives until the Leafs put one into the empty Montreal net to secure the win. Earlier in the series many thought Bower was all but finished, but incredibly he gave up only 1 goal over the final two games to get the Leafs back to the finals.

It was much the same against Detroit (led by the incomparable Gordie Howe and a group of veteran Red Wings such as Delvecchio, Pronovost, and Bill Gadsby in the finals when Bower had to backstop the Leafs to win the final 2 games to clinch a third-straight championship. The final game was very tight until the third period with the Leafs up 1–0. Bower kept the Red Wings off the board and then Toronto poured in 2 goals in the final frame to win the seventh game 4–0. Bower was interviewed afterward thanking Leaf fans for their support. "I'd like to thank the people of Toronto for having so much patience with us," Bower said. "I know we did have a few bad games. It certainly is wonderful to win the Stanley Cup and I certainly give a lot of credit to the Detroit Red Wings who played so well. The city of Toronto deserves the Stanley Cup more than anybody else!" Bower put everything in terms of the team, but it seemed as though he was really thanking Maple Leaf fans for not turning on him when the club struggled.

Toronto coach and general manager Punch Imlach often referred to Bower as the greatest athlete he had ever seen. By the time his NHL career was over, Bower had won four Cups (he won his final championship in 1967) and the Vezina Trophy two times (he shared one Vezina with Terry Sawchuk). His great career would be honored with his induction into the Hockey Hall of Fame. The more Bower played for the Maple Leafs the more popular he became and the city has never forgotten his contribution to four titles. He is often at the Air Canada Centre and draws the loudest cheers whenever he is introduced to the adoring crowd. It does not seem to matter how old the fans are because they all love Johnny Bower!

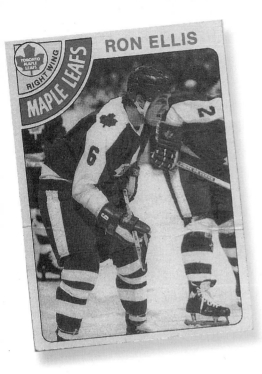

Ron Ellis

Leaf Record:
332 Goals,
308 Assists,
640 Points

Maple Leaf Moment: March 12, 1975

Sturdy right-winger Ron Ellis was popular with Toronto fans dating back to his time with the Marlboro junior club. The Leafs recruited the Lindsay, Ontario, native as a youngster and assigned him to their junior team in 1960–61. By the time he played his final year with the Marlboros, the steady Ellis scored 46 times in the regular season before his team went on to win the Memorial Cup. As a rookie with the Leafs in 1964–65, Ellis notched 23 goals. He would go on to score over 20 goals in eight of his next nine seasons. One of his best goal-scoring years came in 1974–75 with one marker in particular lifting the fans right out of their seats.

Fans and pundits alike believed that the 1974–75 Maple Leafs were going to be solid contenders not just for a playoff spot but for the Stanley Cup. They had finished the previous year in good fashion with a good mix of youngsters, such as Darryl Sittler and Lanny McDonald, and wily veterans, such as Dave Keon and Norm Ullman. Leafs management thought they had strengthened the team with wingers such as Bill Flett and Gary Sabourin. Instead, the season turned into another dismal year with the team finishing with a 31–33–16 record, good enough for a playoff spot but not much else. As the season went on, the team showed spurts of good play and their record (8–2–4) in March was the most impressive of the campaign. In the middle of this winning stretch, the Montreal Canadiens came into town on March 12, 1975. It was a memorable contest with a memorable finish that ended in a 3–3 tie.

To understand why a draw on home ice was special to the Leafs, one has to go back to the 1971–72 season. The Leafs played the Habs at the Montreal Forum on January 19, 1972. The game was tied 0–0 with six seconds left to play and the face-off in the Leaf end. Toronto center Jim Harrison was beaten on the draw by Henri Richard who got the puck over to Peter Mahovlich. The "Little M" as he was known slipped the puck past Leaf goalie Bernie Parent with just two seconds to go. The devastating loss caused the Leafs to lose the next five in a row, contributing mightily to their seven-game losing streak.

Ron Ellis won a Memorial Cup with the Toronto Marlboros in 1964 and a Stanley Cup with the Maple Leafs in 1967. He scored the opening goal the night Toronto won the Cup on May 2, 1967, during a 3–1 Leafs win over Montreal at Maple Leaf Gardens.

Going forward to the 1975 contest at the Gardens, the Leafs found themselves down 3–2 but they had one last chance with an extra attacker. The draw was now in the Canadiens end. Ironically, the face-off came when Peter Mahovlich iced the puck in an attempt to hit the empty Leaf net. Sittler then beat Mahovlich on the face-off and the puck came to Ellis at the side of the Montreal net. Ken Dryden, in the Montreal net, sprawled across the ice, but Ellis calmly lifted the puck over the lanky netminder to even the score with just three seconds to play. The game played in '72 at the Forum was never mentioned, but Leaf fans who had watched both games could not help but smile even if it was only a tie game. Revenge was sweet on this night although it took more than three years to realize!

Ellis chose to comment on the current state of the team rather than on his game-tying goal (his twenty-sixth of the year). "We're solid," he said. "There's been no changes and I think it's paying off," he then said about how coach Red Kelly was trying to stabilize the team.

Kelly was impressed with how the Toronto club was playing late in the year. "They kept persisting. Where they might have quit earlier in the season, they went the full game. We've never had the same drive [before]."

Years later Ellis would recall his role in the 1974–75 season. "From a professional point of view, the season was very enjoyable. I played on a line with Darryl Sittler and Tiger Williams. We had a great line. It was the Leafs number-one line." A surprise victory over the Los Angeles Kings in the best of three salvaged some respect for the Leafs but a second-round loss to Philadelphia quickly ended their year.

Ellis scored a total of 32 times in 1974–75 (the second time in his career he had 30 or more), but decided to retire before the start of the next season. After two years away from the game, Ellis was welcomed back to the Leafs for the 1977-78 season, a year that saw him score 26 times and be a part of a playoff team that saw Toronto win their first best-of-seven series since 1967. He stayed with Toronto until the 1980–81 season and his entire 1,034-game NHL career was spent as a Toronto Maple Leaf. Ellis is still one of the best-liked and most-respected players in team history because of his steady and consistent play.

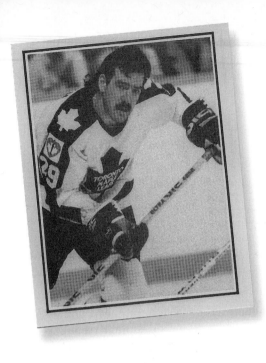

Brad Smith

Leaf Record:
13 Goals,
6 Assists,
19 Points

Maple Leaf Moment: April 16, 1987

Brad Smith put up pretty good numbers (172 points in 136 games) when he played junior hockey in Windsor and Sudbury, Ontario. And that got him drafted fifty-seventh overall by the Vancouver Canucks in 1978. Tall and lean at six foot one, 195 pounds, Smith was not a very good skater and that made it difficult for him to be a regular NHL player. He bounced around in the minors for the most part, but got some NHL action with Vancouver, Atlanta, Calgary, and Detroit. Fans everywhere appreciated his honest and usually physical efforts, but he was a little short on skill to make a major impact.

The Maple Leafs decided to give him another chance when they signed him as a free agent in the summer of 1985. He had a career-best 22 points for Toronto in 1985–86 and was with the team for the 1986–87 season when he racked up 172 penalty minutes in just 47 games to go along with 5 goals and 7 assists. As a result, not much was expected of Smith when the '87 post-season began.

When the Leafs returned home for the sixth game of the 1987 Norris Division semi-final against the St. Louis Blues, they certainly must have been thinking about their previous years' confrontation with the team. In 1986 the Leafs had the Blues down 3–0 during the fifth game of the series only to lose 4–3 in overtime. They won the next game at home, but lost the series with a 2–1 loss in the seventh. Not wanting another repeat, the Leafs were determined to oust the Blues on the night of April 16, 1987, in front of 16,382 hometown fans.

The best way to put a team down is to score early and then play with the lead. That is exactly how the Leafs played it on this night and Smith was the man who posted the opening goal. Smith took a pass from Wendel Clark and motored in on Blues goalie Greg Millen. Smith had his head up as Millen tried to sprawl and sweep the puck away and simply sidestepped past the goalie to put the puck into an empty net with only 2:55 gone in the game. It was Smith's first and only goal of the series, but it would turn out to be the winning tally this night. The Gardens crowd roared as the fan favorite whooped it up after scoring the goal. "That's the move I usually do in practice," Smith said later. "That's the only time it works. It's the only move I have." The game stayed 1–0 for the Leafs until the start of the third period.

Brad Smith played in a total of 222 career NHL games (22 goals, 34 assists) while playing for five different teams. Smith joined the Colorado Avalanche organization as a scout in 1995 and he remains there as the director of player personnel. His name is on the Stanley Cup for his part in the Avalanche championship of 2001.

The Leafs were not about to let the Blues off the hook and scored three more times in the third (on goals by Bill Root, Russ Courtnall, and Peter Ihnacak) to win the game 4–0 and the series by 4 games to 2. After the Leafs had built up their 4-goal lead, the Gardens crowd began cheering for Smith to get more ice time. In such an important game Smith was usually stuck on the Leaf bench. "We want Smith," they chanted but Leaf coach John Brophy was not listening to the hometown partisans. However, during a break in the action, Smith came on to the ice and went out to hug Leaf netminder Ken Wregget, another hero for the Toronto side that series. Smith made it a point to say players like him need to do their part in the playoffs. "The so-called slugs like me, Mike Allison, Greg Terrion, and Dan Daoust... we're the foot soldiers of this army. While the other team is focusing on Rick Vaive or Wendel Clark—they've got to, of course—we go ahead and beat them."

The victory over the Blues provided some sweet vindication for a Leaf team that had suffered an incredible amount of injuries during the season. "Everybody's got to understand the only trouble we got into was when we had all the injuries in January," said Brophy. "I wish someone would write about that. At that time we were at the top of our division. I remember playing Detroit one time and we had five defensemen [out of the lineup]." The Leafs would play the Red Wings in the next round and built up a 3–1 series lead only to lose the next 3 games, once again failing to win the Norris Division in the playoffs.

As for Smith, he never played in the NHL again after the end of the 1987 playoffs. "Motor City Smitty" was able to go out in a blaze of glory, however, listening to the fans chant his name. Most players never get such a send off!

Brad Marsh

Leaf Record:
2 Goals,
28 Assists,
30 Points

Maple Leaf Moment: November 15, 1989

Defenseman Brad Marsh may have been one of the slowest skaters in NHL history but he knew where he had to be and was always very determined to get there. He was actually a very high draft choice (eleventh overall) of the Atlanta Flames in 1978 and moved with the team when it was relocated to Calgary. He caught a big break when he was dealt to the Philadelphia Flyers in exchange for Mel Bridgeman. He was a steady Flyer for seven seasons and appeared in the Stanley Cup finals on two occasions (1985 and 1987).

Marsh rarely contributed to the attack, but was known for his work in his own end of the ice. His consistent efforts to help out his team were widely admired and a main reason the Leafs picked him up on waivers before the start of the 1988–89 campaign. Toronto fans quickly warmed to the hard-working blue liner and for two seasons in blue and white, Marsh was clearly a fan favorite.

If one looked at the box scores of every game Marsh played in, his line would most often show zeros across the board, that is no goals, no assists. On occasion, however, Marsh would suddenly rise up and add something to the offence. Such was the case November 15, 1989, when the St. Louis Blues visited Toronto. The 1989–90 Leafs were still trying to develop an identity under new coach Doug Carpenter. After a very slow start, Toronto had posted 9 wins, but were still below the break-even point with 10 losses over 19 games. The Leafs wanted to prove themselves a serious contender by playing an aggressive, offensive style. But it was the defensive-minded Marsh who was going to lead the charge against division rival St. Louis (the Blues were 8–5–3) on this night.

Brad Marsh played a total of 1,086 career games and played his last season in 1992–93 for the expansion Ottawa Senators. His junior sweater number 22 was retired by the London Knights of the Ontario Hockey League (OHL), making Marsh one of only seven players to receive the team honor.

The Blues had some good goal scorers themselves and found the back of the net twice in the first period, jumping out to a 2–0 lead on markers by Peter Zezel and Brett Hull. Toronto defenseman Al Iafrate got one back before the first period ended to get the Leafs on the board. It was in the second period that Marsh went to work. First, he sent a cross-ice pass to Dan Daoust to even the score at 2–2 with less than two minutes gone. The short-handed goal made the Leafs feel better about how this game was playing out. Later in the period, Marsh dropped a pass back to winger Mark Osborne who bounced a shot in off the pad of Blues netminder Greg Millen to give the Leafs a 3–2 lead. They added 2 more (by Eddie Olczyk and John Kordic) in the final period to make the final 5–2.

When the three stars of the game were introduced after the contest, it was Marsh who was named the evening's number-one performer. When he came out to take his bow, the thirty-one-year-old dashed hard around the entire center-ice face-off circle twice before skating off. The 16,041 in attendance at Maple Leaf Gardens roared their approval for a player they saw as an everyman, a hard worker with the enthusiasm of a young boy. "Stars are few and far between for me," Marsh said after the game. "You've got to enjoy them. I have fun doing it [his post-game skate]."

As for the goal that tied the game, Marsh gave all the credit to Daoust. "If he doesn't yell for the pass, I just dump the puck in and that's that [since the Leafs were killing a penalty]."

Marsh's efforts did not go unnoticed by Leafs coach Carpenter. "I don't know if there are any words to describe what Marsh means to this club. I think you have to watch him to see how important he is to us. His influence is rubbing off and he leads by example."

On a team that did not pay much attention to defense (and was saddled with very average goaltending provided by Allan Bester and Mark Laforest), Marsh's plus-14 ranking at the end of the season was not only the best mark on the team, it was also a truly amazing accomplishment for the skating-challenged defenseman.

One year later Marsh's lack of mobility made him expendable according to new Leaf coach Tom Watt. Marsh was sent to the Detroit Red Wings (for an eighth-round draft choice) after just 20 games in the 1990–91 season. There was no doubting, however, that Marsh left an imprint on Leaf fans despite his short tenure with the club.

Guy Larose

Leaf Record:
10 Goals,
7 Assists,
17 Points

Maple Leaf Moment: February 8 and 11, 1992

When the Maple Leafs acquired Guy Larose in a minor-league swap on December 26, 1991, there was not much fanfare to go with it. After all, the smallish (five-foot-nine, 180-pound left-winger had never been drafted by an NHL team (he signed as a free agent with Winnipeg) and had played very few games (10 in total) at the big-league level. If there was any interest about the player, at least from a Toronto point of view, it stemmed from the fact that his father, Claude, had been a member of the Montreal Canadiens when the Habs and Leafs staged some epic battles in the sixties. In fact, many of the greatest games between the two rivals came in the playoffs when the elder Larose was at his agitating best. Perhaps Guy would have been more suited to the famous red, white, and blue of the Canadiens, but such was not the case. And it made for a nice story when he excelled ever so briefly with the Toronto Maple Leafs.

Larose played well on the Leaf farm team (7 goals and 7 assists in 14 games in 1991–92) after the trade and earned himself a promotion to the big-league team. Injuries and a suspension to Leaf star Wendel Clark also helped open the door to a player who had yet to score an NHL goal. Ironically, the Montreal Canadiens were scheduled to be in Toronto February 8, 1992, for a game that would see Larose make a significant impact. The Leafs had been playing much better hockey (and were hoping to win their seventh game in eight starts) now that they had picked up forward Doug Gilmour, defensemen Jamie Macoun and Ric Nattress -- plus goalie Rick Wamsley, all from Calgary. However, the Habs had Patrick Roy in goal and besting him was no easy task.

The game was tied 2–2 going into the third when Larose scored his first career goal just over two minutes into the final frame. Montreal quickly tied it but Larose gave the Leafs another lead at the 5:42 mark when he poked a puck past Roy giving Toronto a 4–3 edge. Montreal again rebounded to even the score, but goals by Nattress and Daniel Marois made it a 6–4 final for the hometown team.

"I'm never secure, I can't be satisfied. My father taught me that," the twenty-four-year-old rookie said later when asked if his two-goal performance would keep him in the big league. "I'll keep working hard, that's all I can do. I just want to play."

After his exciting run to end the 1991–92 campaign, Guy Larose played in only 26 more games for the Maple Leafs over the next two seasons (1G, 4A) before he was claimed on waivers by Calgary on January 1, 1994. He would play out the rest of his career in the minors and in Europe.

Two nights later the Detroit Red Wings came to Toronto for a Tuesday-night game presenting another strong challenge to a Leaf club trying to get into the playoffs. Although the Leafs scored first, Detroit notched two before the end of the first. The Red Wings scored the first goal of the second, but then Larose stole a puck in the Detroit end and went in to score on goaltender Tim Cheveldae to give the Leafs some spark. It was all Leafs in the third period with Larose swatting home a pass from Claude Loiselle to tie the score 3–3. Then with just two seconds to play, Toronto's Brian Bradley scored the winner on a Leaf power play to secure a 4–3 victory.

Throughout the night the 15,845 Toronto fans at the Gardens chanted "Guy! Guy!" whenever Larose took to the ice, and his two goals helped make him the first star of the game. "It's nice to be recognized for your hard work," he said about the fans calling out his name. "It's a great feeling to hear that. It gives the whole team a boost." The fans had a new hero to warm up to and they loved using the cheer normally reserved for Hall of Fame legend (and Montreal great) Guy Lafleur. It was odd to hear the name called out for a Leaf player, but it energized Leaf hopes of making it into post-season. Larose scored a total of 9 goals and totaled 14 points (in 34 games played) to finish the 1991–92 NHL season, but the Leafs were not able to catch the Minnesota North Stars for the final playoff spot in the Norris Division. However, that did not take away from the efforts of Larose, a new but brief fan favorite who helped bring new life to the Leaf team.

Gary Roberts

Leaf Record:
83 Goals,
74 Assists,
157 Points

Maple Leaf Moment: May 4, 2002

When Gary Roberts became a free agent in the summer of 2000, he saw an opportunity to play close to home. The North York, Ontario, native had played for the Calgary Flames and Carolina Hurricanes, but wanted to put on the Maple Leaf sweater before his career was over. Roberts had suffered a near career-ending neck injury at one point but an entire year off (missing all of the 1996–97 season) and thorough rehabilitation got him back to the point where he could resume his career. A proven goal scorer (he once had a 53-goal season in Calgary), Roberts was known for a physical, all-out style of play that earned him the respect of both teammates and opponents alike. He kept up that type of game when he joined the Leafs and quickly became a fan favorite.

Roberts scored 21 times and added 27 assists during the 2001–02 season, but his real value to the Maple Leafs came in the playoffs that year. The Leaf lineup was depleted by injuries (regulars out included Mats Sundin, Dmitry Yushkevich, and Mikael Renberg who were dinged early in the post-season; Karel Pilar, Jyrki Lumme, and Darcy Tucker were hurt later on). Now more than ever the Leafs needed Roberts' leadership and experience to help guide the team onward. Fans were not disappointed.

Roberts was very good during the opening series win over the New York Islanders to open the '02 playoffs and shone even brighter when the Leafs faced the Ottawa Senators in the second round.

The Sens absolutely crushed the Leafs 5–0 in the opening game in one of the worst playoff games in team history. Toronto had to rebound quickly or face another humiliation. The next game at the Air Canada Centre on Saturday, May 4, 2002, would prove to be a very long night (the contest was not settled until the early hours of Sunday morning). But ultimately, it was a satisfying one for the spirited Maple Leafs.

Gary Roberts finished the 2002 playoffs with 19 points (7 goals, 12 assists) in 19 games played. He was so battered and bruised that he needed surgery on both shoulders afterwards, forcing him to miss the start of the next season!

The Toronto side got off to a great start by scoring the first 2 goals (by Travis Green and Darcy Tucker) before the halfway point of the first period. Ottawa, however, battled back and tied the score 2–2 in the third. The game headed to overtime with the Leaf season essentially on the line.

There was no scoring in two overtime periods (even though each team had a chance on the power play) and both goalies (Curtis Joseph for Toronto and Patrick Lalime for Ottawa) were determined not to give up another goal. Early in the third overtime period, coincidental minors to Shayne Corson of the Leafs and Chris Neil of Ottawa opened up a little more ice. A face-off in the Ottawa end saw Roberts out with center Robert Reichel. The draw was scrambled somewhat, but the puck hit an Ottawa skate and became available to Roberts. He picked up the loose disk, and slid a shot along the ice that went right through Lalime's pads for the winning goal. The Leafs poured over the boards to congratulate the goal scorer, relieved they had won the biggest game of the year so far. The Toronto crowd went wild and the scoreboard posted the score: Toronto 3, Ottawa 2.

After the game, the Leafs spoke highly about goalie Curtis Joseph who had been under fire for uneven playoff performances in the past. "I missed [a two-on-one rush] and thanks to Cujo I got another chance.

Our whole team felt for him," Roberts said.

Other players spoke about Roberts' play. "Everybody has had to take a little more of a leadership role, but I think Gary's on-ice skill and his ability to lead by example has shown itself," said linemate Alyn McCauley. "I guess you could say Gary has been thrust into being the captain without the 'C' on his sweater."

Roberts acknowledged that he had to show something in the leadership area. "I'm just trying to lead by example which I always try to do, and hopefully everyone in this room can elevate their game in the absence of Mats [Sundin] to help our team win hockey games."

The Leafs were a more determined group than the Senators and won the tough series in seven games. Toronto fans would acknowledge the work of the physical left-winger by chanting his name. "Ga-ry Rob-erts" was increasingly heard more and more throughout the Air Canada Centre as the playoffs moved along. The Leafs finally ran out of energy and lost the Eastern Conference final to Carolina in six games. Nevertheless, Roberts' remains one of the most popular players in team history and his playoff performance is a long-remembered talking point among Leaf diehards.

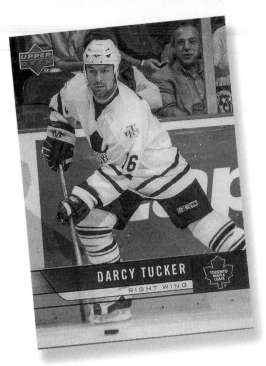

Darcy Tucker

Leaf Record:
148 Goals,
171 Assists,
319 Points

Maple Leaf Moment: May 25, 2002

Little Darcy Tucker had pretty good success in junior playing for three Memorial Cup–winning teams with the Kamloops Blazers of the Western Hockey League. The five-foot-ten, 178-pound left-winger scored plenty in Kamloops (150 goals, 229 assists in 223 career games) and that got him noticed by the Montreal Canadiens who selected him 151st overall in 1993. He did not play much in Montreal (mostly in the minors) and was eventually traded to Tampa Bay. The Lightning soured on Tucker as well, but the Maple Leafs offered two players (including the highly regarded Mike Johnson) and two draft picks for the pesky player. Leaf fans soon took a liking to the agitating Tucker who had some timely scoring from the lower part of the roster. Tucker's second season in Toronto saw him score 24 goals while recording 59 points in 2001–02. The Leafs were pleased with his grit and no wonder—Tucker admired former Toronto star Wendel Clark while playing junior hockey.

The 2002 post-season found Tucker surrounded by great controversy. During the opening round series against the New York Islanders, Tucker threw a low-bridge check at the knees of New York captain Michael Peca that injured his leg, ended his season, and sent Peca to a long rehabilitation program. If Peca had not been injured, no one would have made anything of Tucker's hit, which was delivered from the front and to a player known for his devastating hits when the opposition was not looking. Tucker was vilified by many (especially by Islander fans), but there was no way he was going to change his approach to the game at this point. The Leafs eventually eliminated the Isles in seven games and then moved on to face Ottawa where, once again, Tucker was involved in a highly controversial play.

Late in the fifth game at the Air Canada Centre, Tucker was boarded from behind by Senators forward Daniel Alfredsson as he tried to protect the puck in the Leafs end. Tucker was badly injured and was sprawled across the ice as Ottawa scored the winner off the turnover. The Toronto crowd went wild at the non-penalty call while Leaf players and coaches found the turn of events incredulous as the Senators walked away with a 4–2 win. Tucker suffered a broken shoulder blade and was likely out for the rest of the playoffs while Alfredsson (a player who could at times be as sneaky as he was talented) was immediately and forever a hated opponent of Leaf fans everywhere.

> The Maple Leafs bought out Darcy Tucker's contract after the 2007–08 season; he then signed with Colorado as a free agent. When he returned with the Avalanche to the Air Canada Centre for the first time on November 13, 2009, there was a video tribute to him played during a time-out. Tucker was clearly moved by the gesture and the reception Leaf fans gave him that night. He scored once and assisted on another as Colorado beat the Leafs 4–1.

The Leafs somehow managed to oust the Senators in 7 games and then moved on to play the Carolina Hurricanes. Surprisingly, Tucker was able to play the second game of the Eastern Conference final, but his return, unfortunately, did not inspire the team. The Leafs lost three in a row to fall behind 3–1 in games before returning to Carolina for a fifth game on May 25, 2002.

Behind an incredible performance by goaltender Curtis Joseph (the first star of the game), the Leafs eked out a 1–0 victory to stay alive. The only goal of the game came from Tucker and it was by no means a thing of beauty. While on a power play, Leaf captain Mats Sundin passed the puck back to Bryan McCabe at the point who let a shot go. The puck hit Carolina defenseman Sean Hill before bouncing off Tucker's skate and past Hurricanes netminder Arturs Irbe. Credit has to go to Tucker who was in the right position for a rebound, despite his still-tender injury. The goal came late in the first period and the Leafs carried the lead all the way home (despite a 16-shot barrage by the Hurricanes in the third period) to give them another chance to win a game on home ice.

Tucker's grittiness was also evidenced by the fact that he played 12:02 of the contest and took 3 of Toronto's 19 shots on goal. He also managed to win the only face-off he took, which was likely very painful considering his damaged shoulder. His marker was Tucker's fourth of the playoffs and it looked like his most important tally of the year. The Leafs, however, could not ride the momentum and lost the sixth game at home by 2–1 in overtime.

Tucker had been brought to Toronto because of his pit-bull play and his truly memorable performance in the '02 playoffs certainly demonstrated his commitment to that style of game. And this was the reason Tucker endeared himself to all Leaf fans over his 541 appearances in a Maple Leaf uniform.

Tie Domi

Leaf Record:
84 Goals,
112 Assists,
196 Points

Maple Leaf Moment: February 25, 2003

The Maple Leafs were certain that the Detroit Red Wings were going to select tough left-winger Tie Domi during the 1988 Entry Draft if they got the chance. Domi was not going to be taken in the first round, but when the Leafs selected in the second round with the twenty-seventh pick, they took Domi to prevent the Red Wings from taking the five-foot-nine, 213-pound Windsor, Ontario, native. The graduate of the Peterborough Petes (which saw him score 22 times in 1987–88) was sent to the Leafs farm team in Newmarket, Ontario, for some professional seasoning. However, a two-game call-up to the big team in 1989-90 included some ridiculous on-ice behaviour (42 penalty minutes) and that eventually got Domi a one-way ticket to Broadway in a deal involving the New York Rangers. He was later dealt to Winnipeg, but always pined for a return to Toronto. The Leafs, under the leadership of general manager Cliff Fletcher and coach Pat Burns, accommodated Domi, and the pugilistic forward was soon back in blue and white in April of 1995. He would finish his career as a Maple Leaf, much to the delight of many Toronto fans.

Domi did not often stray from his fourth-line tough-guy role, but there were some notable exceptions. For example, his best scoring season took place in the 2002–03 campaign when he set career bests for goals and points. The 2002–03 Leafs were a strong contender with Mats Sundin leading the team in goals (37) and the multi-talented Alex Mogilny posting a team-leading 79 points; however, no other player broke the 20-goal barrier, which made Domi's contribution to the Leafs attack timely, if nothing else. The Leafs won 44 games and recorded 98 points during the regular season and one of those victories came against the New York Islanders on February 25, 2003, at the Air Canada Centre. The contest produced one of Domi's best career moments.

Tie Domi holds the Maple Leafs' all-time record with 2,265 penalty minutes that he earned in 777 games played for Toronto.

Domi hit the game sheet in typical fashion by getting called for cross-checking (his 3,146th career penalty minute) just 3:31 into the game. The Leafs killed the penalty off and the period ended at 0–0. Martin Lapointe got the Islanders' first goal but then the Leafs responded with three straight (two by Sundin) before the second stanza was over. The then Leafs scored a goal by Travis Green to make it 4–1 before New York got one back. In case the Islanders had ideas of getting any closer, Domi scored his fourteenth of the season (with assists from Green and Tomas Kaberle) to put the game out of reach. He had never scored more than 13 goals before this night. Domi was right on the edge of the Islanders goal crease when he poked the puck past goalie Garth Snow. At least two Toronto newspapers featured a large photo of Domi celebrating his milestone. The Leafs were actually outshot during the game (30–28), but Toronto goalie Ed Belfour was superior to the Isles' rather leaky Snow. It was the Leafs thirty-sixth win of the season, which was the third highest total in the Eastern Conference when the game ended.

Since there were 19 games left to play, the possibility remained that Domi could score 20–quite an achievement for the pugnacious winger. "It would be a nice accomplishment," Domi said. "But on the other hand, it's nice to a part of this ride right now. Mats [Sundin] said to me he wants to have 20-40 goal club between us. I said 40 for him is realistic, but I don't know about 20 for me." He was rightly reserved about the future because he scored only 1 more goal, the rest of the way (Sundin did not hit 40 either). Domi's 15 goals were the most he ever scored in any season and his 29 points also represented a high-water mark for him. His 15-goal total was the fourth highest total on the team for the 2002–03 season.

Domi had 13 regular season fights in 2002–03 and added one more in the playoffs to keep his name prominent on the game sheets and beloved by fans who embrace that element of the game. While the Leafs were not intimidated whenever Domi was on the ice, the fact that he was so high on the Leafs goal-scoring list was a true sign of trouble for the team. That was clearly proven in the playoffs when the Leafs lost a 7-game series to the Philadelphia Flyers in the opening round.

Domi remained a popular figure throughout the rest of his stay as a Maple Leaf and his sweater number 28 was always a best-seller wherever Leafs paraphernalia was sold.

The 1951 Stanley Cup champions gather around the silver trophy after beating Montreal in five games.

HARD ROCKS AND TOUGH GUYS

Bill Barilko • Bob Baun • Orland Kurtenbach • Pat Quinn
Jim Dorey • Dave "Tiger" Williams • Pat Boutette • Bob McGill
Lou Franceschetti • Felix Potvin • Colton Orr

MAPLE LEAFS FOUNDER AND long-time manager Conn Smythe once said, "If you can't beat them in the alley, you can't beat them on the ice." It was one of Smythe's most infamous and most repeated quotes of all-time and the notion had a profound effect on how he selected men to play for the Maple Leafs. They were a dominating team when Smythe was in power, and the organization never forgot this axiom that the Leafs lived by for so many seasons. Toronto fans have enjoyed the result, watching hard rocks and tough guys battling for the blue and white—after all a good scrap provides a great memory. Leafs supporters are often termed sophisticated hockey fans, yet they enjoy a rousing fight as much as any other National Hockey League fan. Sometimes they even like a good beating more than a goal. Tough, hard-nosed players are always welcome in Toronto and if they have a little bit of skill, so much the better. The following Leaf players distinguished themselves with some talent and a willingness to use their bodies and their fists to leave a mark on Toronto's hockey history:

Bill Barilko

Leaf Record:
26 Goals,
36 Assists,
62 Points

Maple Leaf Moment: April 21, 1951

As the 1946–47 season moved along, the Maple Leafs decided they needed some reinforcements along the blue line. So they tapped into an unusual source to find defenseman Bill Barilko. The five-foot-eleven, 180-pound rearguard was playing for the Hollywood Wolves of the Pacific Coast Hockey League (PCHL) when he was recommended to the Leafs by Tommy Anderson, a former NHL player. Leaf manager Conn Smythe was always partial to boys from Northern Ontario and the Timmins-born Barilko fit the bill perfectly. He was not a smooth skater and was, as a youngster, forced to play in net because he did not have to skate so much while playing goal. But he wanted to be a hockey player more than anything and made himself a better skater through hard work and determination. His apprenticeship in the PCHL was part of Barilko's development—and a time when he also learned how to dish out devastating bodychecks.

When the call came to join the Maple Leafs, Barilko quickly made an impression on his teammates with his infectious smile and his robust style. He played his first game as a Leaf on February 8, 1947, when they faced the Montreal Canadiens. Toronto got beat badly by an 8–2 score but Barilko showed he was here to stay with some crushing hits against any and all of the Habs. Soon "Bashin Bill" as he became known, teamed with fellow blueliners such as Wally Stanowski and Garth Boesch to form a strong Leaf defense. Other Leaf defensemen in this era included Jim Thompson, Gus Mortson, Phil Samis, Bill Juzda, and Fern Flaman—by far the toughest group of NHL blueliners from 1947 to 1951. They could make life miserable for all forwards who dared to enter the Toronto end of the ice.

Barilko never recorded less than 85 minutes in penalties in the five years he was with the Leafs. In fact, he led the entire NHL with 147 minutes in his first full season. The stout defenseman also helped the Leafs become Stanley Cup champions in 1947; a far cry from just one year earlier when they didn't even make the playoffs. Smythe decided he had seen enough of the 1945–46 Leafs so changes were made, with Barilko being one of the most important new players added to the squad. As usual, Smythe was right, and the Leafs also took the Cup in 1948 and 1949.

Bill Barilko's remains from the plane crash in Northern Ontario were not found until June 1962, the same year the Leafs won their first Stanley Cup since his famous goal against Montreal in 1951.

In 1951, the Leafs wanted to recapture the Cup, but they had to play two tough playoff series before they could put their hands on the silver trophy. The Leafs managed to get past Boston in 5 games and were fully expecting to meet first-place Detroit in the final. However, the Red Wings were upset by the Montreal Canadiens and that meant a classic confrontation between the two great Canadian cities for all the marbles. Each game went into overtime. The Leafs won 3 games while the Habs only had one victory going into the fifth game of the series at Maple Leaf Gardens. It was the night of April 21, 1951.

With goalie Al Rollins on the bench, Toronto's Tod Sloan tied the game 2–2 in the final minute of regulation. That meant another overtime session, but this time the Cup was on the line if Toronto could score first. The Leafs were determined to win it in front of their fans and came out strong to begin the overtime. Soon winger Howie Meeker was behind the Montreal net doing some good work battling the six-foot, 180-pound Montreal defenseman Tom Johnson for the puck. The loose disk got out to Leaf forward Harry Watson who took a swipe at the puck. Watson's drive did not make it through but the puck was still up for grabs in the face-off circle. Barilko decided to clomp in from the blue line, defying orders from Leafs coach Joe Primeau not to take unnecessary chances. With a sweeping backhand drive, Barilko's shot went over the shoulder of Montreal goalie Gerry McNeil for the Stanley Cup winner!

Barilko was never known as a goal scorer (7 goals and 17 points in 1949–50 was his best offensive season), but he had good hockey sense and on this night it paid off in the Leaf championship just 2:53 into overtime.

Barilko scored the winner with a broken nose courtesy of a Bert Olmstead check, but he was not going to leave the game over such a small injury. He also stopped a Maurice Richard shot to keep the Leafs in the game, ultimately making him the hero of this gritty group of Maple Leafs. The game winner was Barilko's fifth and final career playoff goal.

Smythe made note of Barilko's play while shaking the hand of the man who scored the winner. "We wouldn't be feeling so good right now if it hadn't been for Barilko. That was really the old college try."

Barilko may have summed it all up even better by saying, "It is something I've dreamed about doing all my life."

Sadly, a plane crash that summer ended the twenty-three-year-old's life. He will always be recalled for his courage, toughness, and of course, for scoring the most memorable goal in Maple Leaf history.

21 | **DEFENSE**

Bob Baun

Leafs Record:
29 Goals,
140 Assists,
169 Points

Maple Leaf Moment: April 23, 1964

Bob Baun was a tough man and he played hockey the same way. One night in 1960 he had his throat slit by a skate and merely put a towel on the wound as he walked to the Madison Square Garden infirmary. Baun and the Maple Leafs were playing the New York Rangers that night and a scramble in front of the Toronto net saw Camille Henry's skate come up and slice Baun across the throat, just missing his jugular. He was stitched up and went back out to play the third period even though he was told not to go back to the game. On the team bus that night, Baun suddenly was unable to breathe because he was hemorrhaging while his tongue was being pushed back down his throat. It was a life-and-death situation, but the Leafs managed to get him immediate medical attention. He required two operations in New York to fix the problem. Baun was finally allowed to go back home and be admitted to hospital in Toronto. It was here that he met his new son who had just been born in the same facility! One week after his release from hospital Baun suited up for the Leafs in a playoff game against Detroit. It was not the last time Baun showed his true mettle.

After a very successful junior career that included winning the

Memorial Cup twice (in 1955 and 1956), Baun nearly made the Leafs on his first attempt after turning pro, but was a late cut. He was upset with his assignment to Rochester of the American Hockey League (AHL), but he stayed there for only 46 games in 1956–57 while he played 20 games as a Maple Leaf that same season. He vowed he would never play in the minors again and he made the Leafs the next season, a year that the club finished last in the six-team NHL. Baun was now considered an important part of the Leafs rebuilding efforts and Toronto owner Conn Smythe told a reporter that "Bob the Bomb" was the best Leafs defenseman since Bill Barilko, the tough defenseman who had been with the Leafs for four Stanley Cup wins. It was hoped Baun could fill the same role as Barilko.

Bob Baun was with the Leafs when they won another Stanley Cup in 1967. He also played for the Oakland Seals and the Detroit Red Wings before returning to Toronto in 1970.

Smythe was always a very shrewd judge of hockey talent and he was right on with his assessment of Baun. The Leafs would develop a group of young players like Baun and mixed in the right amount of veterans to become a consistent contender. In 1959 and 1960, the Leafs were already playing in the Stanley Cup finals and two years later, they took their first championship since 1951. The Leafs repeated as winners again in 1963, capping a great end to the 1962–63 season that saw them finish in first place. Baun was a low-scoring defenseman who made life miserable for opposing forwards who dared to challenge him in the Toronto end of the ice. Paired with the talented yet enigmatic Carl Brewer, the hard-rock defenseman was always ready to be physical, but Baun could also carry the puck out of danger as well.

The Leafs were hoping for a third consecutive Cup in 1964, but had a much harder time than in the two previous seasons. They edged Montreal in seven games in the semi-final (with Baun scoring a rare but important goal in the sixth game, one the Leafs desperately needed to stay alive). Detroit, however, was ready for Toronto in the finals and were up 3–2 in games when they next met on April 23, 1964, at the Detroit

Olympia.

The Leafs opened the scoring, but Detroit took a 2–1 lead before Toronto tied it again. Gordie Howe put the Red Wings up 3–2 but Billy Harris tied it for the Leafs late in the second period. The third was scoreless although Detroit worked very hard to end it before their hometowns fans. At one point Baun took a Howe shot on the ankle and although he tried to keep playing on it, he eventually collapsed on the ice and was carried off on a stretcher. Incredibly, Baun returned before the final period was over. His ankle was now taped tightly and it was frozen with a needle. For most other players their season would have ended there and then, but not for Baun.

When overtime began, Baun was ready. On his first shift, the puck came to him at the point in the Detroit end. It was rolling a little and Baun did not try to stop it. He let a shot go that hit a Red Wing stick in front of the net and then went over the shoulder of Detroit netminder Terry Sawchuk. Just 1:43 into overtime and the game was over. The Leafs had forced a seventh game with their 4–3 win.

"I forgot all about the pain when I saw my blooper shot hit the shaft of [Bill] Gadsby's stick and shoot up into the top of the Detroit goal," Baun said later in the dressing room. "I just managed to make it to the blue line in time or it would have thrown our guys offside. Then I fired in the general direction of the goal." When asked if he would play in the seventh and deciding game in Toronto, he answered, "You think a little thing like this is going to make me miss the last chapter?"

The "little thing" as he described it, was a broken bone in his lower leg and while extremely painful, Baun was assured he could do no more damage to it. Once again he was taped and given a pain killer, and he took to the ice, receiving a roaring ovation from the Toronto crowd who jammed Maple Leaf Gardens on this Saturday night, April 25, 1964. The Leafs scored early and then hung onto a 1–0 lead into the third. The Leafs then proceeded to add three more goals to make it a 4–0 final and take their third straight Stanley Cup. Baun did not miss a single shift although his ankle had to be frozen again during the final period.

"I couldn't feel a thing from the knee down," he revealed after the game. "I stopped a couple of shots with my skate and didn't even feel the puck hit the blade. The only time it bothered me was when I tried to skate backwards." People often wondered how Baun was able to play in such agony, but the Leaf realized later on that he had an uncommonly high pain threshold. He was also able to block out the pain mentally, which helped him to overcome his injury.

Years later Baun wrote about his famous playoff goal, "[It] was the high point of years of determination, dedication and desire." There was no way a man like Baun was going to let a little broken bone in his leg stop him—not with the Stanley Cup on the line!

ORLAND KURTENBACH   forward

Orland Kurtenbach

Leafs Record:
9 Goals,
6 Assists,
15 Points

Maple Leaf Moment: 1965–66 Season

Punch Imlach, the Maple Leafs coach and general manager, was always reluctant to let go of a veteran such as Ron Stewart who had helped them win three Stanley Cups (1962, 1963, and 1964). But when the Leafs lost the Cup in 1965, Imlach decided to move a few long-time Leafs in the hopes of injecting new life into the club. Stewart was dealt to Boston for defenseman Pat Stapleton, forward Andy Hebenton, and center Orland Kurtenbach. Stapleton was picked up by Chicago in the intra-league draft while Hebenton was sent to the minors. These moves made Kurtenbach the key acquisition in the deal and that was just fine with Imlach.

"I'm convinced Kurtenbach can match muscles and trade punches with any man in the NHL," Imlach said of the deal that brought the six-foot-two, 180-pound center to Toronto. "He gives me a policeman for my bench, something we've lacked. We lacked muscle when we most needed it last spring [in the '65 playoffs]." Kurtenbach had worked his way back to the NHL after starting his career with New York and Boston between 1960 and 1962. The Bruins sent him back to the minors for the 1962–63 season and he dominated the Western Hockey League (WHL) (winning the most valuable player award) with the San Francisco Seals and solidifying his reputation as a feared fighter. He came back to the Bruins for two more NHL seasons before the Leafs picked him up.

Kurtenbach would only play one season as a Maple Leaf and although he appeared in all 70 games played by the team that year, there was one Kurtenbach contest that left an indelible impression on all Toronto fans. It came at Maple Leaf Gardens on the night of March 2, 1966, when the mighty Montreal Canadiens came into to town for a Wednesday-night contest. The game was tied 1–1 when a brawl broke out early in the second period. While other players were engaged in separate scraps, Kurtenbach squared off with Montreal defenseman Terry Harper.

Orland Kurtenbach was named the first-ever captain of the Vancouver Canucks where he played for four seasons. His career totals include 332 points in 639 games.

The husky (six-foot-one, 200-pound Montreal blueliner was a very good defenseman, but he had a habit of agitating the opposition. On this night Kurtenbach showed he was in no mood to be bothered and instead put a severe beating on the Canadien. The two went at it three different times during their encounter and out of it emerged Harper with sixteen stitches worth of damage pounded out by Kurtenbach's fists. Harper's bloodied face was not a pretty sight for the nearly 15,000 in attendance that night.

However, the Leaf center did not gloat over his rather decisive win, but made it clear that Harper always pushed the limits. "Harper is always coming in late when a skirmish starts, pushing and shoving. We pushed a little then started swinging," he said after the game. Reporters asked if he had ever taken any boxing lessons, but Kurtenbach said he never had, adding that he had never been in a street fight either. Harper might have disagreed with that considering the damage inflicted by a player he outweighed by 20 pounds! All said, the game ended in a 3–3 tie, but all everyone talked about was the fight.

Kurtenbach scored nine times for the Leafs and considering he was on the lower end of the team depth chart, that was a pretty good total. He scored his final goal of the season on night March 24, 1966, when the Leafs visited one of Kurtenbach's previous teams, the New York Rangers. Kurtenbach scored the game winner with less than six minutes to play in the first period. It was a power-play goal with the assist going to Leaf defenseman Kent Douglas. The goal put the Leafs up 2–1 and they went on to a rather easy 5–1 victory. Kurtenbach scored a total of 3 game-winning goals during that 1965–66 season.

The Leafs finished third during the regular season, which meant meeting the Montreal Canadiens in the first round of the playoffs. The Leafs were normally ready for post-season play, but this time they were wiped out by the Habs in four consecutive games. Brawling, fighting, and toughness did the Leafs absolutely no good in the playoffs (although it was not for a lack of trying) and Montreal, the defending Cup champions, went on to win their second-straight title to complete the '66 post-season.

Despite his good performance in his one year as a Maple Leaf, for some reason Imlach left Kurtenbach available in the June 1966 intra-league draft and he was snapped up by the Rangers. He stayed in New York for the next four seasons before his rights were claimed by the expansion Vancouver Canucks in 1970.

Pat Quinn

Leafs Record:
2 Goals,
12 Assists,
14 Points

Maple Leaf Moment: April 2, 1969

Defenseman Pat Quinn was known for his impressive size (six foot three, 215 pounds) and his rugged style, but he had only played minor-league hockey until he was twenty-five. The Hamilton, Ontario, native played junior hockey in his hometown then moved out West to play for the Edmonton Oil Kings. He was on the team that won the Memorial Cup in 1963 (12 points in 19 playoff games) and was then sent to Knoxville in the Eastern Hockey League (EHL) for one season. Detroit (who owned his professional rights) loaned him to Tulsa of the CPHL and he also played minor-league hockey in Memphis, Houston, and Seattle before returning to the Tulsa Oilers who were the Maple Leafs' minor-league affiliate. The Oilers won the championship in 1968 with Quinn a vital member of the defense. In March 1968, Toronto acquired Quinn's NHL rights from the St. Louis Blues (with the Leafs sending the rights to Dickie Moore back to the Blues as compensation) and he was eventually called up to the big-league team for 40 games during the 1968-69 season. It was obvious Quinn had improved his skill level to the point where he was no longer just a tough guy but a bruising blueliner who could clear the front of the net and add a little to the attack.

"Quinn is a welcome addition to any team," said Leaf captain

George Armstrong. "The players all know that if they get into any trouble on the ice, big Pat will be there to help." What Armstrong did not add was that Quinn was also pretty good at getting into trouble all on his own. In his 40-game stint with the Leafs in 1968–69, he quickly accumulated 95 penalty minutes, but that helped the Leafs get back into the playoffs that year by playing an aggressive brand of hockey. Quinn, however, would be at his hard-hitting best in the opening game against the Bruins to start the '69 post-season. The game scheduled for April 2, 1969, in Boston would prove to be one of the worst nights in Leaf playoff history, but at least Quinn would make it memorable on another account.

The Bruins were heavy favorites and they blitzed the Leafs with three consecutive goals to open the game. It was more of the same in the second stanza when the Bruins added four more goals to make it 7–0. They were killing the Leafs with great play and power-play goals led by Phil Esposito who lit the red light four times before the end of the second! Perhaps out of frustration or anger or both, Quinn decided to take matters into his own hands. Late in the second he caught Boston superstar Bobby Orr with his head down. At full speed and with his elbow high, Quinn launched his entire body off the ice and into the Bruin defenseman. Quinn's elbow landed squarely on Orr's head, knocking the unsuspecting puck carrier out cold on the ice. Orr was motionless with his eyes closed. A glove was put under his head for support. Quinn was given a five-minute major for elbowing and the enraged Boston fans tried to get at him in the penalty box. The Leafs came off the bench to get their teammate to safety (with the help of the local constabulary) while Orr was sent to hospital for observation. Wild brawling continued in the third period, but the Bruins poured it on even more to make it a 10–– final.

Afterward, there was as much talk about Quinn's hit as there was

Pat Quinn would coach the Maple Leafs to 300 wins between 1998 and 2006. Only Punch Imlach recorded more victories (365) as a Maple Leaf bench boss. Under Quinn the Leafs won 41 or more games six times and hit the 45 win total three times. He also coached Philadelphia (1980) and Vancouver (1994) to the Stanley Cup finals.

on the lopsided score. "It was a nice, clean check," Quinn said. "Maybe some people thought it was dirty. But like I said, I like to hit." Incredibly, Orr played the next night (recording one assist but indicating he was experiencing headaches) and Boston won 7–0 behind their great attack led by forwards such as Esposito, Ken Hodge, Johnny Bucyk, and Derek Sanderson. The only hope the Leafs had going home was in the fact that Boston had not won a game in Maple Leaf Gardens since November 1965!

It was a different story in these playoffs, however, and the Bruins won 4–2 and 3–2 to end the series in the quickest manner possible. Orr was in the lineup for both games and while still having trouble with headaches, he managed to record two assists over the final pair of games. His puck control was unbelievable throughout. Orr and Quinn shook hands at the end of the series and later, Orr blamed himself somewhat by saying he had his head down. Orr was surely concussed, but he was still allowed to play because that is how concussions were dealt with in this era of hockey.

In addition to Quinn's tremendous hit (which at least showed that the Leafs were not going to go down without a fight), there was more drama to come. Shortly after the embarrassing four-game sweep, Leafs coach and general manager Punch Imlach was pulled into a small office at Maple Leaf Gardens and unceremoniously fired right on the spot by Leaf owner Stafford Smythe. Imlach had guided the team through eleven great seasons of some of the best Leafs hockey ever played and gave the city four Stanley Cups.

Quinn played one more year for the Leafs before going to Vancouver and then to Atlanta to complete his 606-game NHL career.

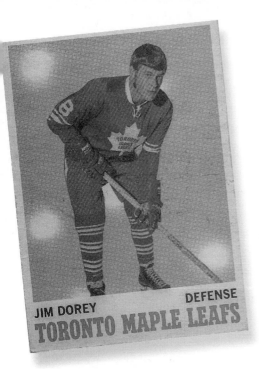

JIM DOREY
DEFENSE
TORONTO MAPLE LEAFS

Jim Dorey

Leafs Record:
25 Goals,
74 Assists,
99 Points

Maple Leaf Moment: February 3, 1971

When Jim Dorey began his NHL career with the Maple Leafs at the start of the 1968–69 season, he was largely an unknown quantity. The Leafs selected the six-foot-one, 190-pound defenseman twenty-third overall in the 1964 Amateur Draft and after he completed his junior career with the London Nationals, Toronto sent the rearguard to Tulsa of the Central Professional League for some seasoning. By October 1968, the Maple Leafs felt the youngster was ready for the NHL. It was good timing as there were now plenty of openings on the Toronto blue line with the team looking to get back into the playoffs. In just his second contest as a Leaf (and his first appearance at Maple Leaf Gardens), Dorey left a lasting impression on everybody (including the defenseman's father who was at the game) that watched the Leafs and Pittsburgh Penguins play to a 2–2 tie. It was October 16, 1968.

Before the night was over, Dorey had recorded 9 penalties, including 2 fighting majors, 2 10-minute misconducts, and one game misconduct. His 48-penalty-minute total also established a new 1-game NHL mark (which was surpassed in 1979 by Randy Holt of the Los Angeles Kings when he recorded 67 penalty minutes in a game against

Philadelphia). As he waited in the dressing room for the game to end, Dorey was certain that his second game would be his last. Instead, Leaf coach Punch Imlach gave him a $100 cash bonus and told him that's the kind of hockey the Leafs were looking for from him! The brash defender then went on to record 200 penalty minutes that very season. Dorey's notable rookie year saw him record 30 points (8 goals, 22 assists, his best performance while in Toronto), which helped the Leafs back into the post-season (if only for 4 games).

The Leafs finished out of the playoffs in 1969, but were back in contention for a playoff berth during the 1970–71 season. The team won 37 games and recorded 82 points, good enough for fourth place in the East Division. Dorey's 1969–70 season was shortened to 46 games because of a knee injury, but he was back for a strong campaign in 1970–71, recording 29 points (7 goals, 22 assists) while playing alongside defensive partner, the tough-as-nails Bobby Baun, who the Leafs had re-acquired in November 1970. In addition to his highly aggressive play (every tough guy in the NHL set their sights on him), Dorey could make a solid contribution to the Leafs attack. The night of February 3, 1971, was a perfect example of what he could do with the puck.

Jim Dorey was a part of the New England Whalers who won the World Hockey Association (WHA) championship in 1973, taking the first-ever Avco Cup. Dorey had 16 points (3 goals, 16 assists) in 19 playoff games for the Whalers in the 1973 post-season. He returned to Toronto in 1974 with the Toros who were in the rival WHA, but played in Maple Leaf Gardens until 1976. Dorey had a good career in the rival league recording 284 points in 431 games played.

The St. Louis Blues were in Toronto that night and got a pair of goals from Bill Sutherland to jump out to a 2–0 lead. On one of Sutherland's goals, Dorey was sitting in the penalty box for another of his many infractions, which totaled 198 penalty minutes that year., Before the first period was over, however, Dorey took a pass from Dave Keon and scored a goal to get the Leafs back in the game. Keon had two Blues defensemen worried about him, which left Dorey wide open. He then walked in on St. Louis netminder Ernie Wakely, deked the goalie down to the ice before depositing a shot in the net.

"Davey had them both suckered," Dorey said of the Blues defenders. "The left defenseman [Bob Plager] was way over, so that left the alley open. I yelled for a pass and broke in." The goal re-energized the Leafs and killed the Blues' spirit. Toronto scored the next 5 goals to win the game 6–2 and Dorey picked up another point on a goal by Brian Spencer.

Dorey's time in Toronto came to an end during the 1971–72 campaign when rumors surfaced that he had signed a contract with the World Hockey Association for the next season. Many other Leafs signed future contracts with the rival league, but only Dorey was dealt away before the season ended. The Leafs received a talented but meek winger (Pierre Jarry) from the New York Rangers in return (Dorey only played in two games for New York because of an injury), but the Toronto club missed his aggressive play and spirited effort. Dorey's 553 penalty minutes in 231 games are proof that the tough defenseman loved battling for the Maple Leafs. Years later Dorey recalled his days in Toronto with considerable fondness. "The Leafs were a contending team. It was an honor to play for them. I knew other players wanted to. I realize that today more than ever."

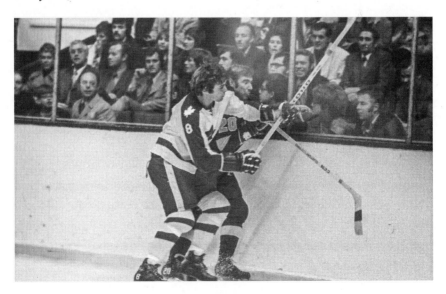

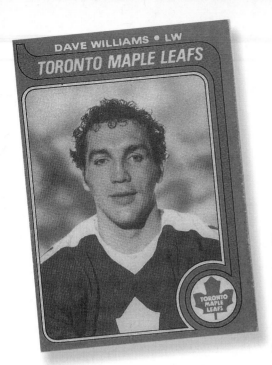

DAVE WILLIAMS • LW
TORONTO MAPLE LEAFS

Dave "Tiger" Williams

Leafs Record:
109 Goals,
132 Assists,
241 Points

Maple Leaf Moment: March 29, 1976

Dave "Tiger" Williams made it to the NHL through sheer will and determination. He was not a large player by any means (five foot eleven, 190 pounds) and not a very graceful skater, but Williams would fight for every inch of ice in junior, minor pro, and then in the NHL. The Leafs took him fairly high in the 1974 NHL draft (thirty-first overall) after he had an outstanding 1973–74 season in the WHL with the Swift Current Broncos (including 52 goals and 310 penalty minutes). The Weyburn, Saskatchewan, native had a burning desire to make the Maple Leafs after his first camp in '74, but he had to start in the minors for the first 39 games of the season. He recorded 27 points for the Oklahoma City Blazers before getting the call to help out a Leaf team that was desperate for some physical play.

Even though Williams had a very strong finish to his rookie year (29 points in just 42 games), nobody was quite sure if he was going to make it as a full-time NHL player. Williams made the Leafs roster to start the 1975–76 season and would end up playing in 78 games. He was even more aggressive in his first full season (totaling 229 penalty minutes), but he also showed another side to his game that made him even more valuable. One measure used to evaluate forward is to see if they can hit the 20-goal mark and in the 1975–76 campaign, Williams proved that he belonged in that prestigious club. The door swung open on March 29, 1976, during a game against the Pittsburgh Penguins.

Toronto started the game strongly by firing 18 shots at the Penguins net and had a 2–0 lead for their efforts on goals by Stan Weir and Bob Neely. Pittsburgh got back into the game with 2 goals in the second before the Leafs responded with 2 more of their own for a 4–2 lead at the end of two periods. Williams was having something of a quiet game (although he did contribute an assist on a goal by line mate Pat Boutette), but in the third he scored his twentieth of the year when Penguins goalie Michel Plasse left one side of the net open for the Leaf winger who snapped a shot home for his milestone marker. The Leafs hung on to win the game 5–4 outshooting the Penguins 35–28. It was the Leafs thirty-second win of the year.

> Dave Williams notched 513 points (241 goals, 271 assists) in 962 career games and also managed to record 3,966 penalty minutes! He also had 12 goals and 35 points in 83 playoff games.

"There have been some people who figured the only thing I could do was punch people in the mouth," Williams said. "But I admit there were times early in the season when I didn't think I'd make it [to the 20-goal level]." It was quite an accomplishment for the Leaf hard rock considering he had only 2 goals in the first 40 games of the season. "I guess I've fought every tough guy in the league, and earned a little respect. They know I can handle myself." It also helped when the Leafs recalled center Jack Valiquette from their Oklahoma City farm team and placed the lanky pivot between Williams and Boutette. The new trio helped take the pressure off the Leafs big line of Darryl Sittler, Lanny McDonald, and Errol Thompson.

Williams added one more goal in 1975–76 to bring his total to 21, but he did not score a single tally in 10 playoff games that year. Williams would not score 20 goals over the next three years but did manage to get 18, 19, and 19 over that time frame. He was, nevertheless, a very important player under coach Roger Neilson who wanted the Leafs to have a very physical presence. However, with Neilson no longer in charge in 1979–80, the Leafs emphasized more offense. Williams would tally 22 goals for Toronto that season before he was dealt to Vancouver in a four-player trade in March. Shocked and hurt, Williams went out to Vancouver and scored eight more goals to bring his season total to 30, a very rare number for such a pugnacious player who brought a tough approach into every game in which he appeared.

Williams racked up 35 goals and 62 points (both career bests) the next season for the Canucks helping the team make the 1982 Stanley Cup finals. The Leafs, on the other hand, continued to flounder without the toughest guy in the NHL.

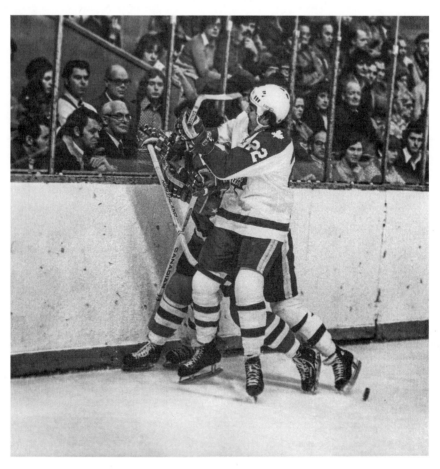

PAT BOUTETTE

Pat Boutette

Leafs Record:
59 Goals,
82 Assists,
141 Points

Maple Leaf Moment: April 9, 1976

Not many U.S.-college-trained players made it to the NHL during the 1970s and Pat Boutette probably faced the longest odds of all. The left-winger was listed at a paltry five foot eight, 175 pounds and was drafted in the ninth round (139th overall) of the 1972 NHL Draft. After he finished playing at the University of Minnesota at Duluth, Boutette was sent to the Leafs farm team in Oklahoma City for two seasons. There Boutette proved he could score at the professional level (68 points in 77 games played in 1974–75). His toughness (163 penalty minutes) also impressed the Leafs enough to give him a shot at the big league.

Boutette certainly made himself noticeable when he joined the Maple Leafs for the 1975–76 season, piling up 140 penalty minutes in 77 games. In addition to his rambunctious play, however, Boutette did find time to score 10 goals and add 22 assists during the regular season. But the feisty Leaf would save his best performance for the playoffs.

The Leafs opened the '76 post-season having to play the Pittsburgh Penguins in a best-of-three preliminary round series. Toronto opened it with a solid all-round performance, taking the game 4–1 on home ice. The Penguins evened the series with a 2–0 win in Pittsburgh forcing a deciding game showdown at Maple Leaf Gardens. It was April 9, 1976, a rare Friday-night game. The Leafs were favored as they had home-ice advantage, but they had to be wary of the high-scoring Penguins who could get their high-octane offense going virtually at will.

Behind Wayne Thomas's superlative goaltending, the Leafs played another strong game before 16,485 fans to win it 4–0 and take the series 2–1. The Leafs looked to be in trouble when Dave Williams took a five-minute major very early in the first, but Toronto managed to kill off the long power play. Then they scored the opening goal late in the first period when Boutette set up defenseman Jim McKenny. Boutette then scored in the second frame to give the Leafs a 2–0 lead. It was only right that Boutette got the goal since he did all the work to get the puck to teammate Ian Turnbull. Pittsburgh netminder Michel Plasse stopped Turnbull's drive, but Boutette put home the rebound. In addition to igniting the Leafs attack, Boutette, along with line mates Jack Valiquette and Williams, shut down Pittsburgh's number-one scoring line (made up of Pierre Larouche, Bob Kelly, and former Leaf winger Rick Kehoe). Borje Salming and Lanny McDonald added the other Leaf goals (Toronto took 36 shots on the Pittsburgh net) while Thomas earned the shut-out, stopping all 26 drives directed at him.

> Pat Boutette was traded to the Hartford Whalers in exchange for Bob Stephenson on December 27, 1979. Stephenson would play all of 14 games for the Maple Leafs, recording 2 goals and 2 assists. Boutette recorded 453 career points in 756 games.

After the game, the Leaf players spoke bravely about having to face the defending Stanley Cup champions in the next round. And they did give the bruising Philadelphia Flyers all they could handle over seven brutal games (it was one of the most violent playoff series in NHL history). But the "Broad Street Bullies" had the last game on home ice and took the contest 7–3 over a depleted Leaf lineup that simply did not have the depth to compete with the champions.

Boutette's penalty-minute totals were always high (107, 120, and 136) over his remaining years as Maple Leaf because the feisty but diminutive winger never took a backward step against anyone. One of his most memorable fights came in Philadelphia on March 7, 1977, when he finished a brawl against Bill Barber by tossing seven straight unanswered shots at the Flyer winger. The Leafs won that game 4–2 and nearly beat the Flyers in the '77 playoffs before defensive breakdowns ended their hopes of pulling off an upset.

Boutette was a very reliable third-line checker for the Leafs, but his talents were not appreciated when general manager Punch Imlach returned to Toronto in 1979. Although he had never scored more than 18 goals in any one season for Toronto, Boutette would record years of 28, 23, and 27 when he departed. The Leafs' media guide compared Boutette to fan favorite Dick Duff in terms of size and style of play. While he could not quite live up to Duff's Hall of Fame standards, Boutette's feistiness and determination will always be remembered fondly by Leaf fans who followed the team in the wild 1970s.

PHOTO BY
ROBERT SHAVER

MAPLE LEAFS
BOB McGILL DEFENSE
DÉFENSEUR

Bob McGill

Leafs Record:
4 Goals,
25 Assists,
29 Points

Maple Leaf Moment: November 4, 1981

Even though defenseman Bob McGill was drafted fairly high (twenty-sixth overall) by the Maple Leafs in 1980, he really had no business being on the big-league team as a nineteen-year-old in the 1981–82 season. A product of the Victoria Cougars of the WHL, McGill was taken because he was a solid stay-at-home type of blueliner who was not afraid to mix it up. In fact, McGill recorded a combined total of 525 penalty minutes in 136 games played over his last two seasons in Victoria. The Cougars (who won the WHL championship in 1981) were a very good team and McGill certainly knew his role with that club. However, playing in the NHL was a completely different story and McGill was simply not ready for the best league in the world at such a tender age.

McGill was willing to grapple with all comers, but the Leafs were such a bad team in 1981–82 (only 20 wins) that every mistake he made stood out. He tried to overcompensate by showing a willingness to fight (picking up 263 penalty minutes which is still a Leafs rookie record), but it was abundantly clear he needed some professional seasoning before he could become an effective NHL blueliner. There was one memorable night for the rookie and that came in his hometown of Edmonton when the Leafs visited the Oilers on November 4, 1981.

The Oilers were just about to embark on their dynasty years having put the pieces together around superstar Wayne Gretzky. The Edmonton club had won 9 of their first 13 starts when the Leafs came into town for the Wednesday-night contest. The Oilers scored forty-six seconds into the game and had a 3–1 lead after just one period. The Leafs lone tally in the opening stanza came from the stick of McGill, his first NHL goal. McGill came out of the penalty box, took a pass from Wilf Paiement and then broke in alone on Oilers netminder Grant Fuhr, a former junior teammate in Victoria. McGill knew Fuhr's tendencies, which might have helped him decide to pick the low corner on his breakaway attempt. The goal showed the Leafs were not going to be run over by the talented Oilers and they tied the game 4–4 by the end of the second period. However, Toronto netminder Michel Larocque could not hold the Oilers off in the third as they scored twice more to win the game 6–4. The Leafs did manage to hold Gretzky to one goal (scored in the last minute of the game) and one assist.

Unsurprisingly, McGill spent most of the next two seasons playing for the Leafs farm club in St. Catharines, Ontario, which did the rugged blue liner a world of good. He re-joined the Leafs on a full-time basis for the 1984–85 season when he recorded 250 penalty minutes with no goals in 72 games played; however, his plus/minus rating was an even zero, an improvement for McGill who had been a minus 24 in just 30 games with Toronto in 1982–83. He continued to improve and although the Leafs were not a strong club, they did make it back to the playoffs in 1986.

The first round of the '86 post-season was a best-of-five series against Chicago and McGill was given the task of shutting down Blackhawks winger Al Secord. He did such a good job that the Leafs

> *Just when it appeared they had stuck with Bob McGill long enough to make him a quality defenseman, the Maple Leafs traded him to Chicago early in September 1987 in a deal that, ironically enough, brought a used-up Al Secord to Toronto! McGill returned to Toronto for the 1992–93 season bringing his penalty-minute total as a Maple Leaf to 998. McGill has been a long-time analyst and reporter for Leafs TV.*

won the series in 3 straight games. By the time it was over, Secord was the most frustrated person in Maple Leaf Gardens. McGill more than handled himself in a fight with Secord in the third game, further deflating the uninspired Blackhawks club. McGill had also fought Secord in the second game in Chicago, leaving no doubt about the Leafs strategy in the series. Coach Dan Maloney had such faith in McGill and his defensive partner, Gary Nylund (a former first-round draft choice), that the pair went up against Chicago's big line, anchored by Denis Savard, for the entire 3-game set. On the strength of McGill's defense, that win in Toronto marked the first time the Leafs won a playoff series since 1979!

The Leaf players all appreciated what McGill had done for the team. Winger Steve Thomas made the point that Secord was an important leader for the Blackhawks and that when he was on, Savard would also be strong. "But when McGill handled Secord, it cooled him out and they had to respect us." McGill, the man they now called "Big Daddy," had indeed come a long way.

Lou Franceschetti

Leafs Record:
22 Goals,
16 Assists,
48 Points

Maple Leaf Moment: March 16, 1990

Toronto native Lou Franceschetti was not new to professional hockey when he was acquired from the Washington Capitals for a fifth-round draft pick in the summer of 1989. The hard-hitting winger had played in the minors for a number of years before becoming a full-time NHLer in 1985–86 with the Capitals who had drafted him seventy-first overall in 1978. Even though he had scored 40 goals and totaled 90 points in his final year of junior with the Niagara Falls Flyers, his role in the NHL was to be a grinding checker who was willing to hit and rack up some penalty minutes in the process.

When a hometown boy gets the chance to play with the Maple Leafs most do whatever they can to make their time in Toronto very special. Franceschetti was certainly thrilled to be a Leaf and made the 1989–90 season his best in the NHL: he had 21 goals and 15 assists for a total of 36 points, all career-high marks for the scrappy left-winger. A big part of his offensive success rested on the fact that the 1989–90 Leafs could score goals (337 in total, good for the third-highest total in the NHL). And Franceschetti proved that he could score at a very good rate if given the chance to escape his normal checking role. While

Franceschetti still found time to record 127 penalty minutes (his fifth straight year over the 100-minute mark), he also scored 4 game winners. None was more memorable, however, than the winner he had on March 16, 1990, in Buffalo's Memorial Auditorium.

Buffalo led this hard, physical game 2–1 by the end of the first; however, Vince Damphousse scored a goal in the second and another in the third (completing a hat trick in the process) to put Toronto on top 3–2. But the Sabres, who historically always give the Maple Leafs a miserable time on Buffalo ice, tied the score when ex-Leaf Rick Vaive tipped home a point shot from Phil Housley. Then, with Damphousse in the penalty box, Franceschetti came to the rescue with a blazing shot that went over the shoulder of goaltender Darren Puppa from just inside the Sabres blue line. It was Franceschetti's twenty-first of the season (he had never scored more than 12 in any previous year) and his first in 13 games. The goal came with more than five minutes to play and Toronto netminder Jeff Reese had to make some outstanding saves in the closing moments to preserve the 4–3 win, a rare victory for Buffalo, the NHL city closest to Toronto.

One of Lou Franceschetti's biggest ambitions when he made it to the NHL (after toiling in the minors for so many years) was to play in at least 400 career games so he could qualify for the lump-sum pension payment of $250,000. He played his 400th career game as a Maple Leaf.

After the game, the man who scored the winning goal said he simply let the shot go. "You don't start picking corners in that situation," Franceschetti said. "It was just a bang-bang thing." About his recent slump, he added, "I think I was looking at 30 goals too much. I've got to get back playing the way I played tonight, taking the body." It was the type of game that got Franceschetti into the NHL and made him a popular figure wherever he played, including especially, Toronto.

Damphousse might have been the second happiest Leaf when Franceschetti scored because it got him off the hook. "I was worried sitting there in the penalty box. But I felt confident we would kill the penalty and when we scored I was pretty happy," said Damphousse who was the first star of the game.

Franceschetti's winning marker was the last significant goal he scored for the Leafs. After only 1 goal the following season, and with the Toronto club struggling badly, the Leafs sent Franceschetti to the Sabres along with defenseman Brian Curran in exchange for Mike Foligno in December. Franceschetti finished out the year in Buffalo and played a few more years in the minors before ending his playing days in 1996. His time in Toronto was brief, to be sure, but for one shining season the hometown kid played some very good hockey for the Maple Leafs. The hard-nosed fan favorite was also the first former Leaf player introduced to the crowd during the closing ceremonies marking the final game played at Maple Leaf Gardens (February 13, 1999).

Felix Potvin

Felix Potvin

Leafs Record:
160 Wins,
149 Losses,
49 Ties,
12 Shut-outs

Maple Leaf Moment: November 10, 1996

It might be hard to believe that a Maple Leaf goalie would be included in a discussion about Toronto tough guys, but netminder Felix Potvin might be the only one that fits in this category. Actually, Potvin might make the category based largely on one spectacular night of work in Philadelphia in 1996, although he mixed it up pretty good against Detroit in the first two games of the 1993 playoffs. (Potvin quickly reformed, though, after coach Pat Burns told him to tone it down.) However in 1996-97 it was a different story—at least for one memorable fight.

The 1996–97 Leafs were going nowhere under coach Mike Murphy. The team used a total of forty-two skaters and three goalies during the regular season only to win 30 games and finish well out of the playoffs. General manager Cliff Fletcher did his best to bring in new players, but little seemed to work. Even the veteran players (such as Mats Sundin, Kirk Muller, Doug Gilmour, Wendel Clark, and Larry Murphy) could do little for a team that started the season with a 4-1 win over Anaheim at home and then promptly lost the next five games. By the time the Leafs landed in Philadelphia on November 10, 1996, however, Toronto had turned it around somewhat and had an 8–7 record on the year.

A game in Philadelphia is always an adventure for the Maple Leafs and this night was no exception. The Flyers opened the scoring on a goal by Pat Falloon, but the Leafs showed some spirit when winger Nick Kypreos dropped the gloves and pounded out a decision over Scott Daniels. Kypreos was tossed from the game for his efforts and the Leafs were then outshot 13–8 in the opening frame. The Flyers put 15 shots on Potvin in the second period, scoring once on a goal by John LeClair. Toronto got one back in the middle stanza from defenseman Mathieu Schneider but the Flyers added another by LeClair in the third to make it 3–1. Potvin stopped 39 of 42 shots and kept Toronto in the game. The Leafs responded to their goalie's good work with a feisty third period. Another fight broke out with just eight seconds to play featuring Toronto winger Tie Domi. But that was not the end of the story.

Felix Potvin, a goalie the Maple Leafs drafted and developed, was dealt away in 1999 to the New York Islanders after they had signed Curtis Joseph as a free agent. Potvin also played for Vancouver, Boston, and Los Angeles before his career ended at the age of thirty-two.

As the final buzzer was about to go, Flyer Daniel Lacroix took a run at Murphy. Potvin responded with a swing of his stick at the legs of the Philadelphia forward. That brought Wendel Clark to Potvin's aid, but Flyers netminder (and noted hothead) Ron Hextall tore down the ice to launch an attack upon Potvin. The Leaf netminder saw the charging Hextall coming at him and was ready to do battle. Everyone watching thought Hextall was going to lay a severe beating on the man known as "The Cat" if only because he was larger and had been involved in more battles than Potvin.

What Hextall did not know was that Potvin had some training in boxing and was not afraid to toss punches. When both facemasks came off it was a flurry of fists, with Potvin landing the more serious blows, cutting Hextall across the forehead. When the fight ended, Potvin was unmarked. "I saw Hexie coming and knew what he was coming for so I was ready," Potvin recounted later. "I had not been in any kind of a fight since my first year of junior. I was just sticking up for my teammate."

Credit should go to Hextall who was able to keep his arms swinging and land some blows even though he was noticeably bleeding. But the Philly goalie did acknowledge that Potvin got the better of him in this scrap. "[Heavyweight boxer Mike] Tyson got beat last night, what can I say?" he quipped. "I'm not looking to fight, believe me. He slashed one of our players and I didn't like it." Those comments were rather amusing considering that Hextall was known for swinging his big goalie stick at opponents—and it certainly appeared that Hextall was indeed looking for a fight seeing that he skated the whole length of the rink to get at Potvin. But no matter. Hextall had played a solid third period by making 12 saves and would have been better advised to stay in his crease at the end of the game.

The Leafs won all the fighting in the contest (a rare occurrence in Philadelphia), but they lost where it mattered most——on the scoreboard. Worse, they took no momentum out of the game and went on to lose seven of their next ten contests; however, all Leafs fans watching the Philadelphia game couldn't help but smile when Potvin won a TKO over a hated enemy. It was one of the few highlights of the rather dismal 1996–97 season with Potvin posting a 27–36–7 mark on the year. His loss total was the worst in the NHL that season, but he did win his only fight.

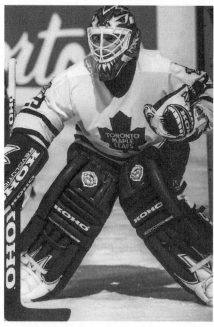

Colton Orr

Leaf Record:
8 Goals,
5 Assists,
13 Points

Maple Leaf Moment: February 11, 2013

By the time the 2011–12 NHL season was over, it looked like the career of tough guy Colton Orr was also at an end. The six-foot-three, 222-pound right-winger had only played in 5 games for the Toronto Maple Leafs that season (recording just 1 point on 1 goal) and was demoted to the Leafs AHL farm club, the Toronto Marlies. Rather than sulk about his plight, Orr focused on getting into better physical condition in an effort to work his way back up to the big league. Orr appeared in 26 regular-season games for the Marlies, and then in 8 post-season games for the AHL club that made it all the way to the Calder Cup finals in the spring of 2012. Marlies coach Dallas Eakins was very pleased with Orr's contributions and lauded the bruising winger's efforts to get his career back on track.

It was never an easy road for the Winnipeg native who was never drafted by an NHL team after a junior career that included stints in Kamloops, British Columbia, and Swift Current, and Regina, both in Saskatchewan. Never a gifted player (his career-best season was eight goals for the Kamloops Blazers in 2000–01), Orr made his mark with his aggressive play and his subsequent penalty-minute totals (570 penalty minutes in 164 games).

The Boston Bruins decided to sign him as a free agent, but he only played in 26 games for them. The New York Rangers then claimed him off waivers in November 2005. He enjoyed some good seasons on Broadway, but became a free agent once again in 2009. That's when Orr was scooped by the Maple Leafs for $1 million a season in a four-year contract. The Leafs were pleased to add any sort of toughness to their lineup while Orr scored 4 times and totaled six points over all 82 games in 2009–10. His 239 penalty minutes in the regular season was the second highest mark in the league; however, Orr did not get much ice time (averaging 6:52 minutes per game) and was proving to be a defensive liability when he did play. His work in his own end was rather poor and soon he was playing less and less for Leaf coach Ron Wilson (down to 4:29 minutes per game). He was eventually put on waivers, which he cleared, and was then sent to the Marlies.

Colton Orr has accumulated 1,076 career penalty minutes in just 422 NHL games played to the end of the 2012-13 season. He has scored 12 career goals and added 12 assists to date.

Orr's resurgence under Eakins got him another chance under new Leafs coach Randy Carlyle and he was on the big-league roster when the lockout-shortened 2012–13 season began. The Leafs had an entirely different look and approach under Carlyle and there was much more emphasis on physical play and fighting. During the Leafs home opener, Orr delighted the Air Canada Centre fans by pounding out a fighting decision over towering (six-foot-eight, 270-pound) Buffalo forward John Scott, setting the tone for the Leafs season. On February 11, 2013, the Philadelphia Flyers rolled in to Toronto looking to keep their dominance over the Leafs intact. Orr and the Leafs wanted to show the Flyers they would not be pushed around anymore and the winger made another type of contribution.

Led by goals twenty-eight seconds apart from Orr and winger Matt Frattin, the Leafs defeated the Flyers 5–2. Orr's goal (his only tally of the season) broke a 1–1 tie early in the second when he rapped a puck into the Flyers net; Frattin followed up immediately afterward to make it 3–1 for the home team. "It feels good for us to contribute," Orr said of his fourth-line duties, "and gives us some confidence out there when we can contribute in other ways than just forechecking and fighting and stuff like that." Orr's main contribution throughout the season, however, still involved his physical play and willingness to drop the gloves when needed.

The win over the Flyers gave the Leafs an 8–5 record on their way to a 26–17–5 finish and their first playoff appearance in nine seasons. Orr led the league in penalty minutes with 155 (in 44 games played) and he appeared in all 7 post-season games for the Leafs.

Orr had shown himself to be a much more responsible and better prepared player throughout the 2012–13 campaign. He was able to cash in on his good performance with a new two-year contract with the Maple Leafs who did not let him become an unrestricted free agent. Orr was rather ineffective for the Maple Leafs in 2013-14 and will have to work hard to retain his role with Toronto or any other NHL team in the near future.

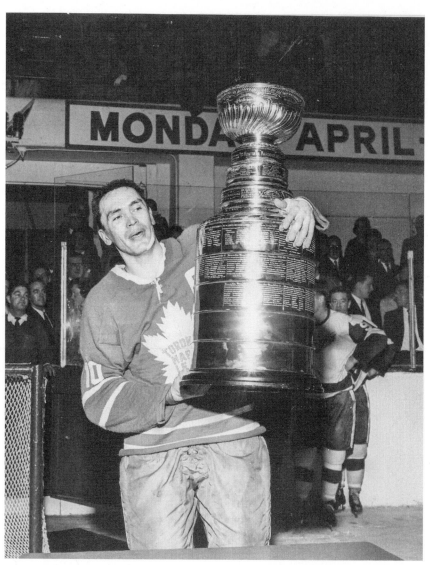

George Armstrong captained the Maple Leafs to four Stanley Cups in the 1960s.

LEADERSHIP

Syl Apps • Walter "Turk" Broda • Ted Kennedy • George Armstrong
Dave Keon • Darryl Sittler • Rick Vaive • Doug Gilmour
Mats Sundin • Dion Phaneuf

THE MAPLE LEAFS HAVE had some great leaders over their long history, many of them named team captain at some point during their stay in Toronto. Maple Leaf leaders are a special breed because they have lifted the team on their shoulders and provided the fans with many memorable performances, including Stanley Cups victories. It is never an easy task to lead when much is expected of you and your every move is scrutinized as soon the blue-and-white sweater is pulled on for the first time. The players listed below proved their mettle and each reached a level of greatness under the spotlight that comes with being a leader on the Toronto Maple Leaf hockey club.

Syl Apps

Leaf Record:
201 Goals,
231 Assists,
432 Points

Maple Leaf Moment: 1942 Stanley Cup Finals

Syl Apps was a natural at just about everything he tried over the course of his life. An outstanding athlete (the Leafs discovered him while he was playing football), scholar, and gentleman, Apps would also turn out to be a great hockey player. He made his first impression as an NHL player in his rookie year when he scored 16 goals and added 29 assists during the 48-game 1936–37 season. Given his style, character and playing abilities, it was only fitting that Apps would take over as team captain by the time Toronto defenseman Red Horner retired in 1940. His appointment as team leader would never be regretted and his leadership skills during the 1942 Stanley Cup finals would only reconfirm the Leafs decision to make Apps team captain.

The Detroit Red Wings were a rather mediocre team during the 1941–42 season and although they got hot in the playoffs, the Wings were not supposed to be any match for the mighty Maple Leafs in the finals. Toronto's strong club was led by all-stars such as goalie Turk Broda, defenseman Bucko McDonald, and high-scoring forwards such as Gord Drillon and Apps. The Red Wings, however, had a shock in store for the

Maple Leafs and their fans.

The first 2 games were at Maple Leaf Gardens; and the Red Wings took both contests by scores of 3–2 and 4–3. The stunned Leafs promptly lost the third game of the series in Detroit and were facing elimination by the fourth contest. If there was a time for great leadership on the Toronto side, the opportunity was now at hand. Years later, Apps recalled sitting in the dressing room prior to game four. "The only thing on our minds was we can't go back to Toronto if we lose this game too. We weren't necessarily thinking about winning the Stanley Cup... we were thinking we couldn't lose four straight and face the people back home."

Even the fear of humiliation did not seem to do much for the Leafs who soon found themselves down 2–0 by the halfway mark of the game. But two Leaf goals tied the game going into the third period. Detroit scored early in the final frame and the Maple Leafs looked to be done, but Apps scored less than two minutes later to even the score once again. With less than eight minutes remaining, Apps set up Nick Metz's winner by outworking two Detroit players for a loose puck. The Leafs had just avoided the embarrassment of a sweep. Apps' goal (his first of the finals) was the most important tally of the night in the 4–3 win and gave the Toronto side new life. It was the Leafs most inspired effort of the series and a number of roster moves by coach Hap Day gave Toronto some fresh legs.

The 1942 Stanley Cup champion Maple Leafs are still the only team in professional sports history to win a final (championship) series after being down 3–0 in games. Syl Apps had his sweater number 10 honored by the Maple Leafs on October 3, 1993.

Back on home ice, the Leafs blitzed the Red Wings 9–3. Apps was on fire, recording 2 points on 2 goals and 3 assists. Toronto was confident they could now force a seventh game back home and a 3–0 victory in Detroit in the sixth contest assured that would happen on Saturday night, April 18, 1942.

After two periods of play, however, the Leafs were down 1–0 and it looked like all that hard work launching an incredible comeback might go for nothing. But the Leaf captain came to the rescue once again forcing Jimmy Orlando of the Red Wings to take a penalty for tripping the Toronto star. Then Dave "Sweeney" Schriner scored on the power play and suddenly the score was tied. Pete Langelle scored the winner—the most important goal of his career—just two minutes later, while Schriner added another to make it a 3–1 final. It was the Leafs first Cup win since 1931, and it all came on the back of the Leafs star captain who had seized the moment and led the way for his team.

The Stanley Cup was presented to Apps who made sure Leaf owner Conn Smythe (on leave from the Canadian army during WWII) was front and center. "Come on out, Conn," Apps was heard saying out loud. "You waited long enough for this Cup. Come and get it." Apps then turned his attention to teammate Schriner who had scored twice on the night. "That was a grand game for us and you did it. You should have had three more goals." Toronto fans celebrated long into the night, their thoughts temporarily away from the war in Europe. Apps may have summarized things best for Leaf fans by saying, "It was a long wait but it was worth it."

Walter "Turk" Broda

Leaf Record:
302 Wins,
224 Losses,
101 Ties

Maple Leaf Moment: 1951 Semi-Finals

Walter "Turk" Broda was one of the best "money" goalies of all time and, incredibly, he backstopped the Maple Leafs to five Stanley Cups during his NHL career.

The portly netminder came to Toronto when the Leafs acquired his rights from the Detroit Red Wings in 1936, but nobody would have bet that he would turn into a legend by the time his career was over. The jovial goalie was popular with his teammates and was a true leader who could backstop them to victories in many important games, particularly in the playoffs when all the money was on the line. The unflappable Broda never let the pressure get to him and did not let jokes about his weight bother him either. Nothing affected his play.

Broda was instrumental in the Leafs successes during the forties, and was in net each time the Toronto side clinched the Stanley Cup in 1942, 1947, 1948, and 1949. In '42, he held off the Detroit Red Wings after they climbed ahead 3–0 in games during the final, giving the Leafs a chance to come back and win the next four contests. The resounding win over Detroit gave Broda a large boost of self-confidence that helped him win three more Stanley Cup titles. By the time the 1950–51 season began, the veteran goaltender was sharing the Leafs net duties with Al Rollins who was charged with starting the '51 post-season. An injury took Rollins out of the lineup and in rode Broda to save the day one last time.

Broda never thought he would see much action when the 1951 post-season began. Rollins had played in 40 of the 70 regular-season games that year. But as the backup, Broda posted a very respectable 14–11–5 mark in 30 appearances.

The second-place Leafs hosted the fourth-place Bruins (led by Milt Schmidt) in the opening round of the playoffs and Rollins was indeed the starter; however, he was hit by Bruins forward Pete Horocek and injured his knee in the first period. Broda was forced into the game (getting dressed in the intermission) and the Leafs dropped the opening game. A second contest was called off with the score tied 1–1 in overtime because of local Toronto curfews (all sporting activities had to stop at midnight on a Saturday night because of a curfew on Sunday sports). That meant the Leafs were going to Boston in need of a win or face the risk of an upset.

> Turk Broda and Ted Kennedy are the only two Leaf players whose names appear on the Stanley Cup five times. Broda's sweater number 1 was honored by the Leafs on March 11, 1995.

The balding thirty-six-year-old Broda needed to show he had something left in the tank on April 1, 1951. As was the case throughout his long career, Broda did not let his team down—and this time before 13,768 rabid Boston supporters. A rough first period saw the team scoreless, but the Leafs took a 1–0 lead in the second on a goal by Cal Gardner. Another tally by Leafs defenseman Fern Flaman put Toronto up by two before the second period was over. A third period marker by Max Bentley sealed a tidy 3–0 victory for the Leafs with Broda turning back 16 Bruin drives on the night. While he did not face a high shot count, Broda was flopping all over the ice to make more than one great save and kept the Bruins off the score sheet. It was the one hundredth professional playoff game of Broda's career (94 were NHL contests) and he earned his twelfth post-season shutout.

Leafs owner Conn Smythe was delighted by Broda's performance, commenting, "And that Broda! He comes out of his hinterland to shut them out." After another Leafs win in Boston, Bruins forward Ed Sandford said of Broda, "That old guy is a marvel. I can't beat him." Toronto took the series with a 6–0 win on home ice. This meant the Leafs would face the Montreal Canadiens in the finals. "Now I can relax for a few days. Al [Rollins)]should be in shape by Wednesday [the day the finals would start)] so I guess it's about time I got a rest."

Broda was still in net the night the Leafs won the opening game 3–2 (his sixtieth and final playoff win), but after losing 3–2 in overtime in the next contest, the Leafs turned back to Rollins for the rest of the finals. The Leafs won their fourth Stanley Cup in five years, but it might not have happened if Broda had not stepped again up and shown the leadership they had relied upon for so many great years.

Ted Kennedy

Leaf Record:
231 Goals,
329 Assists,
560 Points

Maple Leaf Moment: 1951 Stanley Cup Finals

"I'd like to become as great a player as Syl Apps. I'd like to be as great a captain as he was and to gain the respect everyone held for Syl," said Ted Kennedy about his mentor Syl Apps

When Syl Apps retired after the Maple Leafs Stanley Cup triumph in 1948, it was thought there might be a leadership vacuum on the club at the forward position, especially at center. Concern also centered around who would wear the captain's "C" on his sweater. There was no need to worry because Toronto had a leader in waiting with Ted Kennedy ready to assume the all-important role. He was announced as the Leafs new captain to start the 1948–49 season.

Kennedy first joined the Leafs during the 1942–43 campaign after his rights were acquired from the Montreal Canadiens. From the moment of his arrival, the gritty center showed class and character, and would help the Leafs win Stanley Cups in 1945, 1947, 1948, and 1949. He was not an ultra-skilled player but he *was* determined. And his leadership skills were unquestioned. The man known as "Teeder" would not hesitate to keep a teammate in line. And he also had a knack for scoring and setting up important goals, most often in the playoffs. In his first year as team captain the Leafs rallied in the playoffs to retain the Stanley Cup with Kennedy recording 14 points (including 9 goals) in 9 games. The next year (1949) saw him score 8 points in 9 playoff games as the Leafs won their third-straight Cup—the first NHL team to do so. After losing to Detroit in the '50 post-season, the Leafs got another chance to win the Cup in 1951. Once again it was Kennedy who stepped up at a crucial moment.

The Detroit Red Wings were the best team during the 1950–51 season with a record 101 points, but they were upset by the Montreal Canadiens in 6 games during the semi-finals. The second-place Maple Leafs disposed of the Boston Bruins in the other first-round series to set up an all-Canadian final, the first since 1947.

Toronto took the opener 3–2 on an overtime marker by Sid Smith, but the Canadiens evened the series when Maurice Richard scored in extra time in

> Maple Leafs owner and general manager Conn Smythe paid the greatest tribute to Ted Kennedy by calling him the quintessential Maple Leaf player.

the second contest at Maple Leaf Gardens. The Habs were now heading home with some momentum on their side and the Montreal Forum crowd of more than 14,000 was ready to jeer the Leafs at every turn on. It was a tense struggle between the two clubs and it once again went to an extra session before it was decided.

Richard opened the scoring on a power play before the game was even three minutes old, putting a Bert Olmstead rebound past Leafs netminder Al Rollins. The Canadiens continued to pour it on but Rollins held firm. Toronto left-winger Sid Smith then tied it up when the Leafs had the extra man to make it 1–1. The game remained tied through the end of the third with both teams taking turns dominating play.

It was now time for the Leafs captain to shine. Early in the overtime Kennedy had to sweep a puck out from behind Rollins to keep the Habs from scoring. Just fifty seconds later Kennedy picked off an errant clearing attempt by Montreal defenseman Calum MacKay. It went right to Kennedy at the face-off dot and he calmly picked the far corner of the net beating goaltender Gerry MacNeil for the all-important 2–1 victory.

The Leafs won the next game in overtime and returned home with a chance to capture their fourth Stanley Cup in five years.

The Habs would not go down without a fight and led the game 2–1 with less than a minute to play. The Leafs had to chase down a loose puck skittering toward their net empty but then managed to get a face-off in the Montreal end. Kennedy, one of the best face-off men in the NHL, was on the draw for the Leafs. He was able to get the puck free to Tod Sloan who slapped in his second of the game to tie the score before a delirious crowd at the Gardens. Overtime again!

The Leafs took the Cup when defenseman Bill Barilko scored on a rush-in from the blue line, perhaps the most famous goal in Maple Leafs history. It was a wild scene in the dressing room as the Leafs celebrated. Kennedy threw his arms around Barilko and slapped him on the back. In typical fashion, Kennedy thought Toronto coach Joe Primeau (under fire during the playoffs) deserved all the accolades. "If anyone deserves credit more than any other, it's our coach."

However, it was really Kennedy who made sure the Leafs fortunes were saved in the third and fifth games of the finals. It was just your typical performance from the greatest of Maple Leaf leaders.

George Armstrong

Leaf Record:
296 Goals,
417 Assists,
713 Points

Maple Leaf Moment: 1964 Stanley Cup Finals

By 1957, hockey legend and Maple Leafs owner Conn Smythe was fading back from the day-to-day operations of the team he helped found in 1927. One of his last acts as boss, however, was to install George Armstrong as team captain to start the 1957–58 season. The native of Skead, Ontario, had long been considered one of the Leafs best prospects and he became a consistent if unspectacular performer from the moment he first joined the club for the 1949–50 campaign. It became clear that Armstrong was not going to be a top goal scorer at the NHL level (he never scored more than 23 in any one season despite being a pretty good offensive player in junior and senior hockey). But Armstrong would prove to be a highly reliable right-winger for a club record 1,187 career games.

Armstrong was extremely proud of his Native heritage and just as proud to wear the "C" on his sweater. He became known as a ferocious checker who could be counted upon for 15 to 20 goals a year and his wicked sense of humor always kept his teammates loose and smiling. Armstrong could work in the corners of the rink like few others, and his good size and strength helped him win many battles along the boards. He would captain the Maple Leafs to four Stanley Cups (the most by any

Toronto captain) and he often saved his best performances for the post-season. One such playoff year stands out in particular.

The 1964 playoffs opened with the third-place Maple Leafs battling the first-place Montreal Canadiens. The tough 7-game series was eventually decided by a Leafs 3–1 triumph at the Montreal Forum. Two nights later on April 11, Toronto hosted the Detroit Red Wings at the Gardens. The Red Wings had just come off a seventh-game victory over the Chicago Black Hawks so nobody knew quite what to expect from them. But the Leafs certainly did not want to get off to a bad start by giving away home-ice advantage.

George Armstrong would be a very successful junior coach leading the Toronto Marlboros to two Memorial Cups (1973 and 1975). He would coach the Maple Leafs for 47 games in 1988–89, posting a 17–26–4 record. His sweater number 10 was honored by the Maple Leafs on February 28, 1998.

As it happened Detroit scored early in the first period on a goal by Bruce MacGregor. But the Leafs were undaunted and Armstrong quickly evened the score when he stood in front of the net to deflect an Allan Stanley drive from the point past Detroit goalie Terry Sawchuk. Gordie Howe put the Red Wings back in front with a goal before the first period came to a close. The second period was scoreless and it looked like the feared fatigue factor from the previous series would put the Leafs down a game to start the Stanley Cup final.

The Leafs, however, would not quit and made a nice play to even the score during a power-play opportunity in the third. Dave Keon chased down a loose puck and got it over to Don McKenney. The puck was then passed to Red Kelly who took a shot on Sawchuk. The Red Wing netminder made the save, but left a juicy rebound for Armstrong who knocked it into the net to knot up the score 2–2. It was the second goal the Leaf captain scored while in good position in front of the opposition net. He often scored big goals by being in the right spot.

A late short-handed goal with just two seconds to play gained the Leafs a big victory and set the visiting Red Wings back after a game they felt they should have won. Armstrong was named the first star of the game and was interviewed on CBC's *Hockey Night in Canada* after the contest. "I was hoping we could hold them off because we were a man short. I thought if we got through the game [regulation time]that we could get a rest, come out and kill off the rest of the penalty, then give it a good shot in overtime." Asked about the Red Wings style of play, Armstrong accurately responded, "Any team that can best Chicago certainly has to be playing good hockey. We had a very tough time."

The '64 finals went to a seventh game with the Leafs winning it 4–0 on home ice. Armstrong scored the fourth goal (his seventh point of the series and thirteenth in the post-season) of the game with a high shot from the face-off dot over a dispirited Sawchuk. Armstrong gathered his team around the Stanley Cup—the Leafs third in a row—which stood large on a table as photographers snapped pictures. Armstrong then carried the silver trophy to an interview with Ward Cornell and told the *Hockey Night in Canada* host, "We've never lost the last game and tonight is no exception." Those were well-chosen words from a respected leader who always gave his best when it mattered most.

DAVE KEON

CENTER

TORONTO MAPLE LEAFS

Dave Keon

Leaf Record:
365 Goals,
493 Assists,
858 Points

Maple Leaf Moment: April 13, 1965

Dave Keon was not expected to make the Toronto roster in the fall of 1960, but he showed enough to earn a spot on the team right out of junior. The Leafs were concerned the five-foot-nine, 160-pound center might face too many hard hits in the minor leagues (where the refereeing was not up to NHL standards) and perhaps ruin his chances to play in the big league at some point. The Leafs concerns, however, were unfounded since Keon could out-skate any opponent. His skill level was so high that he could also play a solid two-way game night after night. But no one could fault the Leafs in trying to protect their young asset.

Keon quickly showed he belonged in Toronto. He had a 20-goal season in 1960–61, winning the Calder Trophy as the NHL's best rookie. The Leafs had rebuilt their team by the time Keon joined and he soon proved to be the kind of clutch hockey player who saves his best for the most important games. A second-team All-Star in just his second season, Keon would help the Leafs recapture the Stanley Cup in 1962 and repeat as champions in 1963 and 1964. He scored many important goals during those championship years, establishing himself as team leader when all the chips were on the table. He scored 2 short-handed goals in the final game of the '63 playoffs (the first player in NHL history to do so in the post-season), and recorded a hat trick against Montreal in the seventh game of the 1964 semi-finals to keep the Leafs dream alive for a third-straight title. Between 1962 and 1964, Keon played in 36 post-season games and recorded 29 points, including 19 goals.

The Leafs hopes for a fourth consecutive Stanley Cup were on thin ice after the Montreal Canadiens had won the first two games of the 1965 semi-finals. They returned home for the third game on April 6, 1965, and knew a win was imperative if they had any hope of retaining the Cup. The Leafs tied the game 2–2 in the third period, but the tension mounted in Maple Leaf Gardens as the game went into overtime.

Less than five minutes into the extra session, Keon jumped onto the ice replacing Red Kelly on a line change. Leafs' Frank Mahovlich caught up to a loose puck that had been misplayed by Montreal goalie Gump Worsley (who had been anticipating an icing call). The "Big M" brushed off an attempted check by defenseman J.C. Tremblay and the puck lay open to the onrushing Keon. The slick Leaf center moved past a surprised Ted Harris of the Canadiens before backhanding a shot past a still-startled Worsley. The crowd went wild celebrating the 3–2 win, while an enterprising young man jumped over the glass and made off with the game-winning puck, but not before a *Toronto Star* photographer snapped a photo of his escape that appeared on the front page of the paper the very next day!

> Dave Keon was the Leafs captain from 1969 to 1974, a time when the team was no longer in championship form. Nevertheless, in 448 regular-season games wearing the "C," Keon managed 371 points, with 166 goals included in that total. Also, in 22 playoff games as team captain, Keon recorded 18 points.

Keon may have missed out on a souvenir but no matter. "I saw Frank knock the puck from Tremblay," he recalled. "I got it, managed to beat Harris and let go a backhander. Some nights they go in, some nights they don't. This was my night. I had better shots earlier." It was Keon's only overtime winner in his illustrious career as a Maple Leaf.

Toronto coach Punch Imlach was now happy to be back in the

series. "Of all my good-luck charms," the superstitious bench boss said, "Keon is the biggest four-leaf clover." The Leafs tied the series with another victory two nights later, but the Canadiens eventually won it by taking the next two games, the final win coming in overtime at the Gardens.

Keon ultimately got some measure of revenge two years later when he won the Conn Smythe Trophy (as of 2013, still the only Maple Leaf player to win the prestigious award) for his outstanding performance in the 1967 playoffs, a post-season that featured the Leafs beating the Habs in the Stanley Cup finals. Keon's work throughout the '67 playoffs (against Chicago and Montreal) was simply marvelous. And although Keon only scored three times, it was clear the native of Noranda, Quebec, was the Leafs best player in the '67 playoffs which saw the Leafs win it all. It was also Keon's fourth and final championship.

When George Armstrong was in his last years with the Leafs, it was decided that Keon wear the captain's "C" on his sweater, a distinction he clearly deserved from the moment he first put on the blue-and-white jersey.

Darryl Sittler

Leaf Record:
389 Goals,
527 Assists,
916 Points

Maple Leafs Moment: October 14, 1978

When Darryl Sittler arrived for his first NHL training camp in 1970, he immediately got the message that the team had great expectations for him. The six-foot, 190-pound first-round draft choice (eighth overall in 1970) also saw that sweater number 27 was waiting for him in his dressing room stall. It was a clear signal that the Maple Leafs thought Sittler could be as good as the player who wore that sweater previously: the four-time Stanley Cup winning left-winger, Frank Mahovlich.

Sittler did not back away from the challenge and in his third NHL season he scored 29 times and recorded 77 points in 78 games.

He was soon the most dominating personality on the team, and his goal total was usually in the 40-plus range. He was a difficult center to play against and his physical style earned him enough room on the ice to operate like a superstar. By 1975–76 the entire team revolved around his leadership and when veteran Dave Keon left for the World Hockey Association in 1975, Sittler assumed the Leaf captaincy. It was never in better hands.

Sittler had a magical year in 1976: he had a ridiculous 10-point night against the Boston Bruins (still an NHL record); notched 5 goals in 1 playoff game versus Philadelphia; and scored the winning goal in overtime against Czechoslovakia to give Team Canada the first- ever Canada Cup Tournament championship held in September. The curly haired Maple Leaf was celebrated all over Canada and his leadership of the Toronto club was unquestioned.

However, the Leaf captain was never more put to the test than during the 1978–79 season. After a surprising upset of the New York Islanders in the '78 post-season, expectations for the team were sky-high the next year. Such hopes might have been unrealistic, but the Leafs captain was more than ready for the challenge as the new season began.

As much as Darryl Sittler loved being a Maple Leaf, he eventually asked to be traded not wanting to stay around and live with the turmoil Leafs owner Harold Ballard always caused. Ballard also refused to give Sittler as much as he was paying star defenseman Borje Salming on a new contract. So Sittler was sent to the Philadelphia Flyers, ironically enough a bitter rival of the Leafs during Sittler's best years in Toronto. He was inducted into the Hall of Fame in 1989 and his sweater number 27 was honored by the Maple Leafs on February 8, 2003.

After an opening night win in Pittsburgh during which Sittler scored twice, the team returned to Maple Leaf Gardens for their home opener against the Islanders on October 14. Everyone expected a low-scoring affair, much like they witnessed in the '78 playoffs. Instead, they would see an entirely different kind of game.

Sittler opened the scoring and set up another in the opening frame to give the Leafs a 2–1 lead. The second period saw an 8-goal barrage during which Sittler added another assist to his total (fans also witnessed Islanders superstar defenseman Denis Potvin score 3 straight goals). In the third, Sittler scored 2 more and added 2 more assists, giving him 7 points on the night in a wild 10–7 Leafs victory. Islander veterans Billy Smith and Glenn Resch shared the netminding on this night, but there was no stopping the Leafs top center, who assisted on goals by Ron Wilson, Lanny McDonald, and two by Dave Williams.

After the game, Sittler was his usual modest self. "It was a case of both teams jumping on just about every scoring chance,"he commented. Sittler became the first player in history to record 7 or more points in 2 NHL games (the other his 10-point outburst versus Boston on February 7, 1976). And no other Leaf player has recorded more than 6 points in 1 game since Sittler's great performances.

Sittler's great start kept him on top of the NHL's scoring race for a while (13 points in the first 7 games), but a knee injury cost him 10 games and he finished with 87 points, good for twelfth best in the league. He was also instrumental in getting Roger Neilson back behind the bench when he had been "fired" by owner Harold Ballard after a game in Montreal. After a first-round win over Atlanta, however, the Leafs were ousted once again by the mighty Montreal Canadiens in the '79 post-season.

If the 1978–79 season was a trying time for the Toronto leader, it was nothing compared to what Sittler endured in 1979-80 when Punch Imlach returned as general manager. To say the two never saw eye-to-eye would be a huge understatement. In spite of all the turmoil off the ice (which included giving up the captaincy late in December after seeing his best friend and line mate Lanny McDonald traded away), Sittler produced a 97-point season—a great testament to his character and leadership skills.

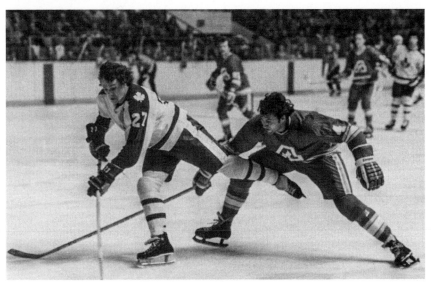

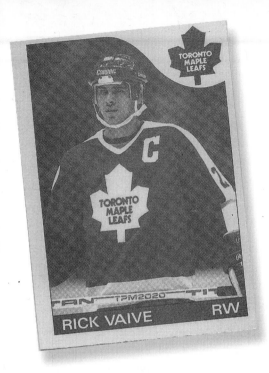

Rick Vaive

Leaf Record:
299 Goals,
238 Assists,
537 Points

Maple Leaf Moment: March 14, 1984

Rick Vaive was a young man when he was traded to the Maple Leafs in March 1980. The hard-shooting right-winger was twenty years old and had already been discarded by the Vancouver Canucks who had selected him fifth overall during the 1979 NHL Entry Draft. The Vancouver club expected plenty from their budding star (Vaive had excelled in his one season with the Birmingham Bulls of the World Hockey Association, scoring 26 times), but gave the six-foot-one winger away, along with Bill Derlago, when the Leafs offered veteran players Dave "Tiger" Williams and Jerry Butler to the Canucks.

The Leafs were a team in transition, but the youngster still managed a 33-goal campaign in 1980–81. Toronto captain Darryl Sittler left the team after a strong dispute with upper management, and the Leafs expected Vaive to fill the leadership void by naming him captain after Sittler was traded during the 1981–82 season. The youngster responded with two 50-goal seasons (including the first-ever by a Leaf when he racked up 54 in 1981–82) despite the daunting demands of being team captain in hockey-mad Toronto. Vaive persevered (although not perfectly) in the leadership role and maintained his status as the best player on the club despite trying circumstances which featured the wretched ownership of Harold Ballard and a team that lacked in star power at practically all positions. The following season, Vaive tried to remain a 50-goal scorer on a team that really needed *his* offense to have any hope of winning most nights.

The 1983–84 version of the Toronto Maple Leafs was not good. Saddled with poor goaltending (a too-young Allan Bester and an aging Mike Palmateer), a very green blue line, and weak forwards, the Leafs managed all of 26 wins over the 80-game NHL schedule while losing 45 contests. Amazingly, the Leafs were still in the playoff hunt until almost the end of the season thanks to the pitifully weak Norris Division. Toronto chased the fourth-place Chicago Blackhawks for the final playoff spot largely on the basis of the Vaive's offensive leadership. The feisty right-winger was the team's only true star and on the night of March 14, 1984, he was trying for the magic 50 mark once again as the Leafs hosted the Minnesota North Stars.

Rick Vaive was the Leafs captain between 1982 and 1986. His captaincy was taken away from him (and never given back) by Toronto coach Dan Maloney after Vaive slept-in during a road trip and missed a practice. It was a rather harsh penalty for a player who had given so much on the ice to his team.

Vaive entered the game with 48 tallies, but managed to notch his forty-ninth just two minutes into the game when he broke in alone on goalie Gilles Meloche and put a backhand drive home. He was assisted on the play by Russ Courtnall and defenseman Jim Benning. Just over six minutes later a falling Gary Leeman managed to slide a puck over to Vaive who then put in a drive off Meloche's leg for his fiftieth. High fives were the order of the day and the Maple Leaf Gardens crowd gave the twenty-year-old a standing ovation. Scoring 50 goals for the third time put the Leaf captain in the elite company of Bobby Hull, Guy Lafleur, Phil Esposito, Marcel Dionne, Mike Bossy, and Wayne Gretzky. And it's safe to say all the other players on the exclusive list played on much better teams than Vaive.

"It was very gratifying for me," Vaive said after the game. "A lot of people felt my first 50-goal season was a fluke. When I got 50 a second time, some of them still weren't convinced. I think they are convinced now." Despite Vaive's inspired performance, the Leafs could only manage a 3–3 tie with the North Stars, further stalling their dim playoff hopes. Vaive noted that, "There is really nothing to celebrate at this point. That will come if we get into the playoffs. That's the most important thing." The Leafs, however, missed the playoffs to close out the 1983–84 campaign and Vaive finished with 52 goals, but he was never as appreciated again during his stay in Toronto. When Wendel Clark joined the Leafs in 1985, Vaive's role on the team diminished to the point where he was considered a tradable commodity.

Vaive never scored 50 goals again (he did record seasons of 35, 32, and 32 goals in Toronto), but the Leafs made the playoffs after the 1985–86 and 1986–87 seasons, winning two series in the process. In September 1987, Vaive was traded to the Chicago Blackhawks in a five-player swap. He scored 43 times in his one season there and then had 29- and 25-goal seasons for Buffalo.

It was a very bleak time for the Toronto Maple Leafs, and Vaive's goal scoring and leadership were greatly missed after he was dealt away.

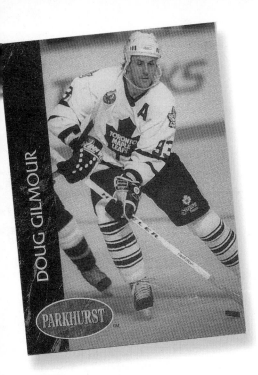

Doug Gilmour

Leaf Record:
131 Goals,
321 Assists,
452 Points

Maple Leaf Moment: May 3, 1993

From the moment Doug Gilmour stepped onto the ice as a member of the Maple Leafs, it was easy to see that the Toronto team was now different. Gilmour came to the Leafs in a massive ten-player deal on January 2, 1992, and his impact was immediate. Gilmour became available when the Calgary Flames refused to meet his contract demands. Fortunately, Toronto general manager Cliff Fletcher knew exactly what he was getting in the feisty Gilmour since he had traded for the center when he managed the Flames years earlier. In fact, Gilmour helped take the Flames to their only Stanley Cup win in 1989.

Immediately upon his arrival, the Toronto Maple Leafs began revolving around Gilmour's superb play. The gifted playmaker did not score a great many goals himself, but he set up others with superior passing skills and the willingness to battle against much larger opposition players to get at a loose puck. The Leafs quickly rallied around their new offensive weapon and the team started to take shape as a contender. New players were brought in to support Gilmour and coach Pat Burns gave his best player plenty of ice time. The Leafs returned to the playoffs after the 1992–93 regular season under Gilmour's point-scoring leadership (notching a single-season team record 127 points) and were ready to be a factor in post-season.

The Maple Leafs defeated Detroit in the seventh game of their first-round series on May 1, 1993. Gilmour had 4 points (1 goal, 3 assists) in the decisive contest, and it was hard to imagine that he could provide any more drama than he already had versus the Wings. However, two nights later Leaf fans learned their smallest (listed at five foot eleven and 177 pounds) but most effective forward had plenty of excitement left to give. Toronto was hosting St. Louis to start the second round of the '93 playoffs.

Doug Gilmour's sweater number 93 was honored by the Maple Leafs on January 31, 2009. He was inducted into the Hockey Hall of Fame in 2011.

The opening game proved to be a very tight contest as goaltenders Felix Potvin of the Leafs and Curtis Joseph of the Blues dominated play. Joseph was especially strong, letting in only 1 goal in the first, as the Leafs poured shot after shot at the netminder. After the Blues tied it 1–1 in the second stanza, the game settled into a nail-biter waiting for some shooter to step forward and end the grueling contest. The stage was set for Gilmour to work his magic and after 3:16 of the second overtime period, the shifty Leaf pivot made his move.

Gilmour found himself with the puck all alone behind the St. Louis net. As teammates Dave Andreychuk and Nikolai Borschevsky occupied the attention of Blues defenders, Gilmour swerved back and forth behind the goal trying to out manoeuvre Joseph and any Blues defenseman trying to check him. A quick spin back in one direction caught the Blues goalie to one side of the net. Gilmour then pounced, stuffing in the puck from the other side for a 2–1 Leafs win! The goal marked the sixty-forth Toronto shot on the St. Louis net. The tense Maple Leaf Gardens crowd went wild.

After the game, Toronto coach Pat Burns spoke for everybody on the Leafs side when he said, "I don't have words left. We deserved to win and that's it." When asked if he was at all concerned about his star player wearing out, he added, "What would I save him for? August? Dougie knows, when he's tired he comes off, when he's not tired, he's out there."

If others were concerned about his stamina Gilmour was not the least bit concerned. He then pointed out that his teammates deserve just as much credit for the Leafs playoff success as he did. "We all have certain roles on the team. My job is to go out and produce points while playing a defensive style as well. Everyone on the team is a leader in their own right. We don't have one leader on this team, we have a team of leaders. I just want to be an impact player. That's what I am thinking about right now." With those words, Gilmour had succinctly summarized his role on the Leafs.

St. Louis coach and former NHL player Bob Berry probably said it a little better: "To me, Doug Gilmour is by far the best player in the league at both ends of the rink right now. He's the best I've seen in a long time." Leaf fans would heartily agree and are forever grateful for the excitement and leadership number 93 brought to the Toronto club during his entire time as a Maple Leaf.

The Leafs nearly made their first final appearance since 1967, but the Los Angeles Kings, led by Wayne Gretzky, edged them out in seven games to end the incredible '93 playoff run for Toronto.

Mats Sundin

Leaf Record:
420 Goals,
567 Assists,
987 Points

Maple Leaf Moment: April 13, 2001

All Toronto hockey fans were shocked on June 28, 1994, when management announced they had traded away captain Wendel Clark, a heart-and-soul player ever since he joined the club in 1985–86. Although there were other players involved, the principal return for the Leafs in the deal with the Quebec Nordiques was a young Swede named Mats Sundin. The six-foot-five, 231-pound Sundin had been drafted first overall by Quebec in the 1989 Entry Draft and even though he had produced four excellent seasons for the Nordiques, they were not prepared to offer him the kind of lucrative contract Sundin believed he deserved. The Nordiques also wanted to change their team makeup and believed Clark would provide a different sort of spark.

Toronto fans were not sure what to make of the superbly talented center they received back in the multi-player swap, but their apprehensions were eased when they watched the smooth Swede in action.

Sundin's best season with the Leafs came when he registered 94 points (41 goal, 53 assists) in 1996–97 and by this time, he was clearly the best player on the team, especially so after team captain Doug Gilmour was traded away to the New Jersey Devils. After careful consideration, the Leafs decided to give the captaincy to Sundin (there was really no other choice). He would wear the "C" on his sweater until the end of the 2007–08 season. Sundin holds many Maple Leaf team records (including most career points), but left the team without ever winning the Stanley Cup or leading the team to the finals. Nevertheless, Sundin performed well in the post-season, with one of his most memorable performances coming at the expense of the Leafs provincial rivals.

The Ottawa Senators won 48 games during the 2000–01 season and finished with 109 points—19 more than Toronto. When the two clubs were paired up in the first round of the playoffs, few expected the somewhat disappointing Leafs (37–29–16) to give the Senators much of a battle. The Leafs, though, *did* have five 20-or-more goal scorers, a top goalie in Curtis Joseph, and a gritty, ill-tempered club which could spark at times under top point (74) producer Sundin. Nevertheless, the Toronto side was a definite underdog when the series started in Ottawa on Friday, April 13, 2001.

Mats Sundin holds many Maple Leaf team records, including the mark for most career game-winning goals with 79! The Leafs honored Sundin's sweater number 13 on February 11, 2012. He was inducted into the Hall of Fame in 2012.

Throughout the game, the Leafs took a number of bad penalties (giving Ottawa six power plays), but they did not allow a single goal thanks mostly to Joseph's stellar work. Trouble was, they could not get one past Ottawa netminder Patrick Lalime who was playing in his first post-season contest.

A scoreless tie went into overtime giving the Leafs a distinct chance to steal the opener. Sundin had always been a top performer in regular-season overtime situations (fourteen such winners for the Leafs over the course of his career in Toronto). But the Leafs captain had scored just 1 game-ending tally in the playoffs. The play in the extra session this night was fairly even (6 shots to 5 for Ottawa). Then Sundin found himself with the puck at the Senators blue line. Thinking that he and his line mates should go off on a line change, Sundin hesitated. It was then he noticed that teammate Steve Thomas had headed to the front of the Ottawa net. Thomas attracted two Senator defensemen providing Sundin with a bit of a screen. The big Swede wound up and rifled a shot that hit the far post and rattled in past a startled Lalime! The Leafs had a 1–0 road win on Sundin's brilliant play—and the only significant playoff winner in his career as a Maple Leaf.

"When you're playing street hockey as a kid, you dream about scoring overtime goals," Sundin said after the game. "That's a lot of fun." He also commented on the goal. "I was actually going to change but [Thomas] yelled he was passing to me. I took a couple of strides and shot it. I heard it hit the post and went in. It was a little fluky one, but I'll take it." The goal seemed to inspire the Leafs to greater heights and they took the Senators out in 4 straight games ruining their rival's great season. The Leafs were eliminated in the next round by the New Jersey Devils, but for a brief moment, the captain had taken his team to a spot no one else could have imagined at the start of the 2001 playoffs.

Dion Phaneuf

Leaf Record:
39 Goals,
104 Assists,
143 Points

Maple Leaf Moment: March 16, 2011

Defenseman Dion Phaneuf was clearly shocked when he was traded to the Maple Leafs on January 31, 2010. He believed himself an important member of the Calgary Flames, a team that drafted him ninth overall in 2003 and nurtured him along to the point where he was a runner-up to Nicklas Lidstrom of Detroit for the Norris Trophy in 2008. That year the big defenseman produced 17 goals and 60 points in the regular campaign. Phaneuf's top performance earned him a new contract worth $6.5 million a year, but the Flames soon came to regret giving the bruising (six-foot-four, 214-pound) blueliner such a lucrative deal. They sought to move him and the Maple Leafs were more than happy to add a sterling defender to their team. Phaneuf quickly got over the shock as soon as he arrived in his new city. He began to make his presence felt in the dressing room—and on the ice—finishing the 2009–10 season with 10 points in 26 games with the Leafs.

Toronto management liked what they saw in Phaneuf and decided to challenge the defenseman even further: He was named team captain on June 14, 2010, the eighteenth player to receive the honor since the club became known as "Maple Leafs" in 1927. The Leafs had sent four players to the Flames to complete the Phaneuf deal and clearly wanted to maximize the return and show fans they had traded for something special—a new leader. Like any other major move in Toronto, the decision to give Phaneuf the coveted "C" was closely scrutinized and harshly reviewed by some media members, but it did not bother the defender who took it all in stride. Phaneuf has always been very willing to stand up in the dressing room and face all the media's questions. And he is not afraid to give an honest answer.

The Leafs acquired Dion Phaneuf, a native of Edmonton, by sending Matt Stajan, Ian White, Nicklas Hagman, and Jamal Mayers to the Calgary Flames. Fredrik Sjostrom and Keith Aulie also came to the Maple Leafs in the multi-player exchange. Since coming to Toronto, Phaneuf has established "Phaneuf's Friends in the Captain's Corner," which provides a private suite at the Air Canada Centre for children (and their families) who are patients at the Hospital for Sick Children so they can watch a Maple Leafs game.

His first season as captain was a little uneven under coach Ron Wilson. The team finished with a winning record of 37–34–11, good for 85 points, but out of the 2011 playoffs. The Leafs were in the running for a post-season spot well into March, and they were still hoping for some playoff action when the club visited the Carolina Hurricanes on March 16, 2011.

Both teams were chasing the last spot in the Eastern Conference playoff race held by the Buffalo Sabres. When the night was done, it was the Maple Leafs, led by Phaneuf and goalie James Reimer (36 saves), who crept closest to the Sabres.

The Hurricanes opened the scoring on a goal by Chad LaRose on a Carolina power play, but Phaneuf one-timed a shot from the point to tie it up before the first period was over. Phaneuf's hard drive deflected in off Carolina defenseman Tim Gleason and then goalie Cam Ward before crossing the goal line. The game remained tied until the second when Phaneuf broke the tie after taking another hard shot that eluded Ward. Just twelve seconds later, Phaneuf gained his third point (a season high for him) of the night when he helped set up a goal by Tyler Bozak to give the Toronto side an insurmountable 3–1 lead that was nursed home the rest of the way. The win gave the Leafs a 5–0–2 mark over their last 7 road games and provided hope they might catch the Sabres. "They're huge points for our team and it's a big win," Phaneuf said after the game.

Although the Leafs failed to catch Buffalo, it was still a pretty good ending for the team, and Phaneuf in particular, since he had missed 16 games earlier in the season when a skate sliced his leg in early November. If Phaneuf had not missed so much time, the team might have made up more ground in the standings. The Leafs' captain, though, did manage 30 points (8 goals, 22 assists) in 66 games played.

Phaneuf's performance over the course of his first full year with the Leafs indicated that the team was going to rely on him for plenty of minutes (an average of 25:18 per night—the most of any Maple Leaf player) and lots of work on the power-play and penalty-killing units. He took the third-most shots on goal (190) for the Leafs and blocked 121 opposition drives. It was readily apparent that the blueliner had become a highly valued club leader who set a good example for his teammates.

Phaneuf continued his fine play in 2011–12 with 44 points (including 12 goals), but the Leafs missed the playoffs once again. In 2012–13 Phaneuf played alongside rookie defensemen Mike Kostka and Korbinian Holzer for a good part of the 48-game schedule and he still managed 28 points. He was also logging a tremendous amount of ice time (25:11 minutes on average without a word of complaint) under new coach Randy Carlyle in the shortened 2012–13 campaign. The Leafs returned to the playoffs in the '13 post-season before dropping a very exciting 7-game series to Boston. His only goal of the playoffs was significant because it helped the Leafs force a seventh contest (after being down 3–1 in games earlier) with a 2–1 win at the Air Canada Centre.

Phaneuf signed a new seven-year contract which made many fans happy and others not so much. His leadership was brought into question when the Leafs missed the playoffs in '14 but it is likely the blueliner will get a chance to redeem himself starting in 2014-15.

Toronto centre Billy Harris is in the middle of the third row of this team photo.

LOCAL BOYS

Billy Harris • Brian Conacher • Mike Palmateer
Bruce Boudreau • Dave Reid • Mark Osborne • Peter Zezel
Mike Johnson • Joe Nieuwendyk • Matt Stajan

THE GREATER TORONTO AREA (GTA) has produced many National Hockey League players over the years. As a result, a good number of these players have had the golden opportunity to perform for their beloved hometown team in front of friends and family. Many years ago Toronto-area boys had to impress Leafs owner Conn Smythe and his scouting staff (which included the legendary Frank Selke) to get contract to play for the renamed (from St. Patricks to Maple Leafs) hockey heroes. Years later (beginning in 1969) a few are very fortunate to get selected by the Maple Leafs during the NHL Entry Draft while others have arrived to play for the blue and white after a trade is completed. Some others have the occasion to come back to Toronto when they become free agents, usually late in their careers, and they seem quite happy to do so. The Leafs have passed on some golden opportunities to get more GTA-born players on the team over the years, but many who grew up in this hockey-rich area and went on to play elsewhere in the NHL still recall many Leaf greats, such as Syl Apps, Dave Keon, Frank Mahovlich, Darryl Sittler, Wendel Clark, and Doug Gilmour, as their childhood hockey heroes. Starring for the hometown team was special, especially for the following players who experienced a moment of great joy when they donned the Maple Leaf sweater

Billy Harris

Leaf Record:
106 Goals,
161 Assists,
287 Points

Maple Leaf Moment: December 2, 1961

Billy Harris clearly recalls growing up in Toronto, listening to legendary broadcaster Foster Hewitt on the radio as the Maple Leafs came back from a 3 games to none deficit to defeat the Detroit Red Wings and capture the 1942 Stanley Cup. Harris's father died in action during the Second World War, but the youngster's dream of being a hockey player carried on and he began playing in the Maple Leaf chain of junior teams in the 1950s. He played Junior B hockey for the Weston Dukes in 1950–51 and recalled how Leafs legend Syl Apps spoke at one of his hockey banquets. Harris eventually joined the Toronto Marlboros and was a key player when the team won the Memorial Cup in 1955. He had 66 points (37 goals, 29 assists) in the 47-game regular season and then added 39 points in 24 total playoff games. Harris broke into the NHL the following year and enjoyed a 22-goal year in 1958–59, a season that saw the Leafs finally get back to respectability after missing the playoffs the previous season. Harris would never score 20 or more again, but he had a strong hand in the Leafs three-straight Stanley Cup wins between 1962 and 1964.

By the time the 1961–62 season began, Harris was pretty much restricted to a backup center role behind Toronto stars such as Dave Keon, Red Kelly, and Bob Pulford. Not one to complain, Harris accepted his position on the team and waited for chances whenever they presented themselves. One such occasion came Saturday night, December 2, 1961 when Keon was out with an injury. Chicago was in town looking to climb up in the standings. The defending Stanley Cup champions opened the 1961–62 season slowly (only 6 wins in 20 games), but they were still a formidable hockey club especially with Glenn Hall in goal, and Stan Makita and Bobby Hull up front.

The Leafs, however, were ready to make a statement of their own with Harris opening the scoring at 4:02 of the first period. After taking a George Armstrong pass, he then broke in on Hall with a Chicago defender on his back. He fired a shot past the Black Hawks goalie to give the Leafs a quick 1–0 lead. Toronto had a 3–0 advantage for before Chicago hit the scoreboard to end the first period.

After a scoreless second stanza, the Black Hawks got closer on a goal by Bronco Horvath, but Harris then scored his second of the game with a backhand drive that eluded Hall. Harris made a neat play to get past Chicago defenseman Dollard St. Laurent before unleashing his drive. The Black Hawks responded once more to make it 4–3; however, Harris restored the Leafs 2-goal lead when he tipped in an Armstrong shot. The third goal of the game for Harris would turn out to be the game winner as the teams exchanged goals to end the contest 6–4 in the Leafs' favor.

Harris's hat trick was the second of his career (his first came against

During the 1964 Stanley Cup finals versus Detroit, Billy Harris scored his only goal of the series during the sixth contest to tie the score 3–3 late in the second period. His goal set the stage for Bobby Baun's dramatic overtime winner and sent the series back to Toronto for a seventh game. Harris picked up 1 assist (on a goal by Keon) and 2 penalties in game seven, a contest the Leafs won 4–0. "Toronto is the greatest city in the world, populated by great people. Torontonians have always loved their hockey team. No matter what. Winning means nothing if you have no one to share it with," Harris said on playing hockey in Toronto for Maple Leaf fans.

Terry Sawchuk when the netminder was with the Bruins in 1957), but this one might have been the most important as it showed he could come off the bench (in his hometown, no less) and make a significant contribution to a powerful Leaf team. The three goals were also timely for twenty-year-old Maple Leaf goalie (and future Hall of Famer) Gerry Cheevers who made his NHL debut that night. The next night, Harris scored the Leafs' only goal in Detroit during a 3–1 loss to the Red Wings. That goal in Detroit gave Harris four goals over the weekend and closed Cheevers' career record with the Leafs at 1–1. (Toronto tried their best to keep Cheevers in their organization but Boston picked him up in the Intra-league Draft in June 1965 while the Leafs hung on to Johnny Bower and Sawchuk.)

Harris would play in 67 games in 1961–62 with a very respectable 15 goals and 25 points during a year that saw the Maple Leafs win their first Stanley Cup since 1951. Harris would never star again as a Maple Leaf as he had in the fifties, but the hometown hero's contribution to three straight championships could never be questioned.

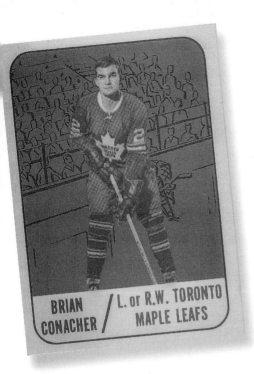

BRIAN CONACHER / L. or R.W. TORONTO MAPLE LEAFS

Brian Conacher

Leaf Record:
25 Goals,
27 Assists,
52 Points

Maple Leaf Moment: April 18, 1967

The Conacher family was famous throughout Canada for its athletic prowess. In the 1930s, Charlie Conacher became the Maple Leafs first superstar while his brother, Lionel, was named Canada's top athlete of the first half century, excelling in a variety of sports, including hockey (he was on teams that won the Memorial Cup, two Stanley Cups, and even football's Grey Cup). Another brother, Roy, won the NHL scoring title during the 1948–49 season. Brian Conacher (Lionel's son) was born into this amazing athletic environment and excelled at football, but eventually hockey won out, and the kid from Toronto followed in the steps of his famous forebears.

Tall at six foot three but a slender 197 pounds, Brian played junior hockey for the Marlboros and then for Canada's national team before deciding to turn professional. He did not have a long career with the Maple Leafs, but one magical season in 1966–67 left an indelible mark on Toronto's hockey history.

Nobody knew what the 1967 playoffs would hold for the Maple Leafs. The team spent the regular season alternating between very good and very bad, which landed them in third place with 32 wins and 75 points over a 70-game schedule. The Leafs faced the first-place team in the last post-season of the Original Six—and that meant a best-of-seven meeting against the Chicago Black Hawks who finished 19 points ahead of Toronto. Led by Bobby Hull, Stan Mikita, Pierre Pilote, Phil Esposito, and Kenny Wharram, the Black Hawks were heavily favored to beat the Leafs rather handily. With that in mind, the veteran-laden Leafs called a team meeting before the playoffs and plotted to control Chicago's attack by closely watching Hull and Mikita. For the most part the Leafs plan worked and the two teams spilt the first 4 games of the series. However, the Leafs won the fifth game in Chicago and came home with a chance to wrap up the series on April 18, 1967 before 15, 977 fans at Maple Leaf Gardens.

Brian Conacher scored 14 goals and added 13 assists during the 1966–67 regular season—his rookie year. He would also play in the NHL for the Detroit Red Wings before his 155-game (28 goals, 28 assists) career came to an end. Conacher also played one season for the Ottawa Nationals in the World Hockey Association recording 27 points in 69 games played during the 1972–73 campaign.

The '67 Leafs got contributions from a variety of unexpected sources (including Pete Stemkowski, Ron Ellis, Mike Walton, Larry Hillman, and Jim Pappin), but Conacher was the biggest surprise of all. After the third game against Chicago, the rookie winger replaced an injured George Armstrong on a line with Dave Keon and Frank Mahovlich. Conacher fit in perfectly with the two future Hall of Fame players and, in the sixth game, they struck first to give the Leafs a 1–0 lead in the opening period. Before the game was six minutes old, Conacher scored his first of the playoffs with Mahovlich and Keon getting the assists. The "Big M" did most of the work on the opening marker giving Conacher a pass he drove past netminder Hall.

On his second goal, Conacher got things going with a heavy check on Chicago defenseman Ed Van Impe. Keon picked up the puck and moved in with Conacher on a two-on-one with only Pat Stapleton back to defend for the Black Hawks. Keon fed Conacher a pass that then went in off Hall to give the Leafs a 2–1 advantage, a lead they would not give up over the 3–1 victory. In the dressing room after the game, Conacher said, "I still can't believe I got two goals in one playoff game. I just fired the puck on those two goals. It was as simple as that." Conacher then elaborated on his style of play. "You go out there and try to play as hard as you can. Some nights you don't play too well but you play as hard as you can. I'm just not a consistent hockey player but I try as hard as I can every night." Conacher may have been a little hard on himself, but the 2-goal effort against Chicago marked the first time in 23 games that he had hit the score sheet.

The contact-wearing (he was often kidded about his poor eyesight) Conacher scored one more important goal in the playoffs at the Montreal Forum during the fifth game of the Stanley Cup finals. It helped ensure another Leaf upset and put the Conacher name back on the Stanley Cup much like his uncle Charlie had done for the Leafs in 1932. Both Conachers were born in Toronto and each helped the Maple Leafs achieve hockey's highest honour.

Mike Palmateer

Leaf Record:
129 Wins,
112 Losses,
41 Ties,
15 Shutouts

Maple Leaf Moment: 1976–77 Season

It seems that goalie Mike Palmateer was destined to be a Maple Leaf from the moment he started playing hockey. The Toronto native played in the Marlboro chain of teams as a youngster and experienced winning on more than one occasion. He helped the Markham Waxers win an Ontario championship in 1972 and then helped the Marlboros win the Memorial Cup in 1973. The Leafs were lucky to land the roly-poly five-foot-nine netminder with a selection in the fifth round of the 1974 draft. They then sent him to the minors for some seasoning in cities such as Saginaw, Oklahoma City, and Dallas. His style was one of flash, drama, and reflex, but he could stop the puck when he had to and the Leafs needed someone to step up and take the net. When they called up the twenty-three-year-old goalie for the first time, Palmateer promptly declared that the Leafs search for a netminder was over!

When the Maple Leafs got off to a poor start (1–5–3) to the 1976–77 season, they turned to Palmateer to give them some stability in goal. Wayne Thomas was not as sharp as he had been the previous season while Gord McRae was only regarded as an experienced backup. Winless in 7-straight games, the Leafs were in Detroit on October 28,

1976, having lost 5–3 to Minnesota the previous night at home. Luckily for Toronto, the Red Wings were not much of a team either (they would only win 16 games that year), but the players wearing blue and white were in desperate need of a win and they pinned much of their hopes on the little rookie netminder.

It was by no means a pretty victory, but the Leafs played a basic game to register a 3–1 win. Defenseman Borje Salming was back in the lineup and set up 2 goals (one by Bob Neely and one by Darryl Sittler) while Dave Williams scored another to give the Leafs a 2-goal margin. The only Red Wing to beat Palmateer was Danny Gare, but the goaltender was otherwise perfect in his first NHL start.

Leaf coach Red Kelly commented after the game: "Palmateer did the job but the guys in front of him played the type of hockey we have to do anything. We had discipline and control in our play, checking hard and waiting for opposition mistakes."

As for Palmateer, he was relieved he had shown well in the opening contest of his career. "This was a big night in my life, the chance to show what I could do in the NHL and to get my foot in the door. I wasn't too nervous but then I had a hectic 24 hours and was a little tired. That helped me relax," he said about his journey to arrive in Motown in time for the game.

> On November 17, 1976, at Maple Leaf Gardens Mike Palmateer and the Leafs shocked the Stanley Cup–champion Montreal Canadiens with a 1–0 victory in one the most exciting contests played that season. The Leaf goalie was at his acrobatic best stopping 39 Montreal shots. Opposing netminder (and another Toronto-area kid) Ken Dryden said, "It was obvious he [Palmateer] played well. It was an honest shutout and he earned it."

The Leafs went 3–2–1 over their next six games and found themselves in Vancouver to end a four-game road trip on November 13 a Saturday-night contest. Palmateer faced 30 Canuck drives (25 in the first two periods) and turned them all aside while Neely, Inge Hammarstrom, and Pat Boutette scored the Leaf markers. Palmateer's shutout was the highlight of some much better play from the team that had been expected to be something of a contender in 1976–77.

The goalie commented after the exhausting road trip that he had seen some great play in front of his net. "I think I've played well and I've learned a great deal since I got here. The guys have been checking and clearing beautifully. I think we've done well because every player has worked his behind off."

Both coaches had good things to say about Palmateer's efforts that night. Leaf coach Red Kelly said, "Palmateer has been exceptional and the shutout shows he won't ease up. He battled hard for it right to the end and his gung-ho attitude lifts the team."

Vancouver coach Phil Maloney focused more on the netminder's style. "He's a gutsy little devil and he's extremely quick.... He doesn't do everything right but he compensates with speed and reflexes." The Leafs record after 17 games was a more respectable 6–7–4.

The Leafs would go on to post a 33–32–15 regular-season mark for the 1976–77 campaign (for seventh-best in the league) mostly on the strength on Palmateer's 23–18–8 record that included four shutouts. All in all an excellent start for the kid who came home to lead the Leafs back to respectability.

BRUCE BOUDREAU

Bruce Boudreau

Leaf Record:
27 Goals,
42 Assists,
69 Points

Maple Leaf Moment: December 16, 1977

Bruce Boudreau was not the largest player (listed at five foot nine, 175 pounds), but he could sure talk a big game, thus earning the nickname "Gabby." When he played junior hockey in his home town of Toronto, Boudreau showed he was more than just a talker by recording 165 points (68 goals, 97 assists) in 69 games. It was the 1974–75 season and the Marlboros won their second Memorial Cup with Boudreau on the club (he was also on the team in 1973). Considered too small and a little slow on his skates by most NHL teams, the Leafs nonetheless selected him forty-second overall in the 1975 draft, but the playmaking center instead signed with the Minnesota Fighting Saints of the World Hockey Association. He was then promptly sent down to the Johnston Jets, a team that was used in the filming of the hockey classic, *Slapshot,* starring Paul Newman. Boudreau played half a season in Minnesota during the 1975–76 season but signed with the Maple Leafs for the following year.

Boudreau first joined the Maple Leafs for 15 games during the 1976–77 season and scored his first goal against goalie Jim Rutherford when the Leafs beat Detroit 6–0 on March 13. It was only 1 of 2 goals Boudreau notched during his stay in the NHL that season. The Leafs were hoping the junior scoring sensation could repeat at the big-league level, but mostly Boudreau toiled in the minors.

The 1977–78 season provided Boudreau another opportunity, but the Leafs (now coached by Roger Neilson) were still unsure of what they had in the Toronto native. A game against the Minnesota North Stars on December 16, 1977, gave Toronto management reason to keep Boudreau up with the big team.

The Leafs had won 5 of their last 6 games when they traveled to Minnesota for a Friday-night contest. It turned out to be memorable for more than one reason. The Leafs won the game 8–5 and Boudreau not only scored the game-winning goal but he also recorded his first career hat trick—with all 3 goals coming against North Star netminder Pete LoPrestri. A big reason for Boudreau's success was defenseman Borje Salming who recorded 5 assists, including a helper on each of Boudreau's goals. One of Boudreau's tallies was set up following an end-to-end rush by Salming who then spotted his wide-open teammate who simply put the puck into the wide-open net. Boudreau marveled at how Salming caught him out of the corner of his eye. "It was an unbelievable play by Borje," Boudreau recounted afterward. "I figured he was going to shoot himself because he never looked at me. Then all of a sudden the puck was on my stick. He must have an extra eye on the side of his head."

After coaching many years in the minor leagues (which included one Calder Cup championship in 2006), Bruce Boudreau was named coach of the Washington Capitals in 2007, a job he held for more than four seasons. He then took over behind the bench for the Anaheim Ducks during the 2011–12 season. "If you were a popular Toronto Maple Leaf in the 1970s, you had the world by the tail. You didn't want to play in any other city. Nobody blamed the players... everyone blamed owner Harold Ballard."—Bruce Boudreau

Boudreau knew his terrific game gave no assurance that he would stay with the Maple Leafs. "I had hoped I could play good enough to stay up here. I'm still playing it by ear and whenever they make a decision, I'll find out if it's been good enough." It turned out to be good enough for about half a season with Boudreau posting a respectable 29 points (including 15 goals) in 40 games. Neilson was primarily a defensive coach and that was not exactly Boudreau's strongest point.

Years later, Boudreau acknowledged that he did not do enough to stay in the big league nor did he heed the advice of team captain Darryl Sittler about his work habits, especially at practice where Boudreau could have spent time refining his game. The Leafs were always on the lookout for a second-line center to play behind Sittler, but Boudreau did not seize the opportunity; instead, it was back to the minors to play in cities such as Johnstown, Dallas, Moncton, St. Catharines, Cincinnati, Baltimore, and Newmarket, among other stops. He played for the Leafs at various points following the 1977–78 season, including a 39-game stretch for the blue and white in 1980–81 when he scored 10 times. He played briefly for the Chicago Blackhawks, but Boudreau would be remembered as a Maple Leaf whenever his NHL playing career is mentioned. No wonder, the kid from Toronto had his best night with the Maple Leafs—a game he would never forget.

Dave Reid

Leaf Record:
33 Goals,
53 Assists,
86 Points

Maple Leaf Moment: 1990–91 Season

Dave Reid always had good size (six foot one, 217 pounds) and speed mixed with a scoring touch, but he was never a star player. The Toronto native played his developmental hockey in local arenas before playing major junior hockey with the Peterborough Petes. He was not considered a top prospect, but still managed 196 points in 198 games played. Reid was selected by the Boston Bruins, but they mostly kept him in the minors in cities such as Hershey, Pennsylvania; Moncton, New Brunswick; and Maine. When they let him go after five seasons, the Leafs brought home another Toronto boy (whose childhood hero was Toronto great, Darryl Sittler) to help get them on track. Reid was never more than a third- or fourth-line checker, but he could be very effective in the role because he was such a good positional player. He totaled 18 goals in his first two seasons in Toronto, but had his best goal-scoring year as a Leaf in 1990–91.

When the struggling Maple Leafs clawed back to a .500 season in 1989–90, it was generally believed that the young team had finally turned a corner. As a result, hopes were high when the 1990–91 season began. It was the second campaign under coach Doug Carpenter and the team was loaded with young offensive players such as Wendel Clark, Gary Leeman, Eddie Olczyk, Daniel Marois, and Vincent Damphousse. The Leafs were generally weak on defense and in goal, but it was thought the natural goal scorers on the team would carry the day. It did not work out that way, however, as the team lost eight of its first 10 games (1–8–1) and Carpenter was replaced by assistant coach Tom Watt. The new mentor stressed defensive play and suddenly, checking players such as Reid became more important. Reid was never going to be a big-time goal getter, but something magical happened to him in what was otherwise another season of despair for Leaf fans.

Maybe it was his sweater number 14 (like Leaf legend Dave Keon) or maybe it was because he just happened to be in the right spot at the right time; whatever the case, Reid somehow managed to equal a team record for most shorthanded goals (8) in one season. When Keon established the mark in 1970–71, the Leafs were a respectable playoff team with a 37–33–8 record. The team Reid played on was a horrible outfit that won just 23 games, finishing well out of the playoffs (and without a number-one draft choice to look forward to since it was traded away to New Jersey for Tom Kurvers!). It was so bad that on November 8, 1990, when Reid scored 2 shorthanded goals, the Leafs still lost 5–3 to the Vancouver Canucks at home! He scored his first goal when he stole the puck from Vancouver defenseman Doug Lidster and then went in alone to score on netminder Troy Gamble. It gave the Leafs a 1–0 lead. His second goal came on a backhand drive to bring the Leafs within one while Marois was in the penalty box. It was to no avail for Toronto.

After the game, Reid commented on the fact that he was enjoying some good luck this year even though the team was not. "Last year I couldn't get any breaks or bounces, but this year I've had a few." He

Dave Reid was let go by the Maple Leafs after the end of the 1990–91 season, but he went on to win a Stanley Cup with the Dallas Stars (in 1999) and with the Colorado Avalanche (in 2001) before retiring after playing 961 career regular-season games. Reid owned and operated a hockey-card shop in the Toronto area when he played for the Leafs.

had scored nine times in each of his two previous seasons as a Maple Leaf, but would finish with 15 for the 1990–91 campaign. This meant that more than half of his goals came while the Leafs were shorthanded. Reid's top penalty killing was one the few highlights of the year and his eight shorthanded tallies were the most in the NHL that season, beating out the likes of Theo Fleury, Steve Yzerman, Craig MacTavish, and Dirk Graham for the top of what is usually a very impressive list of NHL talent.

Reid tied Keon's mark on March 23, 1991, when he scored his final shorthanded goal of the year. It came against former Leaf netminder Allan Bester with assists going to Dave Ellett and Dave Hannan and tied the game 1–1. The Leafs went on to beat Detroit 4–1, giving Reid a victory to celebrate along with his share of a team record. It was a great time for the Toronto boy to be a Maple Leaf, and his mark is still in the team record book.

Mark Osborne

Leaf Record:
94 Goals,
160 Assists,
254 Points

Maple Leaf Moment: October 23, 1993

Mark Osborne is the type of player the Maple Leafs always seemed to miss in the draft. Born in Toronto and a member of the Young Nationals as a sixteen-year-old (20 goals and 48 points in 58 games), the six-foot-two, 205-pound winger could have helped the Leafs. Instead Osborne went to Detroit in the third round (forty-sixth overall) in the 1980 NHL Entry Draft after a pretty good junior career with the Niagara Falls Flyers. He did not have the hands to be a great goal scorer, but Osborne did score 26 times for Detroit in 1981–82, his rookie year. He was a Red Wing for two more years before being dealt to the New York Rangers in a multi-player swap. New York general manager Phil Esposito liked Osborne, but felt the left-winger would do better if he had a chance to play for the Maple Leafs in his hometown. A trade was completed that saw the Leafs send young forward Jeff Jackson to the Rangers in exchange for Osborne, and Esposito turned out to be something of a prophet. Osborne did seem to thrive at home and had a career-best 93-point season (including 50 assists) for Toronto in 1989–90. The Leafs included Osborne in a trade with Winnipeg just one year later, but managed to re-acquire him in March 1992. Everyone was glad to see

"Ozzie" back in Toronto. He was shifted to a checking line and for two seasons starting in 1992–93, Leaf fans finally got to watch a winning team.

While all of Toronto was preoccupied with the Blue Jays, who were poised to win their second-straight World Series, the 1993–94 Maple Leafs started the NHL season with a terrific run. They won their first eight contests (equaling the NHL record) and were in Tampa Bay on October 23, 1993, looking for their ninth consecutive victory. The Tampa Bay club was only in their second year of existence, but the Lightning were not going to be a pushover by any means. They had won three of their first nine starts and playing at home in front of a large crowd (22,880) was only going to give them more incentive.

> Mark Osborne helped the Leafs equal an NHL record on May 8, 1994, when he had 1 of 2 shorthanded goals (Dave Andreychuk had the other) in one period (third) of a playoff game. The record came against the San Jose Sharks during an 8–3 Toronto win. Osborne scored another shorthanded tally against the Sharks in the same series to tie a team playoff series record held by Dave Keon (1963) and Bob Pulford (1964).

The first period was scoreless with Tampa holding a slight edge in play. Halfway through the second, Osborne stole the puck from a Lightning defender before putting it past goalie Daren Puppa at the edge of the Tampa crease. The Leafs took the 1–0 lead into the third before Osborne scored his second goal of the contest. At 8:55 of the final frame, Osborne was trying to center a pass when it was deflected into the net off a Tampa forward. For Osborne, the 2-goal effort was typical of how hard the checking winger had to work for every point. The goals were the first 2 of the season for Osborne (who would score 9 times during the regular season). Toronto goalie Felix Potvin blanked the Lightning the rest of the way (24 saves in total) for a 2–0 Leafs victory.

Although the Leafs were playing second fiddle to the Blue Jays, the team had accomplished something no other NHL had ever done with 9 straight victories to start the season. The World Series win overshadowed the Leafs' accomplishment, to be sure (only the 1934–35 Leafs and 1975–

76 Buffalo Sabres had previously won their first 8 games). But it didn't stop the Leafs who defeated Chicago 4–2 in the next contest to bring their record up to an even 10 games (a mark that was later equalled by the Sabres in 2005–06). One of the reasons for the Leafs early success was the contributions of players such as Osborne who chipped in timely goals and was a significant part of the Leafs penalty-killing unit.

Toronto leveraged their great start to post a 43-win, 98-point season, and another trip to the Western Conference final to end the 1993–94 season.

Osborne was one of those players who thrived playing in Toronto. On the day he was first acquired back in 1987, Leafs coach John Brophy said, "He's big, he can play pretty physical hockey and, with regular ice time, he might help us." Brophy did not last long behind the Toronto bench, but he did have it right about Osborne who was always a player that gave it his all as a Maple Leaf.

Peter Zezel

Leaf Record:
50 Goals,
78 Assists,
128 Points

Maple Leaf Moment: May 16, 1994

Peter Zezel was a very good soccer player as a youngster and there were plenty of places to play the"beautiful game"in Toronto; however, playing professional soccer in Canada offered little in the way of a lucrative living. Fortunately, the sturdy (5'11", 227 pounds) center was also a very good hockey player. He played for the renowned Don Mills Flyers as a sixteen-year-old and scored 43 goals and added 51 assists in just 40 games with the team. He then played for the Toronto Marlboros for two seasons (recording 207 points in just 134 games). But the Maple Leafs passed on the Toronto prospect in the 1983 Entry Draft. Instead, Philadelphia selected Zezel forty-first overall and he stayed with the Flyers for almost five full seasons (including two trips to the Stanley Cup final) before he was dealt to St. Louis. Zezel had a great time centering Brett Hull of the Blues (recording 72 points in 73 games in 1989–90), but he was traded again, this time to Washington before the 1990–91 campaign started. The Leafs brought him home in 1991 when they made one of their best trades, landing Zezel and Bob Rouse in exchange for the enigmatic Al Iafrate. Zezel was a main cog in getting the Leafs to the Western Conference in 1993 and once again in 1994.

When the Leafs knocked off the San Jose Sharks after seven grueling games during the second round of the 1994 playoffs, it was very uncertain whether Toronto had anything left in the tank for the next battle against the well-rested Vancouver Canucks. The Leafs-Canucks series (the first ever between the two Canadian clubs) would be played in a 2–3–2 format with Toronto hosting the first two contests. The only hope the Leafs had rested in their ability to get off to a good start at home, perhaps catching the Vancouver club a little rusty considering they hadn't played in five days. The series started on May 16, 1994, and everything went pretty well for the hometown heroes at Maple Leaf Gardens.

After a scoreless first period, the teams exchanged goals in the second to create a 1–1 tie. Early in the third, Zezel scored his first of the playoffs to give the Leafs the lead. The goal came on a backhand drive (putting in his own rebound) just thirty-eight seconds into the final frame. The Leafs nursed the lead all the way until the last minute of the game, when disaster struck. Toronto's Mike Gartner (usually a very clean player) was in the penalty box (after a highly debatable holding call) when Vancouver captain Trevor Linden scored with just thirty seconds to go to even the game once again. The Leafs were furious over the penalty, but there was nothing they could do about it.

Peter Zezel played in 873 career NHL games (207 were with the Leafs) and recorded 608 points. Zezel passed away from a rare blood disorder on May 26, 2009. He was forty-four.

In overtime, the Leafs got a big break when a Vancouver shot by Sergio Momesso hit the crossbar behind Toronto netminder Felix Potvin and bounced out. Potvin then had to make a tremendous save off Canucks superstar Pavel Bure, who was sent in alone. The Leafs good fortune continued when Vancouver netminder Kirk MacLean misplayed a loose puck well outside his net at the 16:55 mark of the first overtime period. Zezel pounced on it then ripped a shot into the far side of an empty net to give the Leafs the 2–1 win.

MacLean was very unhappy about the game winner. "I got to the puck first. It was just bad luck. I chipped it up and over [Leaf winger Bill

Berg's] stick but Zezel got lucky and caught the inside of the post," the Vancouver goalie lamented.

"I just shot it at the net," a relieved Zezel said in response. "It's definitely one of the biggest goals I've scored."

The game was especially satisfying to Zezel and his line mates Berg and Mark Osborne who were assigned to check the Canucks best line of Linden, Bure, and Greg Adams. "Their job is to check," said Leaf head coach Pat Burns, "and when they score its gravy on the potatoes." Despite the great night to open the series, Zezel knew his line was still in for a long battle. "I think we're still going to have to keep watching them," he said with a grin knowing full well that the Leafs were a tired bunch.

It turned out Zezel was exactly right. The Canucks flew past the Leafs in five games with Adams scoring the winning goal in double overtime in the final contest. The Leafs '94 playoff run came to an end. It was Zezel's last big moment as a Maple Leaf and his last goal for the team he grew up watching. For the hometown hero, it was a great way to leave Toronto—with a lasting memory for all Maple Leaf fans.

Mike Johnson

Leaf Record:
48 Goals,
72 Assists,
120 Points

Maple Leaf Moment: March 29, 1997

The 1996–97 Maple Leafs underwent major change when they traded away Doug Gilmour to the New Jersey Devils. Gilmour's departure meant the successful teams of the 1990s were a thing of the past and the club had to start re-organizing once again. Part of the renewal involved the addition of young players, including the three acquired in the Gilmour trade: Steve Sullivan, Jason Smith, and Alyn McCauley. Another important young player was the college free agent acquisition, Mike Johnson. The Toronto native (born in the suburb of Scarborough) was twenty-two when he inked a deal with the Leafs. He was also an undrafted player coming out of the University of Bowling Green after a four-year stint there (scoring a total of 64 goals). He had played some junior hockey in Richmond Hill and Aurora, Ontario, and his good numbers (68 total goals over two seasons) caught the attention of university recruiters. The Leafs had to fight off other NHL suitors for Johnson's services, but being his hometown team gave the blue and white a bit of an edge.

The youngster felt his maturity was going to be a factor in him making the NHL quickly. "I think it helps that I'm a little older," Johnson reasoned. "I don't see myself as a project who has to develop for a few years. My time is now." By this time, he had filled out to stand six-foot-two and weigh 202 pounds. As a youngster, however, he was much smaller and that kept him out of major junior hockey. While at Bowling Green (where he studied for a business and finance degree), he discovered he could be an effective college-level hockey player despite his size. Things were different now and the Leafs saw a smart player who had some speed and a scoring touch. He was signed on March 16, 1997 and played his first game that night against the Tampa Bay Lightning. Five days later, Johnson scored his first goal against the Pittsburgh Penguins, but his first major contribution came in Colorado on March 29, 1997.

Mike Johnson scored three goals in the 1999 playoffs for the Maple Leafs. Since he retired from hockey, he has become a color analyst for TSN, frequently working out of their Toronto studio.

The Avalanche were a very good team in 1996–97 and would record 49 victories in the regular season. The Leafs were a team going through the motions late in the campaign, which saw them win only 30 games by the time it was over (but were 5–5–5 since the Gilmour deal). It was not expected that the Leafs would offer much competition this night, but Colorado had to start Craig Billington because star goalie Patrick Roy was out with an injured shoulder. After a scoreless first, the Colorado club scored the first two goals of the game in the second period. Wendel Clark got one back for the Leafs to get them to within one before the period ended.

Sergei Berezin scored to even the game with less than six minutes to go and then Johnson made the big play of the night. With the Leafs trying to kill off a penalty to Todd Warriner, Johnson stole the puck from Valery Kamensky and streaked down the ice. He broke away from the Colorado defense to go in all alone, beating Billington with the game-winning tally to give the Leafs a 3–2 win. It was a very impressive shorthanded effort by the lanky Johnson, and seemed to give him a boost of confidence going forward with the Leafs. Johnson showed he was ready to make key plays at the NHL level and to perform better than many who were drafted in the first round!

Johnson scored 15 times in his first full season in 1997–98 and then added years of 20 and 21 before the Leafs decided they would rather have Darcy Tucker who was with Tampa Bay at the time. Despite averaging 46 points over his first three full years with Toronto, he was included in the deal that brought Tucker to the Maple Leafs. Johnson was never the aggressive power forward teams covet, but he was effective in his own right. The Scarborough kid left his hometown team never to return to the blue and white. He went on to play for Phoenix, Montreal, and St. Louis before his 661 NHL game career was over.

Joe Nieuwendyk

Leaf Record:
22 Goals,
28 Assists,
50 Points

Maple Leaf Moment: April 20, 2004

A way back in 1985, the Toronto Maple Leafs had a chance to select Oshawa, Ontario, native Joe Nieuwendyk in the second round of the NHL Entry Draft. He grew up in the nearby town of Whitby and enjoyed a stellar career as a lacrosse player, but hockey was going to be his professional game. The Leafs held the first pick of the '85 draft and made a great choice in selecting Wendel Clark. They also had the twenty-second selection (the top pick in the second round) and wasted the choice on defenseman Ken Spengler who would never play a single game for the blue and white. Five picks later, the Calgary Flames surprised everyone by selecting the six-foot-two, 205-pound Nieuwendyk who had attended Cornell University. There he had scored 47 goals in 58 games over two seasons as a center. The superbly talented pivot went on to score 51 goals as a rookie and helped lead the Flames to their only Stanley Cup in 1989. Nieuwendyk went on to win two more Cups (with Dallas and New Jersey) before he became available to Toronto as a free agent.

One of the main reasons the Maple Leafs signed the thirty-seven-year-old Nieuwendyk was for his playoff savvy and experience. It took about $2 million to get him, but the Leafs felt he would be worth every penny, especially if he could help them win a playoff series or two.

It was the 2003 post-season and Toronto was in tough against their Ontario nemeses, the Ottawa Senators. Despite clearly having the better goaltending (Ed Belfour was far superior to Ottawa's Patrick Lalime), the Leafs were still forced to a game seven at the Air Canada Centre on April 20, 2004. This was exactly the type of situation in which Nieuwendyk had excelled so often in his illustrious career, and why he has three Stanley Cup rings. This game would once again show why Nieuwendyk was such a clutch hockey player.

The Sens were built around a lightning-quick attack, but often found themselves short on toughness when the playoffs rolled around. On this night, their offense was largely irrelevant when the Leafs struck quickly in the deciding contest. Toronto's Chad Kilger opened the scoring at the 6:19 mark of the first then a little over a minute later Nieuwendyk scored with a seemingly stoppable wrist shot from well out that got by Lalime. seconds. If that did not demoralize the Senators enough, Nieuwendyk let another shot go late in the first that Lalime also blew to give the Leafs an insurmountable 3–0 lead going into the first intermission. It was Nieuwendyk's fifth goal of the series.

Joe Nieuwendyk was not re-signed by the Maple Leafs after the lockout year, but he did play two more NHL seasons with the Florida Panthers before retiring. He was inducted into the Hockey Hall of Fame in 2011 and was named the general manager of the Dallas Stars in 2009 (a position he held until 2012) after he had worked in the Leafs front office for a short time.

The Senators had scored a league-leading 269 goals (recording 43 wins and 102 points) during the regular season, but could only score one time in this important contest to make the final score 4–1. The win marked the fourth time in the last five years that Toronto had knocked out Ottawa of the playoffs. What was even more impressive from a Toronto point of view was that they were without their captain Mats Sundin for the last three games of the series; however, there was no reason to be concerned with Nieuwendyk in the Leafs dressing room.

In the post-game media interviews Nieuwendyk took the time to praise Belfour first. "I've played with Eddie a long time," Nieuwendyk said. "He's a warrior and loves this time of year. He has it going right now." The classy veteran also refused to gloat over Lalime's misfortune. "I think he [Lalime] had a terrific series and I think I got a couple tonight that maybe shouldn't have gone in, I don't know. I think he got overshadowed by a pretty hot Eddie Belfour." As for his second goal of the game, Nieuwendyk figured Lalime was thinking about the first one he put past the Ottawa goalie. "It was late in the period and I just thought 'Why not take a shot with what has already happened? Maybe he's second guessing himself.'" It turned out to be a good move and put the Leafs comfortably in front.

The Leafs lost a close series to the Philadelphia Flyers in the next round and they struggled when Nieuwendyk missed games due to nagging back spasms. A completely healthy Nieuwendyk could have been the difference, but the kid from Oshawa still gave the Leafs something special, even if it was for only one season, and one memorable game seven!

Matt Stajan

Leaf Record:
87 Goals,
136 Assists,
223 Points

Maple Leaf Moment: April 5, 2003 and April 13, 2006

When Matt Stajan was a little kid he received a Maple Leaf sweater for Christmas. It had number 93 on the back just like the one Toronto hockey hero Doug Gilmour wore at the time. Stajan's family also had access to Leafs season tickets and Stajan got to attend a few games every year. The Mississauga, Ontario, native was naturally a Leafs fan and began playing hockey as a five-year-old. He would play on many of the well-known teams in the GTHL and excelled to the point where he could advance to play major junior. His childhood was filled with great minor hockey memories and he was eventually drafted into the Ontario Hockey League with the Belleville Bulls. He scored more than 30 goals twice for the Bulls and showed enough talent that the Maple Leafs selected him fifty-seventh overall in the 2002 Entry Draft. Stajan's father, Mike, had also been a Leafs fan and admired the way Leaf legend Dave Keon played for Toronto between 1960 and 1975. When Stajan joined the Maple Leafs in 2003, he wore number 41 but then switched the digits to 14—the same as Keon!

Stajan signed with the Maple Leafs in April 2003 and was in the lineup on the fifth. Injuries to regulars such as Mats Sundin gave Stajan an opportunity to start his career on the CBC's *Hockey Night in Canada* on the final night of the regular season versus the Ottawa Senators. Both teams were playoff bound so there was nothing significant on the line; however, the moment was not lost on Stajan who managed to score his first NHL goal during the contest. Playing center between wingers Owen Nolan and Gary Roberts, he scored the goal about halfway through the first. Ottawa defenseman Chris Phillips gave up the puck in front of the Senators' net and Stajan made no mistake, beating Ottawa goalie Martin Prusek. He became the twenty-ninth player in Leaf history to score a goal in his first game with the team. "What a big thrill," Stajan said after the game. "Every kid dreams of scoring his first goal on *Hockey Night in Canada* and I had the chance to do it."

Although Matt Stajan played in 445 career regular-season games for the Maple Leafs, he only played in three playoff contests (in 2003–04) for Toronto and did not record a point.

Stajan launched his career in impressive fashion and, although he was a solid player throughout his stay in Toronto, his flair for the dramatic was occasional; however, on April 13, 2006, he once again made a sudden impact. The Leafs had a faint hope of making the playoffs as the 2005–06 season was coming to a close. They absolutely had to win on Long Island, but it took an overtime session to keep Toronto's post-season hopes alive. The Leafs opened the scoring early on when Darcy Tucker scored at 2:04 of the first. The Islanders tied it just before the end of the first and then took the lead in the second.

Leaf captain Mats Sundin tied it once again on a power play and then Stajan scored his thirteenth of the season on a wrist shot from the slot to put the Leafs up 3–2. Jeff O'Neill (who made a nice play along the boards to spring Stajan for his drive) and Alex Steen earned assists on Stajan's marker, but the Isles came right back to tie the game 3–3. The game went into overtime and it looked like the contest was headed for a shoot-out. However, at the 3:52 mark of the five-minute overtime, the Leafs grabbed the puck in the New York zone. Tucker went to the front of the net while Stajan put a low, backhand drive past Islander netminder Garth Snow for a 4–3 Toronto victory. It was one of Stajan's best games in a Toronto uniform and it would mark his only overtime winner as a Leaf.

"The way we are going now, we have the confidence to beat anyone in the league," an excited Stajan said at the end of the game. His 2-point night gave him 8 (5 goals, 3 assists) over his last 9 games, which saw him moved back to his natural position at center.

The Leafs did not make the playoffs when the 2005–06 campaign ended 3 games later, but they did make a very respectable run at it (mostly behind J.S. Aubin's goaltending) to give Toronto fans some hope for the next year. Stajan ended the year with 15 goals and 27 points and would go on to record seasons of 39, 33, 55, and 41 points as a Leaf. He then became part of the deal that saw the Leafs acquire Dion Phaneuf from the Calgary Flames. He has since struggled to find his game in the Western Conference. Perhaps the young man from Mississauga simply misses playing for his hometown team.

Frank Mahovlich started his time in the Maple Leafs organization at St. Michael's.

MAJORS, MARLBOROS, AND MARLIES TO MAPLE LEAFS

Les Costello • Frank Mahovlich • Brit Selby • Peter Stemkowski
Jim McKenny • Stew Gavin • Bill Berg • Steve Thomas
John Mitchell • James Reimer • Jake Gardiner

WHEN CONN SMYTHE AND Frank Selke took over management of Toronto's NHL franchise in 1927, they both agreed the Maple Leafs needed a development system to bring along young talent. The executives decided to add the Toronto Marlboros (also known as "Marlboroughs" from an established athletic club in Toronto that first organized a hockey team in 1904) to their newly renamed team. The Marlboros soon became one of the best junior organizations in the history of the game and they developed many a star for the blue and white. Smythe also sensed that it would be easier to attract Catholic boys to the Toronto organization if they could continue their education in the separate school system. The Leafs turned that task over to St. Michael's, a Catholic high school in Toronto where young talent would play for the team known as the Majors.

Neither junior team exists in the Leaf system today, but the Marlboros name is now associated with the Leafs minor pro team in the American Hockey League, known as the Marlies, who still play out of Toronto. Here, the tradition of turning young talent into future Maple Leafs still continues. The following players began their time learning what it takes to be a Maple Leaf and an NHL-worthy player by first donning a Major, or a Marlboro, or a Marlie uniform:

Les Costello

Leaf Record:
2 Goals,
3 Assists,
5 Points

Maple Leaf Moment: 1948 Playoffs

When Les Costello began playing hockey at St. Michael's as a sixteen-year-old, he was on a very good Majors club. The 1944–45 St. Mike's team featured future Leafs such as Gus Mortson, Jimmy Thomson, and Johnny McCormack. The five-foot-eight, 158-pound Costello was on the smallish side, but the native of South Porcupine, Ontario, was speedy and skilled. He had 16 points in 14 playoff games helping the Majors to the Memorial Cup championship in '45. Two years later, he was on a second winning team that included Red Kelly, Rudy Migay, Fleming Mackell, and Johnny McLellan, all of whom would go on to play for the Maple Leafs. During the 1947 Memorial Cup playoffs, Costello scored 12 goals in 10 games and totaled 21 points. In 70 regular-season games played at St. Mike's, Costello had recorded 121 points (57 of them goals) making him a good prospect for the Leafs. Not quite ready for the NHL just yet, Costello would play the entire 1947–48 season in Pittsburgh for the Leafs farm team. He scored 32 times for the Hornets and had 54 points in 68 games. Then the unexpected happened: he was called up to the big league for the Stanley Cup playoffs.

The Leafs had actually been impressed with Costello at training camp in September 1947, however, they believed that the youngster would benefit from playing a year in the American Hockey League. It is very rare that a rookie gets thrust into the Stanley Cup playoffs without ever having played a regular-season NHL game, but that is exactly what happened to the twenty-year-old Costello in April 1948.

The Maple Leafs had finished in first place during the 1947–48 season and were heavy favorites to repeat as Stanley Cup champions. The team was especially loaded at center with Syl Apps, Ted Kennedy, and Max Bentley, who finished 1–2–3 in Leafs scoring that year; however, the Leafs were not afraid to make changes or add fresh faces for the post-season.

The Leafs were pretty much ripping through the Boston Bruins in the first round when they added Costello at forward and Phil Samis on defense (both from Pittsburgh) for the fifth game of the series. Leaf general manager Conn Smythe said of the two youngsters, "[They are] kids with legs and the fire of youth. They should be skating faster than ever at the end of the playoff[s]."

On April 3, 1948, Costello put on a Leaf uniform for the first time and contributed one goal in the Leafs 3–2 win to eliminate the Bruins. The score was tied 1–1 in the first period when Costello battled in the corner to get the puck over to Bentley. He scrambled to the front of the goal where he knocked in Bentley's rebound. The Bruins tied it in the second period, but Kennedy scored the winner in the third. Smythe was impressed with the rookie's speed and made it quite clear Costello was going to stay in the lineup. "He skated them dizzy and was making use of passes Bentley had been wasting all season," Smythe said.

In the opening game of the finals against Detroit, Costello secured

Les Costello, however, did not hang up his skates and instead became one of the founding priests who started a hockey team in 1962 known as the "Flying Fathers." The team of priests would play charity hockey games and entertain fans with some impassioned play and funny, crazy antics on ice. Tragically, Les Costello died in 2002 from injuries suffered when he struck his head (he never wore a helmet) on the ice prior to the start of a hockey game.

his first NHL assist when he set up Joe Klukay for a first-period goal in the 5–3 Leafs victory. In the second contest, he was instrumental in getting the puck to Bentley for the winning goal in a 4–2 Toronto triumph. Klukay and Costello both made nice passes before Bentley finished off the play with the important goal. The youngster was held off the score sheet in the next game, but was able to make a nice contribution the night the Leafs clinched the Cup.

The final game of the Leafs 4-game sweep came on April 14, 1948, and really, Detroit had no chance in this contest. The Leafs jumped out to a 3–0 lead after one period and then added 3 goals in the second to make it 6–1. Costello finished off a good play by Bentley to give the Leafs their seventh tally in the 7–2 win. After the final game, Smythe complimented his team. "This is the greatest team I have ever had. They have never failed me... I've had some great stars on other [Leaf] teams but I've never had a team like this." For a raw rookie like Costello to make a solid contribution to a star-studded club's run for the Cup spoke well for his future with the Maple Leafs.

However, Costello played only part of the 1948–49 season (15 games to be exact) and then after one more playoff game, he never played in Toronto again. He did play three full seasons in the minors with Pittsburgh and was very productive (135 points in 184 games), but he had other plans. In May 1950, Costello decided to become a Catholic priest and went into the seminary. He told his brother Murray (a Hockey Hall of Fame member in the builder category) that he could no longer resist God's calling. The St. Michael's graduate was now going to put his Catholic education to use for the rest of his life!

27 LEFT WING

F
R
A
N
K

M
A
H
O
V
L
I
C
H

Frank Mahovlich

Leaf Record:
296 Goals,
301 Assists,
597 Points

Maple Leaf Moment: 1964 Semi-Finals

The Maple Leafs beat out the Detroit Red Wings to sign the tall (six-foot, 205-pound) youngster Frank Mahovlich from Timmins, Ontario, in the mid-1950s. The Leafs felt they had a potential superstar on their hands and convinced his family to go with Toronto where he could attend St. Michael's high school. In his last two seasons as a St. Mike's Major, the swift-skating Mahovlich scored a total of 76 goals and 138 points in just 79 games. The Leafs could not wait to get the "Big M" into their lineup, which was rather weak by 1957.

The left-winger did not disappoint, winning the Calder Trophy as the NHL's best rookie in 1957–58. He scored 20 goals that year and became a league All-Star by 1961. He would lead the Leafs in goals scored for six consecutive years (he had 48 tallies in 1960–61) and helped the Leafs capture four Stanley Cups starting with their triumph in 1962 (12 points in 12 games played in the playoffs). He was vital to the Leafs playoffs hopes every season—and Mahovlich rarely disappointed. He was especially good in 1964 when the Leafs had to play two seven-game series to retain the Cup.

Mahovlich had not been his stellar self in the Leafs 1963 Stanley

Cup win (only 2 assists in 9 games), but the team was so strong they really did not miss their top talent too much on route to their second straight championship. He was injured in the '63 post-season and was out of the lineup for one game (he was also fighting the flu), but the Leafs had plenty of depth to overcome any deficiencies. The 1964 playoffs proved to be a different story and the Big M had to be vital if the Toronto club had any hope of winning its third consecutive NHL title.

The 1963–64 Maple Leafs team struggled during the regular season and although they managed a third-place finish, all that assured them was a semi-final meeting with the first-place Montreal Canadiens. The Habs were hungry to get back to the finals. They hadn't got that far since 1960 and felt they had a good chance to beat the veteran Leafs this time around. Montreal netminder Charlie Hodge had been excellent throughout the season (he won the Vezina Trophy that year), and he was especially good against the Leafs, so the Canadiens felt pretty confident that they could ride his hot hand versus Toronto.

Years after Toronto traded Mahovlich to Detroit, the big winger was traded once again—this time to the Montreal Canadiens during the 1970–71 season. Mahovlich recorded 27 points in 20 post-season games to help lead the Habs to a surprise Stanley Cup win in 1971. He would win another championship in Montreal in 1973 before leaving to play for the Toronto Toros of the World Hockey Association (WHA). The Maple Leafs honored Frank Mahovlich by raising sweater number 27 to the rafters of the Air Canada Centre on October 3, 2001.

In the opening game of the series, the stellar Hodge and his teammates shut the Leafs out 2–0 at the Montreal Forum. The Leafs needed to win the second game, on March 29, 1964 in Montreal, if they were going to have any chance of getting past the Habs.

Mahovlich took over the game quickly, resulting in a 2–0 lead for the Leafs after one period. First, he set up linemate Red Kelly for the opening goal then he notched one himself after jumping off the Toronto bench to join Kelly on a rush to the Montreal zone. Kelly fed a perfect pass to Mahovlich who slammed it home to put the Leafs up by a pair.

The Habs scored a goal in the second period, but the Leafs held on for a 2–1 victory.

After the game all the talk was about Mahovlich's play. "That was the finest game the Big M has played for us in two seasons," enthused Leafs assistant general manager King Clancy. "He owned the puck and with any luck he would have had three goals."

Montreal coach Toe Blake was just as impressed. "The Big M was the difference....He had us off balance from the first shift on the ice. We couldn't contain him; he was just too much hockey player."

"I feel good, want the puck and have plenty of zip," the first star of the game commented as he compared his playoff readiness to the year before. "Skating is not an effort but a pleasure."

Montreal won the next game in Toronto, but it was another superb effort by Mahovlich in the fourth game that evened the series again. The Leafs beat the Habs 5–3 on April 2, with Mahovlich scoring twice and adding three assists. In short, he was a one-man wrecking crew. Named the first star of the game once again, Mahovlich helped the Leafs get off to a good start by setting up goals by Andy Bathgate and George Armstrong to give the Leafs a 2–1 first-period lead. He also helped Kelly score a second-period marker before scoring twice himself.

After the game, the Maple Leaf star talked about his teammates rather than his own 5-point evening. "Our forward lines got the job done," he said. "But most of the credit belongs to our penalty killers [featuring the efforts of Dave Keon, Bob Pulford, Ron Stewart, and Armstrong]. They were tremendous and the Canadiens were never able to exploit an advantage in manpower."

Even though Montreal won the next game, the Leafs roared back to take the next 2 and win the series in 7 games—the last win coming at the Forum. It took another 7 games to win the Cup against Detroit in the finals with Mahovlich leading the way with 8 points. The Majors graduate had shown he was indeed worth all efforts needed to get him signed and to St. Michael's for without his great play, the Leafs would not have won three consecutive championships.

BRIT SELBY
MAPLE LEAFS
WING

Brit Selby

Leaf Record:
29 Goals,
30 Assists,
59 Points

Maple Leaf Moment: January 15, 1966

A native of Kingston, Ontario, left-winger Brit Selby first joined the Toronto Marlboros for 2 games in 1960–61. He was fifteen years old. He then played in 3 games the following year and scored his first goal. He was a regular on the junior club starting in 1962–63 and would go on to score 93 goals in 133 games played over the next three seasons. Selby was also part of the powerful Memorial Cup–winning team in 1964 (featuring the likes of Ron Ellis, Peter Stemkowski, Mike Walton and Jim McKenny, who would all go on to play for the Leafs). In his final year with the Marlboros (1964–65), he scored 45 times and totaled 88 points in just 52 games. And he was Toronto's captain during his final year of junior play.

The five-foot-eleven, 175-pound Selby scored twice in a 3-game call-up to the Maple Leafs during the 1964–65 campaign. He scored his first NHL goal in his second game when the Leafs beat the hometown New York Rangers on January 3, 1965. It is not surprising, then, that the Leafs had high hopes that this Marlboro graduate was going to have a long NHL career in Toronto.

Selby joined the Maple Leafs for the start of the 1965–66 season and took on sweater number 11 because the superstitious coach, Punch Imlach, believed it was a lucky number for Leaf rookies (especially since Bob Nevin in 1960–61 and Ron Ellis in 1964–65 enjoyed great first years wearing number 11). The twenty-year-old Selby would, in fact, have a good year in 1965–66 with 14 goals and, amazingly, that was good enough to win the Calder Trophy as the NHL's best rookie. His best moment that season came on January 15, 1966, when Boston came into Maple Leaf Gardens for a Saturday-night contest.

The Bruins were in their customary spot—at the bottom of the standings—but they could always get up for a good performance on *Hockey Night in Canada*. The Leafs were up 1–0 when Selby skated hard to take a pass from Ellis before whipping it past Bernie Parent in the Boston net. Selby had to withstand a slash across the back of the legs from Bruin tough guy Ted Green, but he still managed to score. Selby then added two more tallies in the second period to give the Leafs a commanding 4–0 lead. He scored both second-period goals by putting rebounds past Parent on drives by Dave Keon and Marcel Pronovost, respectively. The Leafs cruised to a 6–1 victory.

Imlach was naturally pleased with the hat trick from his prized rookie but was even happier with how Selby responded when

Brit Selby suffered a concussion while with the Maple Leafs during a game on February 1, 1970, against the Boston Bruins. He could not remember much of the match after the fight he had with Boston forward Johnny MacKenzie. He was taken to a Toronto hospital for a checkup when the team returned from Boston. Selby was given tests similar to the ones they gave boxers in Ontario when they needed to get a fight license. X-rays showed no damage and Selby was declared fit to play after passing all the tests administered. He played in the Leafs next game three days later against St. Louis, but he was wearing a helmet. Leaf coach Johnny McLellan benched Selby during the contest against the Blues and while Selby complained about adjusting to the helmet, he also said he felt fine. This is an example of how concussions were treated in this era of hockey and also how much more serious such an injury has become in the current game since the hits are being delivered by larger players going at higher rates of speed.

challenged by Green throughout the game. "Green was testing him and the kid didn't back up an inch," Imlach stated. "Green bumped him; Selby bumped right back. That's the kind of stuff that shows you've got a professional hockey player."

Selby agreed with his coach and assessed things this way: "With a guy like Green, you've got to prove yourself. If you don't, you're done."

Most felt Selby would be a good player for a long time. He showed some scoring prowess and was trained to play a two-way game. Against the Bruins, for example, he was able to keep Boston forwards such as Ron Stewart and Johnny McKenzie in check, not an easy task. Leaf captain George Armstrong took note of the rookie's good play as well. "He's always in position," the Leaf leader said. "You can't get in much trouble or in a serious slump, if you play your wing the way he does." Scoring three times against Boston may not have seemed like a great accomplishment at the time, but few rookies recorded hat tricks in the six-team era and all his goals did come against future Hall of Fame netminder, Bernie Parent.

However, Selby only scored three times the rest of the season. One year later he was in the minors and soon he was traded away to Philadelphia only to be re-acquired by the Maple Leafs (late in the 1968–69 campaign) for a 99-game stint which ended early in the 1970–71 season. Although Selby was only a Leaf for a total of 129 games, he is still considered one of the great Marlboro players on the '64 championship squad who made the Leafs. He would go on to play pro hockey for 12 seasons, spending his last four years in the World Hockey Association (recording 74 points in 153 games played) before retiring after the 1974–75 season.

Peter Stemkowski

Leaf Record:
29 Goals,
64 Assists,
93 Points

Maple Leaf Moment: 1967 Playoffs

Center Peter Stemkowski first came to hockey prominence when the seventeen-year-old played for his hometown Winnipeg Monarchs. He scored 22 times for the Monarchs in 1960–61 and then potted 31 goals the following year. His strong play got him into major junior hockey with the Toronto Marlboros where he had his best junior season in 1963–64, winning the Memorial Cup. Stemkowski recorded 103 points that season and then added 43 more over the course of the playoffs to complete his junior career.

The six-foot-one, 196-pound Stemkowski spent half of the 1964–65 season in the minors with the Rochester Americans (39 points in 35 games played), and the other half with the Maple Leafs (20 points in 36 games). It was hoped he would be ready for the big league on a full-time basis for the following 1965–66 season. He did get into 56 games for the Leafs that season, but only posted 16 points with just 4 goals. The big center, however, was better prepared for the 1966–67 campaign and he scored 13 times while totaling 35 points in 68 games played. Toward the end of that season, the Leafs put Stemkowski on a line with Jim Pappin and veteran Bob Pulford. The unit clicked as the Leafs improved their standing to third place to close out the year. While no hockey expert expected the Leafs to beat the Chicago Black Hawks in the opening round of the playoffs, the line centered by Stemkowski would prove to be very effective, scoring many key goals.

The Leafs were badly outplayed in the opener as the Black Hawks recorded an easy 5–2 win on home ice. The second game was played three days later on April 9, 1967 in Chicago and the Leafs knew they had to at the very least put up a more respectable showing. Stemkowski opened the scoring after his line got things going in the Chicago end. Pappin got the puck over to Stemkowski who backhanded a shot past Glenn Hall in the Black Hawk net. It was Stemkowski's first-ever playoff marker. The Leafs made it 2–0 before the first period was over and they checked Chicago at every opportunity to win 3–1. The series went back and forth, but the pivotal contest was the fifth game, which was played in Chicago on April 15 with each team having already won twice.

Chicago fully expected to run the Leafs out of the building and take control of the series, but the veteran Toronto club did not give up by any means. Even though the Leafs opened the scoring, shaky netminding by Johnny Bower was such a concern that he was replaced by Terry Sawchuk to start the second period with the score tied 2–2. Sawchuk was rocked by a blast from the stick of Bobby Hull, Chicago's best player and top goal scorer. The thirty-seven-year-old Leaf netminder struggled back to his feet and carried on despite a bruised and battered body. The Leafs were inspired to win it for their goalie and it was Stemkowski who scored the winning goal early in the third. The winning tally was set up on a pass from Pappin and Stemkowski merely had to push it home. One more goal gave the Leafs a 4–2 win and, incredibly, they then took the sixth game 3–1 to make it to the Stanley Cup finals.

The Leafs started the series against Montreal much like they had against Chicago with an embarrassing loss in the opener, only this time

Peter Stemkowski was part of one of the biggest trades in NHL history when he was dealt to Detroit, along with Frank Mahovlich, Garry Unger, and the rights to Carl Brewer for Norm Ullman, Floyd Smith, and Paul Henderson on March 3, 1968. Stemkowski may not have been the biggest name in the trade, but he would finish with 555 career points (including 206 goals) in 967 games played. The Maple Leafs could have used his size and scoring abilities at center ice during the last ten years of Stemkowski's NHL career.

the score was 6–2. With their backs to the wall once more, the Maple Leafs dug deep to win the second game in Montreal 3–0 with Bower back in net. Again, it was Stemkowski who opened the scoring with his fourth goal of the playoffs. This time it was Pulford and Mike Walton who set him up on a first-period power play to give the Leafs the all-important first goal. Stemkowski was speared by Montreal defenseman Terry Harper, but returned to the game in the third when he set up the final Leaf tally by Tim Horton. Stemkowski also starred in the third game of the series when he scored once and helped set up Pulford's overtime winner in an exciting contest at Maple Leaf Gardens.

The Leafs won the fifth game of the finals in Montreal and took a 3-2 series lead home with the chance to win the Cup on May 2, 1967. The Leafs opened the scoring in the second period on a goal by Ron Ellis and nursed the lead until the last minute of the middle frame when Pappin let a shot go at the Montreal net from the far boards. The puck appeared to hit Stemkowski's or Harper's skate and bounced past Gump Worsley in the Montreal net.

Stemkowski unselfishly told the official scorer that it had bounced off a Hab skate so Pappin would get credit and end up the leader of all 1967 playoff goal scorers with 7. "Pappy wanted to beat out Beliveau [who had 6 playoff goals]," Stemkowski said after the game. "I told the referee the puck hit [a Montreal defenseman], not me." Stemkowski was given an assist on the play for his twelfth point of the playoffs which placed him second in playoff scoring behind Pappin's 15. There were some tense moments after Montreal made it 2–1, but an empty-net goal by captain George Armstrong sealed the Leafs eleventh Stanley Cup victory.

"I haven't been this happy since I passed my economics course!" Stemkowski quipped during *Hockey Night in Canada* post-game interviews. "Guys play 20 years and never win one [Stanley Cup]. It's only my third year and I won one. I'm tremendously happy." The twenty-three-year-old Stemkowski now had an NHL championship to go along with his Memorial Cup title. Now he could look forward to more impressive achievements as a Maple Leaf, but that was certainly not the way it would work out!

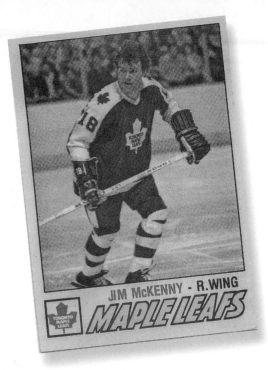

JIM McKENNY - R.WING
MAPLE LEAFS

Jim McKenny

Leaf Record:
81 Goals,
246 Assists,
327 Points

Maple Leaf Moment: January 31 and February 1, 1970

Jim McKenny played for the Neil McNeil Maroons (high-school hockey) in Toronto as a sixteen-year-old defenseman and scored 5 goals and added 12 assists in 37 games. The Ottawa native's performance caught the Maple Leaf's eye and they selected McKenny seventeenth overall in the very first amateur draft conducted in June 1963. The Leafs then assigned him to the Toronto Marlboros junior club. The five-foot-eleven, 192-pound blueliner had three stellar seasons (126 points in 150 games) with the Marlboros capped off with a 1964 Memorial Cup win. Those who watched McKenny play junior hockey thought he was a blue-chip prospect. In fact, he was often compared to superstar Bobby Orr who was excelling in Oshawa as a junior star. McKenny's playmaking skills made him a natural for the power-play unit and his puck-handling abilities were as good as any player in the Ontario Hockey League.

McKenny's arrival in professional hockey was much anticipated by the Leafs because of his rather storied junior career. Yet he had trouble making the team in his first few tries. He did play in 6 games for the Leafs in their Stanley Cup winning season of 1966-67 (scoring 1 goal), but McKenny was still primarily a minor-league player until the age of twenty-three. He became a Leaf regular for the 1969-70 campaign, when Toronto fell out of the playoffs once again. The Leafs were trying to rebuild their defense (along with other youngsters such as Pat Quinn, Mike Pelyk, Brian Glennie, Rick Ley, and Jim Dorey) with McKenny providing some much-needed offense from the blue line. He scored 11 times in his first full year with the Leafs and added 33 assists for a highly respectable 44 points. One of the highlights of the season for McKenny came on a weekend: Saturday, January 31 and Sunday February 1, 1970.

The first game was played in Minnesota and the Leafs came away with a 4–3 victory. McKenny got the Leafs going by setting up George Armstrong for a first-period goal just 2:57 into the game. Even though the Leafs were up 2–0, the North Stars battled back to make it 3–3. Not long afterward, McKenny sent in a pass to the North Stars goal mouth that was re-directed in by Ron Ellis to give the Leafs the win.

Jim McKenny worked as a sportscaster for CITY-TV in Toronto for many years before retiring. His 327 career points as a Maple Leaf rank him twenty-ninth on the all-time Toronto list.

The next afternoon in Boston proved to be a wild affair featuring a good old-fashioned donnybrook. The Bruins were up 4–1 when McKenny went to work and set up 3 straight goals to even the score. Two of the markers (by Norm Ullman and Mike Walton) came on Toronto power-play opportunities to which the Bruins responded quickly with 2 goals to regain the lead. However, before the second stanza ended, McKenny scored a goal of his own (shooting home a drive after taking a beautiful pass from Ullman) to bring the Leafs back to within one at 6–5.

The melee took place in the middle of the second period and both teams seemed to gain momentum as a result of all the fisticuffs. The main event featured the Leafs' Pat Quinn going up against the Bruins' Bobby Orr. The bench clearing brawl featured four major penalties and one 10-minute misconduct and that was followed up by a fight between Toronto defenseman Tim Horton and Boston winger Ken Hodge.

The recharged Leafs tied the game at 6-6 when Dave Keon scored early in the third but Boston scored once more on a goal by Johnny

McKenzie to make the final 7–6. The loss took some of the lustre away from McKenny's great weekend, which saw him record a total of 6 points (1 goal, 5 assists). By contrast, Orr only had 4 points (1 goal, 3 assists) for the Bruins over the weekend and, while it may not seem like much of a difference, it was one of the few times that McKenny bested the greatest player in the game—a contemporary he was unfairly compared to during his entire hockey career.

Years later in 2011, McKenny commented, "There were such high expectations of me. Basically I view myself as a failure." When asked about a playoff goal he scored in 1971 on a great rush down the ice against the New York Rangers, he said, "Yeah, but Bobby [Orr] used to do that every night." If the comparisons to Orr had never been made perhaps the Leaf blueliner might have handled the pressure better (he freely admits to being a recovering alcoholic, but has been dry for more than twenty-five years) and become a star in his own right. Sometimes the weight of high expectations can bring a player down, and while most Leaf fans expected better play from McKenny, he still had a respectable NHL career that lasted 604 games, all but 10 as a Maple Leaf.

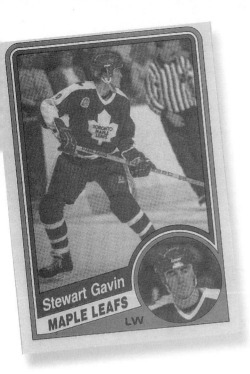

Stew Gavin

Leaf Record:
34 Goals,
48 Assists,
82 Points

Maple Leaf Moment: March 10, 1984

Drafted in the fourth round (seventy-fourth overall) by the Maple Leafs in 1980, left-winger Stew Gavin felt quite comfortable in the Toronto organization. The six-foot, 190-pound Gavin was also well known to Leafs management since he played three seasons with the Marlboro, a team that also played in Maple Leaf Gardens. The Ottawa native played minor hockey for the Nepean Raiders before coming to the Marlboros in 1977–78. Never a high-powered offensive player, the speedy Gavin still managed to record 146 points (including 67 goals) in 196 games for the Marlboro club. (He worked on the maintenance crew at the Gardens in the off-season.) He spent some time on the Leafs farm teams in Moncton, New Brunswick and St. Catharines, Ontario, before sticking with the big team for the 1982–83 season where he scored 6 goals in 63 games played. The Leafs were now expecting Gavin to be a regular contributor to their re-building club.

The 1983–84 Maple Leafs were not very good under head coach Mike Nykoluk; they had just 26 wins to show over the 80-game regular schedule. However, even as late as March, the Leafs were still in contention for a playoff spot in the very weak Norris Division that featured Detroit, Chicago, St. Louis, and Minnesota. Only the North Stars were above the .500 mark while the rest wallowed in mediocrity. That said four out these five Norris teams would still make the playoffs! So it was no real surprise that the Leafs still had a shot at the post-season when the almost equally dreadful Red Wings came into Toronto for a Saturday-night contest on March 10, 1984.

The Maple Leafs led the game 2–1 after the first period with goals by Rick Vaive and Russ Courtnall. Then former Red Wings star Dale McCourt gave the home side a 3–1 lead going into the third. Detroit scored 2 third-period markers to send the game into overtime. The Leafs had not done very well in extra time (five minutes of five-on-five play) during the 1983–84 season despite eleven chances to win a game in overtime (0–3–8). On this night, however, the Leafs finally won an overtime contest and they did so in dramatic fashion.

Stew Gavin was with the Minnesota North Stars when they made it to the Stanley Cup finals in 1990. He had 3 goals and a total of 13 points in 21 post-season games that year.

Early in the extra frame, the Leafs faced off in their end in front of goalie Allan Bester. McCourt took the draw for the Leafs and got the puck back to defenseman Borje Salming. The sublimely talented defenseman fired a quick pass to a breaking Gavin who took the puck on his stick, beat Detroit defenseman Greg Smith with his speed, and suddenly found himself in alone. Red Wings netminder Corrado Micalef came out to challenge Gavin but the Leaf player had his head up and went to his backhand to put home a shot, that gave the Leafs a 4–3 victory.

It was Gavin's eighth goal of the season and he admitted he was rather nervous as he approached the Detroit net. "I'm not great on breakaways," Gavin said. "I knew at center that I was clear of the defenseman and that there was no one backing me the rest of the way. When I saw the goalie move out, I went to the backhand. We needed the win very badly because we would have been in a really desperate space if we had lost. Now if we can get a little winning streak together, we can get into the playoffs." It was certainly the biggest goal of Gavin's career to this point as well as the most important goal in the Leafs 1983–84 campaign.

Even though Chicago and St. Louis were within reach, the Leafs did not build off Gavin's goal and promptly lost 4 of the next 5 games, and would win only 2 of their next 10. Gavin scored twice more to bring his season total to 10, and it looked like the former Marlboro was going to be a solid if unspectacular contributor to the Leafs for years to come. However, after a 12-goal season in 1984–85, he was dealt away to Hartford for defenseman Chris Kotsopoulos on October 7, 1985. He enjoyed two consecutive 20-plus goal seasons with the Whalers (he scored a career-high 26 in 1985–86) before joining the Minnesota North Stars. The Leafs certainly missed his speed and strong checking game for a good number of years, while Gavin went on to play out his 768-game NHL career outside of Toronto.

Bill Berg

Leaf Record:
21 Goals,
21 Assists,
42 Points

Maple Leaf Moment: January 13, 1993

Bill Berg first started toying around with a hockey puck when he was a little kid and was enthralled by the great Canadian sport. The left-winger and native of St. Catharines, Ontario, played in the nearby town of Beamsville when he was fifteen. From there he went on to play Junior B with the Grimsby Peach Kings for two seasons and then on to the Toronto Marlboros by age eighteen.

Berg was never a goal scorer, but he was industrious and willing to do whatever it took to drive opponents to distraction. The New York Islanders saw enough in Berg to select him fifty-ninth overall in 1986 and he was on a minor-league championship team in Springfield in 1990. His playoff performance in '90 (17 points in 15 games) helped Berg finally land a role on the big team for the 1990–91 campaign where he managed to score 9 goals in his first NHL season.

When the Maple Leafs claimed Berg off waivers on December 3, 1992, Toronto general manager Cliff Fletcher said the virtually unknown six-foot-one, 205-pound Berg "was a versatile player who has been both a defenseman and a winger, he's young [at twenty-five] and he has good skating speed." Despite the GM's enthusiasm, coach Pat Burns was decidedly unsure about the young player, claiming he would not recognize Berg if he ran him over him with his car! The feisty Berg, however, had something to play for since he was on an expiring contract that would end after the 1992-93 season and his strong efforts that year certainly reflected his desire for a new deal.

Berg was not having a bad year on Long Island (6 goals and 9 points in 22 games), but he was probably best known at the time as the Islander who accidently shot the puck into his own net. The Leafs were hoping to add a little spice and scoring on the left wing where there was not much behind the oft-injured Wendel Clark at this point in the season. Veteran Mike Krushelnyski and youngster Kent Manderville would get better as the year went along, but they did not have Berg's checking abilities. It took a little bit of time for Berg to get going for his new team, but the night of January 13, 1993 proved to be a turning point.

Bill Berg had 8 goals and 19 points for the Leafs in 1993–94 and scored 1 more in the post-season. He was with the Leafs for one more year before he was dealt to the New York Rangers in a deal that saw Toronto acquire Nick Kypreos on February 29, 1996. Berg also played for the Ottawa Senators in 1998–99 before retiring after 546 career games.

The Leafs had not won a game when trailing after two periods so far during the '92-'93 campaign, but the game against the St. Louis Blues at Maple Leaf Gardens would prove to be different. Down 2-1 as the final frame began, the Leafs got a big short-handed goal by defenseman Bob Rouse to tie the score. A little more than six minutes later, Berg took a pass in the slot and fired one past Blues goalie Guy Herbert. A large smile came to his face as he raised his arms to celebrate the goal – his first in a Leaf uniform.

It was also his first goal in 18 games since joining Toronto and a big relief for number 10. "I kept going back home after every game banging my head against the wall wondering if I was ever going to score," Berg said afterward. "My wife kept telling me that I was doing my job defensively and that they didn't bring me here to score 50 goals. But you play the game to score goals and this one was a long time coming."

The Leafs made it 4–2 on a goal by Jamie Macoun, but the Blues got one back for a 4–3 final. The win put the Leafs seven up on the Blues for fourth place in the Norris Division and only three behind third-place Minnesota.

Berg ended up on a line with veterans Peter Zezel and Mark Osborne forming an effective checking line for a Leafs team in desperate need of such a trio. The line could drive opponents crazy with effective play in the neutral zone and they were all very willing to use their bodies in executing their *very* defined duties. The Leafs would go on to win 44 games and make the playoffs after having missed the post-season the previous two years. Berg had seven goals and 15 points in 58 regular-season games as a Leaf (and 24 total points, his best NHL season) and then chipped in 2 points in an amazing 21-game run by the team in the '93 playoffs. Although they fell just short of the Stanley Cup finals, another Marlboro had come home to make a very important contribution to a very good Maple Leaf team.

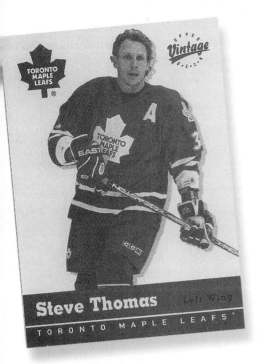

Steve Thomas

Steve Thomas

Left Wing

TORONTO MAPLE LEAFS

Steve Thomas

Leaf Record:
118 Goals,
173 Assists,
291 Points

Maple Leaf Moment: February 20, 1999

Even though Steve Thomas was born in Stockport, England, he grew up in the Toronto area and played minor hockey for the renowned Markham Waxers club. As an eighteen-year old, Thomas scored 68 goals in just 48 games for the Markham-based Junior A squad. His solid performance finally gave him a chance to play major junior, and he landed a job with the Toronto Marlboros for the 1982–83 season. He scored 18 goals that year. The next season Thomas pounded in 51 goals and recorded 105 points in 70 games played yet no NHL team drafted the stocky five-foot-ten, 180-pound left-winger with a howitzer of a shot. Finally, the hometown Maple Leafs took a chance on the Marlboro grad and signed him as a free agent. He was assigned to the farm team in St. Catharines and promptly scored 42 times in 1984–85, winning American Hockey League (AHL) rookie of the year award. The next season, he split his time between the Saints and the Maple Leafs. Despite splitting his time, Thomas scored 20 NHL goals that season and by the end of it his minor-league days were over. Thomas would score an impressive 35 goals the next year, but the Leafs foolishly traded him (along with Rick Vaive and Bob McGill) away to Chicago the following season. He would play for the Islanders and Devils before coming back home.

When Thomas scored only 14 goals for the New Jersey Devils in 1997–98, many thought that his career was on the definite downside. Toronto assistant general manager Mike Smith brought the thirty-five-year-old back for the 1998–99 season, but nobody knew exactly what to expect from the man they affectionately called "Stumpy." When regular season began, it was clear the Leafs had made a very good free-agent signing with Thomas scoring 26 goals and totaling 73 points in 78 games. Naturally, it helped playing alongside Leaf captain Mats Sundin, but Thomas was a solid addition to the Leafs' top line. He enjoyed coming back to the city that gave him his NHL start with his most memorable moment of the year certainly coming on the night Toronto opened up a new hockey palace.

Steve Thomas had a 10-point game (6 goals, 4 assists) with the Toronto Marlboros during a 10–4 win over the Kingston Canadians on March 11, 1984, at Maple Leaf Gardens. Thomas also played in the Stanley Cup final in 2003 as a member of the Anaheim Mighty Ducks.

The Leafs had been embarrassed one week earlier when Maple Leaf Gardens hosted its final NHL contest, losing a one-sided game to the Chicago Blackhawks by a 6–2 score (Thomas got one of the Leaf tallies). The Leafs had a chance to redeem themselves on February 20, 1999, when the Montreal Canadiens came into town to play the very first hockey game at the Air Canada Centre. Todd Warriner of the Maple Leafs scored the first-ever goal in the new building to give Toronto a 1–0 lead, but Montreal tied it up before Sundin put the Leafs back up by one. It stayed that way until the Habs tied it early in the third and it was still 2–2 when the third period ended.

An overtime loss to Montreal would have been an especially sour defeat for the Leafs on a night like this, so there was a wonderful opportunity for a hero to emerge. Thomas had a knack for scoring overtime goals and this game would only add to that legacy. With the five-minute overtime period winding down, Thomas knocked a backhand shot into the Montreal net past goalie Jeff Hackett to give the Leafs a 3–2 win sending Leaf fans home happy. Ladislav Kohn made a cross-ice pass to Thomas to start the winning play which ended with his twenty-second goal of the year.

"It was an incredible feeling to score the winning goal, especially in the first game in this building,"Thomas said."If you've ever scored a goal in overtime in any sport, it's an incredible feeling. I was just lucky to be that guy tonight. We needed those two points desperately,"he added, reminding everyone there was still a season to complete.

In his career with the Leafs, Thomas scored 7 overtime-winning goals during the regular season (second only to Sundin who had 14), but he found it hard to explain why he was so good in extra time."I don't know why that is; why I've been able to get so many overtime goals." However Thomas then added, "When I go out I want to score that overtime goal. That's my mindset."Thomas was a very good player whenever the game was on the line and scored 78 game-winning goals over his 1,235-game career. He scored 11 more in the playoffs.

The 1998–99 Leafs surprised the hockey world by finishing with 97 points, scoring the most goals in the league (268), and winning two rounds in the playoffs. Thomas had 6 playoff goals to bring his total for the year to 32—quite a season for a player nobody expected much production from anymore. Then again, few thought Thomas would ever score 421 career goals!

John Mitchell

Leaf Record:
20 Goals,
35 Assists,
55 Points

Maple Leaf Moment: November 1, 2008

The Maple Leafs do not often get players drafted as late as the fifth round that come up and join the big-league squad, but that is exactly what happened with Oakville, Ontario, native John Mitchell. The six-foot-one, 204-pound center/winger grew up a Leafs fan. He played in Waterloo, Ontario when he was sixteen for a team known as the Siskens of the OJPHL. Here he recorded 44 points in 48 games. He then played four seasons of major junior hockey with the Plymouth Whalers and notched 230 points (including 80 goals) in 258 games. Never an aggressive player, the Leafs took a chance on Mitchell by selecting him 158th overall in 2003 and then waited for him to develop in the American Hockey League.

It was a slow process, but Mitchell put a good season together for the first time as a professional when he had 51 points for the Toronto Marlies in the 2007–08 regular season. He then added 12 points (8 of them goals) in the playoffs as the Marlies made it to the final four in the 2008 Calder Cup playoffs. His excellent performance and his hard, rising shot served as a springboard to the Maple Leafs team which he made for the 2008–09 campaign.

Mitchell did not get off to a great start and as November rolled around, he remained scoreless. The New York Rangers, the best in the NHL, were scheduled to play the Maple Leafs at the Air Canada Centre on Saturday, November 1—not exactly the best circumstances for Mitchell to break out, nor for Toronto to get a win.

The Leafs did get something of a break when backup netminder Steve Valiquette (and not regular Henrik Lundqvist) got the start, nevertheless, Toronto was down 2–0 going into the third period. In fact, the game was halfway through the final frame when Mitchell stepped out of the penalty box and found himself following the play to the Rangers end. Matt Stajan got the puck over the New York blue line and it rolled to Mitchell. He found an open spot before letting a high drive go that found the net.

John Mitchell scored 5 goals and recorded 16 points for the New York Rangers in 2011–12, a team that finished first in the Eastern Conference. He signed as a free agent with the Colorado Avalanche in 2012–13, recording 20 points (10 goals, 10 assists) in 47 games played.

It was Mitchell's first NHL goal and he was thrilled to say the least. "I just fist pumped as many times as I could," Mitchell recounted. "I was so excited that nothing was really running through my mind, just, 'I scored, I scored, I scored.' It was great." Teammate Niklas Hagman retrieved the puck for the excited Leaf player.

The Leafs tied the score moments later on a goal by Jason Blake, and defenseman Pavel Kubina added another to suddenly give the Leafs a 3–2 lead. Mitchell scored his second of the night at the 16:06 mark when he let go a low, hard shot to the far side of the Rangers' goal. Another late marker gave the home side a 5–2 win over the high-flying Rangers. It was quite a demolition by the Leafs and all in the last eight minutes of the contest. The 19,179 spectators in Toronto loved every second of the comeback and quickly got behind the team when they started rolling.

Mitchell was named first star of the game and reflected on the Leafs play of late. "I think we just try to make it hard on ourselves. Being down 2–0 is not something that we like but it seems to be working." He was talking about how the team often found itself down in a game, but seemed to find a way back. However, they weren't able to climb back all of the time and the 2008–09 Leafs finished with a 34–35–13 record and out of a playoff spot.

Mitchell turned in a pretty good season for a rookie (12 goals and 29 points) who averaged 13:48 of ice time per game. He produced slightly fewer points (23 in 60 games played) in 2009–10, but after only 23 games the following season, he found himself back in the American Hockey League for the balance of 2010-11. However, the Rangers liked Mitchell and on February 28, 2011, they picked up his rights for their seventh-round draft choice in 2012. The Leafs essentially gave away a player they had spent time developing—and for nothing. Mitchell successfully re-established himself in the AHL and was brought up to the Rangers for the 2011–12 season. He has been with Colorado since 2012 and scored 21 goals over the last two seasons.

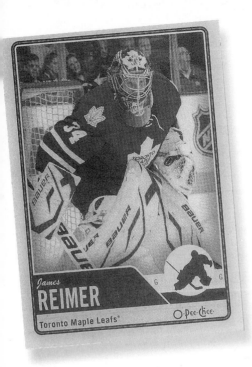

James Reimer

Leaf Record:
65 Wins,
48 Losses,
15 Ties,
11 Shutouts

Maple Leaf Moment: January 1, 2011

Goaltender James Reimer came to hockey a little later than do most youngsters who live in Canada. The Manitoba native was already twelve when he first strapped on goalie equipment, only doing so because his older brother Mark needed someone to shoot at! Reimer quickly became competitive and after a good performance during a church hockey tournament, he caught the eye of hockey agent Ray Petkau. Reimer went on to excel for two seasons in AAA hockey for the Interlake Lightning. His impressive performance got him drafted by the Red Deer Rebels of the Western Hockey League (WHL) for the 2005–06 season when he was seventeen years old. Reimer did not do well initially, but fortunately, was given another chance thanks to Carter Sears, the director of player personnel for the Rebels. Reimer had only one good season for the Red Deer club (posting a 26–23–7 record in 2006–07), but the Maple Leafs liked him enough to select the six-foot-two, 208-pounder ninety-ninth overall in 2006.

Reimer did not begin his pro career with the Leafs top farm team; instead, he was assigned to the East Coast Hockey League where he played for two teams in 2008–09. He ended the year as playoff MVP with the champion South Carolina Stingrays. The Maple Leafs took notice and he was with the Toronto Marlies of the AHL for most of the 2009–10 season. A bad ankle injury caused him to miss eleven weeks of action, so he only played 26 games; nevertheless, he posted an impressive 14–8–2 record. He started the next season with the Marlies (9–5–1 overall in 2010–11), but got called up to the NHL when Maple Leafs suffered injuries.

It was not known at the time when or if Reimer would get a start with the Leafs. But Reimer stayed calm and cool on the bench as he backed up Jonas Gustavsson, patiently waiting for his chance. Then, when the Leafs headed into Ottawa for a game on New Year's Day, coach Ron Wilson let the raw netminder know he was going to get his first NHL start in two days. The information was not made public until game day when Reimer was ready to play. By the time the night was over, the Leafs had cause to celebrate the New Year with a 5–1 triumph over their hated provincial rivals.

James Reimer was born and grew up in Morweena, Manitoba, a tiny town (population 1,100) two hours north of Winnipeg. While he has come a long way to meet the challenges of playing in hockey's most passionate market, the Leafs have given Reimer another concern with the acquisition of goalie Jonathan Bernier from the Los Angeles Kings in June 2013. The off-season plan in the summer of '13 was to have both goalies battle for the number-one position in net for the 2013–14 campaign.

It was a strong performance from a Leaf team that had only won twice in their last 7 games. "It felt great and this is one of the best games I've seen us play since I've been here," said a very happy and relieved Reimer. He had been waiting for about two weeks to start a game but it was worth it to secure such an important victory.

It was a big night for other Marlies players on the Leafs roster who gave Reimer some excellent support in his first victory. Darryl Boyce scored his first NHL goal while winger Joey Crabb recorded 2 assists on goals scored by Tyler Bozak, another Marlie graduate. The only Senator to beat Reimer was defenseman Sergei Gonchar on a 5–3 Ottawa advantage. Otherwise, the large netminder stopped 31 of 32 shots and looked good doing so.

Reimer admitted to having some pre-game jitters. "I was nervous in the afternoon but once the game started, I settled down and tried to keep it like any other," the twenty-two-year-old said afterward. His wife and parents came in for the game, providing the red-headed netminder with lots of moral support. The young goalie did not consider himself high on the Leafs depth chart, but an injury to veteran J.S. Giguere gave him an opening— and he was prepared to take advantage. In 37 games for the Leafs, Reimer posted a 20–10–5 record with 3 shutouts and a .921 save percentage. He also gave the team an outside chance to make the playoffs. The Leafs fell short of their goal that year but a new goaltending star might have been found.

Reimer suffered a serious concussion early in the 2011–12 season and finished with a 14–14–4 record in 34 games. He started the 2012–13 season trying to re-establish his credentials as a starting netminder at the major-league level once again. He did very well to post a 19–8–5 record during the regular season and helped the Leafs get back into the playoffs. However, a third period melt down during the seventh game of the opening round against Boston (he allowed 4 straight goals, including one in overtime, after the Leafs had established a 4–1 lead in the third period) once again raised questions about his ability to be a number-one netminder.

Reimer did not have a great season in 2013-14 and was playing a secondary role to the newly acquired Jonathan Bernier. He faltered badly in the last month of the '13-'14 campaign but a new two-year contract might give him another chance to stay with the Maple Leafs although it might be in a back-up role.

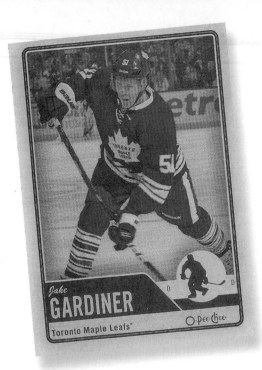

Jake Gardiner

Leafs Record:
17 Goals,
48 Assists,
65 Points

Maple Leaf Moment: January 24, 2012

When the Maple Leafs signed defenseman Francois Beauchemin as a free agent in 2009, the team was hopeful the veteran would provide stability and leadership to their blue line. However Beauchemin never seemed to find a comfort level in Toronto. During the middle of his third year as a Leaf, it was obvious he was not the same player and he was never going to be as effective as he had been for the Anaheim Ducks. It was also evident the Leafs were going to have trouble making the playoffs while the Ducks wanted the defender back to give their team a boost going into the post-season. A deal was worked out on February 9, 2011, that saw Beauchemin return to California in exchange for winger Joffrey Lupul and the former first-round draft choice (seventeenth overall in 2008) Jake Gardiner, a promising defenseman who had yet to play in the NHL.

Anaheim did not wish to part with Gardiner, but felt that since they had Justin Schultz (drafted in the second round, fortieth overall in 2008) waiting to join their blue line, they could afford to send Gardiner to Toronto. Ironically enough, both young defenders had been teammates at the University of Wisconsin and neither ended up with the Ducks after Schultz signed as a free agent with the Edmonton Oilers. The Leafs, on the other hand, were quite pleased with how the deal worked out and assigned Gardiner to the Toronto Marlies of the AHL for 10 games during the 2010–11 season. The twenty-year-old recorded three assists during his brief stay and it looked like he was going to be a Marlie to start the 2011–12 campaign.

Gardiner, however, so surprised everyone with his good play at training camp and in pre-season that he made the big team to start the year. Coach Ron Wilson clearly showed great faith in the still green defenseman. A gifted skater and puck handler, Gardiner is most effective when he has the puck and carries it out of his own end or makes a sharp pass to clear the zone. He is also good at manning the point and creating offensive chances for his team. He was racking up some points with assists, but it took until January 24, 2012, to register his first NHL goal.

A total of 110 players who played with the Marlies (in junior or the AHL) have gone on to play for the Maple Leafs. To date, six of them—Charlie Conacher, Harvey Jackson, Joe Primeau, Red Horner, George Armstrong, and Bob Pulford—have gone on to Hall of Fame careers in the NHL.

The Leafs were down 2–0 to the New York Islanders before getting one back late in the second. Early in the final frame, Gardiner let a wrist shot go from the point to even the score 2–2. It was his first-ever NHL goal (playing in his forty-third game of the season) and he was not done yet. A Gardiner pass to Mikhail Grabovski helped set up winger Clarke MacArthur to give the visiting Leafs a 3–2 lead. But the Islanders forced overtime on a goal with just thirteen seconds to play. However MacArthur scored his second of the game to give the Leafs a 4–3 overtime triumph.

"Pretty awesome, a once-in-a-lifetime thing," said a very happy Gardiner about his first career marker. "It was kind of a lucky play, but it feels good. Dion Phaneuf and Phil Kessel were screaming at me to shoot the puck tonight … so I threw it on net and it went in." Gardiner's father, John, had been following the Leafs in person for a while, but went home just two days before the goal versus the Islanders. The youngster believed his dad would give him a phone call soon. "He's always supported me and I'm sure it's an emotional night."

Gardiner would go onto to score a total of 7 goals as a rookie and added 23 assists to complete his first NHL season. When the Leafs missed the playoffs in 2012, Gardiner was assigned to the Marlies once again and he helped the AHL team make it to the Calder Cup final by recording 11 points in 17 post-season games.

The shortened 2012–13 season was not an easy one for Gardiner who had to start the year with the Marlies (since he was eligible to do so during the lockout) where he suffered a concussion. Marlies coach Dallas Eakins was very impressed by Gardiner's play and he saw plenty of ice time prior to the head injury. When the NHL season started, Leafs coach Randy Carlyle was not nearly so enamoured with Gardiner's play, stressing that defensive responsibilities were just as important as putting up points. Thus he was sent back to the farm club where he got an opportunity to better recover from his concussion and work on his game.

Gardiner eventually got the message and played better as the year went along. He was very good in the '13 playoffs (5 points in 6 games) but was still a minus 3 over the same number of games. It is obvious Gardiner has much to learn but it still looks like the Leafs took a good number-one draft choice away from another team, which is quite a shift in fortunes for the blue and white. Gardiner's development also shows that their AHL affiliate is still doing a solid job of preparing future Maple Leafs.

Jake Gardiner was born in Minnetonka, Minnesota, where he played high-school hockey. He attended the University of Wisconsin where he recorded 75 points (including 56 assists) in 121 games played over three seasons.

Gardiner was one of many Marlie players who were on the Maple Leafs roster during the 2012–13 season. The others who spent time with the Marlies over recent seasons include Tyler Bozak, Joe Colborne, Mark Fraser, Matt Frattin, Carl Gunnerson, Ryan Hamilton, Korbinian Holzer, Nazem Kadri, Leo Komarov, Mike Kostka, Colton

Orr, James Reimer, and Ben Scrivens. This impressive list is a strong indicator that the Marlies produce effective NHL-caliber players, and that more will be on the way to the Maple Leafs in the near future.

Gardiner finished the 2013-14 season with 10 goals and 31 points and was then rewarded with a new five-year contract that totaled over $20 million. It would appear the Maple Leafs are counting on Gardiner's continued improvement going into the future and helping them get back to the playoffs.

Gardiner finished the 2013-14 season with 10 goals and 31 points and was then rewarded with a new five-year contract that totaled over $20 million. It would appear the Maple Leafs are counting on Gardiner's continued improvement going into the future and helping them get back to the playoffs.

Wendel Clark was named captain of the Maple Leafs in August of 1991.

FIRST ROUNDERS OR FIRST PICKS

Rick Kehoe • George Ferguson • Lanny McDonald
Randy Carlyle • Joel Quenneville • Wendel Clark
Vincent Damphousse • Rob Pearson • Carlo Colaiacovo
Nazem Kadri • Morgan Rielly

SINCE 1969 WHEN THE National Hockey League adopted a universal draft system to decide who would get the next group of incoming talent, the Maple Leafs have selected their fair share of studs and duds. The Leafs have generally chosen well in the first round of what is now known as the Entry Draft, but have failed for the most part to unearth talent in the subsequent rounds of selection. The first player chosen by the Leafs always gets an inordinate amount attention and, in some cases, far too many chances to prove that the general manager and scouts made the right choice. In other cases, it has worked out very well. The Leafs have had some of their greatest difficulties since 1969 after they traded away their first pick (a story of poor management that did not appreciate the value of a top-round draft selection). However, when the Leafs have managed to keep their best choices, the draft always brings them new hope and an opportunity to take a potential superstar who can change the long-term fortunes of the team. The following players were either selected in the first round of the draft or were the first choice the Leafs had in a particular year:

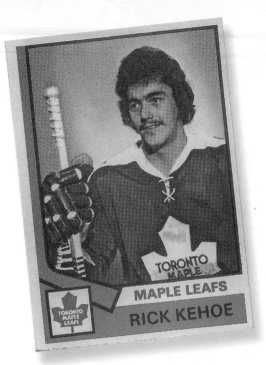

Rick Kehoe

Leaf Record:
59 Goals,
72 Assists,
131 Points

Maple Leaf Moment: 1972–73 Season

The Hamilton Red Wings were not an especially good team during the 1970–71 season, winning just 22 games in the regular season (while losing 35), although they did earn a playoff spot. The best player on the club that season was right-winger Rick Kehoe who led the team in assists (41) and points (80) while scoring 39 goals, the second-best mark on the team. Kehoe was voted MVP of the Red Wings who had acquired him one year earlier from the London Knights of the OHL. The offensively gifted five-foot-eleven, 180-pound Kehoe was not selected in the first round of the 1971 NHL draft, but the Leafs took him twenty-second overall with their first selection, the eighth pick of the second round.

The Leafs projected that Kehoe would be a good goal scorer, but assigned him to Tulsa of the Central Hockey League for some seasoning to start the 1971–72 campaign. He proved a quick study, scoring 18 goals and totaling 39 points in 32 games played. Kehoe's good work in the minors got him promoted to Toronto to close out the 1971–72 season, scoring 8 goals and totaling 16 points in just 38 games. It appeared for a change that the Leafs had made a great selection with a second-round pick!

The 1972–73 edition of the Toronto Maple Leafs was one of the worst in team history. Their lineup was essentially wrecked by players who defected to the World Hockey Association (including star netminder Bernie Parent) after the 1971–72 campaign. The Leaf defense was made up mostly of youngsters who were not going to be permanent NHL players, and the forwards featured only a few gems such as Dave Keon, Darryl Sittler, Norm Ullman, Ron Ellis, and 1972 Canada-Russia series hero, Paul Henderson (who played in only 40 games in the 1972–73 regular season). The only rising young star at this stage was Kehoe who had showed some promise as a right-winger.

The Leafs were still looking for their first win of the season when the Los Angeles Kings came in for a Saturday-night contest at the Gardens on October 14, 1972. It was just the third game of the season but the Leafs needed a win to give their team a boost.

Rick Kehoe would go on to score 312 goals for the Penguins, bringing his career total to 371. He would also play in two NHL All-Star Games (1981 and 1983).

Kehoe was hoping to show the NHL that he was a big-league talent who could play an entire season in the top circuit. The Leafs opened the scoring on a rare goal by defenseman Bob Baun, but the Kings came back to lead 2–1 by the end of the first. Henderson tied it for Toronto and then Kehoe scored his first of the year with assists going to Sittler and Denis Dupere. Los Angeles goalie Gary Edwards stopped Kehoe on a breakaway, but the twenty-one-year-old stayed out in front of the net and eventually slapped the puck home after taking a pass. The Kings again came back to tie the score, but Ellis gave the Leafs the lead again before the middle frame was over.

Kehoe scored what turned out to be the game winner when he found the back of the net early in the third and then Ullman scored to ensure the home side of a 6–4 win. "Kehoe was really flying," said Leaf coach Johnny McLellan after the game. "In fact that whole line looked great again. That's the third game in a row they've played well," the coach continued about the Sittler, Kehoe, and Dupere line. Sittler and Kehoe formed an effective pair the whole season and finished 1–2 in Leafs scoring with 77 and 75 points respectively. Kehoe's best night of the season (2 goals, 2 assists) came on November 25 when they shellacked Oakland 11–0 on home ice, taking advantage of former Leafs goalie Marv Edwards who was in net for the Seals. Kehoe finished 1972–73 with 33 goals (second only to Keon's 37), but the Leafs still finished a dismal 27–41–10, well out of the playoffs.

It was expected Kehoe would continue at his productive pace, but he only managed 18 goals the following season and feuded with new coach Red Kelly. Kehoe requested a trade and was soon dealt away to Pittsburgh for Blaine Stoughton (the Penguins' seventh overall pick in 1973) and a number-one draft choice (used by the Leafs to select defenseman Trevor Johansen twelfth overall in 1977). Stoughton contributed little to the Leafs (he did have a 23-goal season in 1974–75), but had a career-best 56-goal season for Hartford in 1979–80. Johansen was gone after just two seasons, although he had helped the Leafs win a couple of playoff rounds in the 1978 post-season. Kehoe, on the other hand, would have many productive years in Pittsburgh including a 55-goal season in 1980–81, when he also earned the Lady Byng Trophy. Obviously, the Leafs let a great draft choice get away and they would regret it for many years.

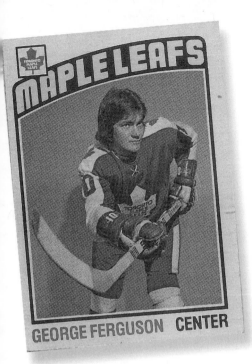

GEORGE FERGUSON CENTER

George Ferguson
Leaf Record:
57 Goals,
110 Assists,
167 Points

Maple Leaf Moment: April 11, 1978

George Ferguson first came to the attention of the Maple Leafs when the Toronto Marlboros acquired him in a trade with the Oshawa Generals, the team that had drafted the talented center into major junior hockey. The six-foot, 200-pound Ferguson had a strong shot, just the right amount of aggressiveness and he was a very good skater. In his final junior year, he scored 36 goals and recorded 92 points for a Marlboro club (45 wins and 93 points in 1971–72) that was one of the best in junior hockey. The Leafs decided to take the native of Trenton, Ontario, with the eleventh pick of the 1972 draft after three of his junior teammates, Bill Harris, Steve Shutt, and Dave Gardner, were selected ahead of him that year.

The Leafs hoped Ferguson would eventually develop as a second center behind Darryl Sittler who had been drafted two years earlier. At times it looked like Ferguson was going to fit into the mold perfectly after playing the entire 1972–73 season in Toronto (scoring 10 goals as a rookie) for a very bad Leaf squad (only 27 wins). However, Ferguson split the next season between Toronto and the minor league team in Oklahoma City where he had 40 points in 35 games. He was back with the Leafs full time in 1974–75, scoring 19 goals and totaling 49 points in 69 games. Veteran centers, such as Dave Keon and Norm Ullman, were now gone from the Leaf squad and the club expected Ferguson to help fill the void. However, after a 42-point season in '75-'76, Ferguson settled into a third-line role where goals and points from his stick were much less frequent. This was especially the case when Red Kelly was replaced as Leafs coach.

The 1977–78 Leafs started off the season in fine style under new coach Roger Neilson. They went 4–1–2 in October and followed that up with eight wins in November and nine more victories in December. The club slowed down by the end of the regular campaign, but still finished with 41 wins (matching the club record) and 92 points. The Leafs had the sixth-best overall mark in the NHL in 1977–78 and faced the Los Angeles Kings in the opening round best-of-three preliminary series. The Leafs would host the opener on April 11, 1978, at the Gardens.

George Ferguson's three goals versus the Kings tied a then post-season record for most goals in one period of a playoff game, making Ferguson the eleventh NHLer at that time to reach the feat. The record is now set at four goals, and was established by Tim Kerr (1985) and Mario Lemieux (1989). Ferguson finished his 797-game NHL career with 398 points.

The Leafs were favoured to win the series since the Kings were a rather unimpressive 31-34-15 during the season. But Toronto certainly did not want to take anything for granted. The Kings had goalie Rogie Vachon in net who was a proven Stanley Cup winner (twice with Montreal in 1968 and 1969). However, the Leafs started quickly and never looked back. Supporting players Stan Weir and Jerry Butler each scored to put the Leafs up 2-0 by the end of the first. The contest turned a little nasty in the second period (two fights) but the Leafs scored twice more on markers by Dave Williams and Borje Salming. The third period belonged to Ferguson who potted three goals in the final stanza.

Ferguson scored twice to open the third, padding the Toronto lead 6–0 before the Kings finally hit the scoreboard. Ferguson responded with his third of the period and although Los Angeles scored a couple of late goals, the Leafs cruised to a 7–3 win with 32 shots on goal. For Ferguson, the playoff hat trick was a moment of redemption. He had scored just 7 times (in 73 games) over the entire season and his status as the number-two center behind superstar Sittler was pretty much a thing of the past.

"There were times this season even when I figured I was checking well when I didn't think I was contributing much to the team because I just couldn't buy any goals," a relieved Ferguson said after the game. "I knew that if I could score a few times it would take the pressure off some of the other guys to produce all the time. But nothing seemed to work and that kept the pressure on me."

For at least one night the pressure was off, and his teammates responded by coming off the bench to congratulate the hard-working Ferguson after his third tally of the night. The Leafs won the next game 4–0 and the Kings were dispatched in two straight games. The Leafs followed up with a seventh game elimination of the New York Islanders in the next round.

Ferguson never could match the scoring prowess he had shown in junior and, after the Leafs success in the '78 post-season, the once-promising center was deemed expendable. He was dispatched to Pittsburgh where Ferguson would record 20 or more goals in the next four seasons—a level of achievement he could not reach in Toronto.

Lanny McDonald

Leaf Record:
219 Goals,
240 Assists,
459 Points

Maple Leaf Moment: 1977 Playoffs

Right-winger Lanny McDonald knew that the Maple Leafs were very interested in drafting him after his great junior career in Medicine Hat, Alberta. In his final two seasons of junior, the hard-shooting McDonald scored 112 goals and Leaf scout Torchy Schell let him know the Leafs were likely going to select him in the first round of the 1973 draft. Denis Potvin went first, as expected, to the New York Islanders while Tom Lysiak (McDonald's line mate in junior) went second to the Atlanta Flames. It was uncertain what Vancouver was going to do with the third pick, but when they announced Dennis Ververgaert, the Maple Leafs breathed a sigh of relief and made McDonald their fourth overall selection. The newest Maple Leaf had a real appreciation for the long and storied history of his new club and looked forward to playing in fabled Maple Leaf Gardens.

Although he was an inspired choice of the Leafs, the six-foot, 190-pound McDonald took his time getting going in the NHL. A 14-goal rookie season was followed by 17 goals the next year. But in 1975–76, McDonald scored 37 times and found himself playing alongside center Darryl Sittler. The two formed a dynamic duo and provided a great deal of excitement for fans and a lot of inspiration for what was at this point, a very young Leafs team. McDonald scored 46 times in the 1976–77 season and the Leafs earned a playoff spot under coach Red Kelly.

Leaf fans were hoping that the team would play better in the '77 post-season than they did during the regular season (33–32–15, good for 81 points). They were also hoping to see the club advance farther in the playoffs this year than they did in '76, after taking defending Stanley Cup champion Philadelphia to 7 games. However, the Leafs had to play the Pittsburgh Penguins in the best-of-three preliminary round before the serious work began. The Leafs took the opener 4–2, but lost the next game 6–-4 on home ice—the same day the Toronto Blue Jays played their first-ever major-league baseball game. The Leafs needed to win back in Pittsburgh to extend their season. As usual, it was the Leafs best players who helped the team advance with a 5–2 win on April 9, 1977.

In 1978, the Maple Leafs won their first best-of-seven series since 1967 on an overtime goal by Lanny McDonald defeating the New York Islanders in a seven-game series.

The game got off to a good start for Toronto when Salming scored the opening goal on a setup from McDonald and Mike Pelyk. McDonald was also in on the Leafs second marker scored by Ian Turnbull, but the Penguins got one back before the first period ended to make it 2–1.

McDonald stole the show in the middle frame with 2 goals to make it 4–1. Both goals came on wrist shots from about twenty-five-feet out and each eluded Pittsburgh goalie Denis Heron. The Penguins got one back on a goal by Blair Chapman, but could get no closer. As the game was winding down, the Penguins pulled Heron for an extra attacker, but Leaf captain Darryl Sittler broke away and then in a classy and unselfish manner passed off to line mate McDonald who shot it into the empty net for the hat trick. It was McDonald's fifth point of the night, a game the Leafs right-winger called the best of his career to that point.

McDonald commented on Sittler's generosity: "I was yelling at Darryl to shoot but he just laughed at me and passed the puck."

Sittler seemed a little bewildered that people were surprised he passed the puck. "Why wouldn't I do it when Lanny had the chance to score three goals in a playoff game?"

The Leafs survived to play another round with the Philadelphia Flyers, the third-straight year the teams would face-off in a best-of-seven series.

Toronto won the first two games on the road, but returned home only to lose two consecutive games in overtime. In the fourth of the series, played on April 17, McDonald scored four times to give the Leafs a 5–2 lead. Unfortunately for Toronto, they ended up losing 6–5 in extra time. "It's just a sad, sad way to lose a hockey game," an inconsolable McDonald said after the Sunday night loss at the Gardens. "It didn't matter who scored the goals. We'll take a day to get our heads together. We know we can win in Philadelphia."

Unfortunately, the Leafs did not win another game in the series though McDonald scored twice more in the final contest. In spite of the series loss to the Flyers, McDonald proved he was a playoff performer notching a club record 10 goals in one playoff year.

Randy Carlyle

Leaf Record:
2 Goals,
16 Assists,
18 Points

Maple Leaf Moment: January 28, 1978

The Maple Leafs did not have a first-round selection in the 1976 Entry Draft and it looked like they had made a mistake taking defenseman Randy Carlyle with their first choice in the second round (thirtieth overall). It had nothing to do with Carlyle's abilities because he was a good prospect; rather, it had to do with the "letter of intent" the youngster had signed with Cincinnati of the World Hockey Association. Cincinnati thought Carlyle's signature on the letter was as good as a contract. The Leafs had another view.

The dispute between the two teams was likely headed for a courtroom battle when a side deal was struck. Toronto agreed to pick up Mike Pelyk's contract (a former Leaf defenseman who was now playing for Cincinnati in the rival league) and in exchange, the Leafs would get the uncontested playing rights to Carlyle. This was one deal that worked out well for the Leafs in every way because they had a young blueliner to add to their team, which included Borje Salming and Ian Turnbull, while Pelyk turned out to be a nice veteran addition to their defensive brigade.

In his last year of junior, the very determined Carlyle recorded 79 points (15 goals, 64 assists) for the Sudbury Wolves. He came to the Leafs' training camp in September 1976 with a couple of job openings available since Dave Dunn and Rod Seiling were both gone from the blueline. Carlyle made a good impression, but was sent to Dallas where he would get some seasoning on the Leafs farm team. He played in Texas for 26 games in 1976–77 then came up to the Leafs for 45 contests (recording 5 assists). He still needed to work on his defensive game (he was a minus 19 with the Leafs), but Carlyle was a confident player, especially when he had the puck. He played in 9 playoff games during the '77 post-season, recording 1 assist.

Roger Neilson took over as Leafs coach the next season, which meant that Carlyle started the 1977–78 campaign back in Dallas; however, he was only there for 21 games (recording a very impressive 17 points) before coming back to stay. He was with Toronto for 49 games during the regular season and scored twice while recording 13 points. He had a multiple point game on the night of January 28, 1978 which first showed Toronto fans that this player had some real NHL talent. It was a wild, offensively charged contest that saw Carlyle and his teammates escape with a 7–5 victory over the Atlanta Flames.

> Randy Carlyle became a Maple Leaf once again in the 2011–12 season when he was named head coach on March 3, 2012. His first game behind the bench came against the Montreal Canadiens, which the Leafs won 3–1. "For an Ontario kid coming back and getting a second chance at this, that's special," he said upon his appointment to the job. He coached the Leafs back into the playoffs for the first time since 2004 during the lockout-shortened season of 2012–13. Carlyle had coached the Anaheim Ducks to a Stanley Cup win in 2007.

The game was tied 5–5 when Carlyle picked up his second assist of the night at the 7:09 mark of the third. It came when Carlyle drove a shot from the point, which hit teammate Bruce Boudreau in front of the net and bounced past Atlanta goalie Yves Belanger (a netminder who had shut out the hometown Leafs 3–0 on New Year's Eve). Toronto's Ron Ellis added an empty-net goal to wrap up the scoring and give the Leafs their twenty-sixth win of the year. Interestingly, Carlyle was not on the ice for any of the 5 Atlanta goals. Neilson commented that the Leafs were, oddly, better when playing away from Maple Leaf Gardens. "We play better on the road," the coach said of his club that was now 15–9–3 away and 11–6–4 at home. "The worst thing that's happened to us all year is losing to some of the poorer clubs at home." How many times has a Leaf coach had the same lament in the post-expansion era?

The Leafs had one of their best years under Neilson and although they closed out the year with 10 loses in their last 12 games, the Leafs still finished the 1977–78 season with 41 victories. They went on to beat Los Angeles and the New York before Montreal beat them in the semi-final. Carlyle appeared in 7 playoff games (1 assist) and helped fill in the gap when Salming suffered a bad eye injury against New York. It looked like Carlyle was going to be a good Leaf defenseman for a number of years until he was traded to Pittsburgh (along with George Ferguson) in a deal for Dave Burrows. Carlyle starred in Pittsburgh (winning the Norris Trophy once) while Burrows did not meet any expectations whatsoever. Carlyle also played nine seasons for the Winnipeg Jets before his long playing career (1,055 NHL games, 647 points) came to a close at the age thirty-six.

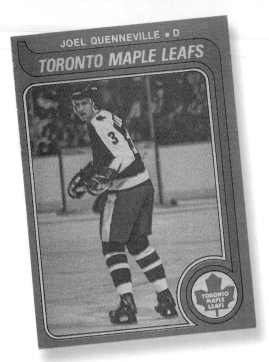

Joel Quenneville

Leaf Record:
3 Goals,
13 Assists,
16 Points

Maple Leaf Moment: March 3, 1979

Defenseman Joel Quenneville scored an impressive 27 goals and totaled 103 points in his final year of junior playing with the Windsor Spitfires of the OHL. He also had 114 penalty minutes during the 1977–78 regular season. Despite this, Quenneville was nervous as he waited for his name to be called at the draft. He did not want to go to a team such as Montreal who were loaded with talent on the blue line and had two picks in the first round. The Canadiens selected Danny Geoffrion (eight overall) and Dave Hunter (seventeenth overall) before the Leafs, with the third pick of the second round, finally selected Quenneville twenty-first overall.

He was relieved and happy to be a Maple Leaf. "I've always liked to watch the Leafs, especially Ian Turnbull. I guess that's the kind of style I like to play—I'm an offensive defenseman," Quenneville said.

"We were drafting so low we had to take the best player available regardless of position," said Leafs general manager Jim Gregory.

Coach Roger Neilson said the six-foot-one, 200-pound blueliner was highly rated by Leaf scouts and that Quenneville could play any position, not just defense.

"And remember when Turnbull stepped into his first training camp nobody heard of him either," added Gregory.

The Leafs sent the young defenseman to their farm team in New Brunswick where Quenneville posted 11 points (10 were assists) in 16 games before he got the call to the big team for the final 61 games of the 1978–79 season. The Leafs were under-performing that year and talk of coach Neilson getting the ax was circulating all around the city. Then owner Harold Ballard (apparently)"fired"Neilson after a loss in Montreal. But the Leafs could not find a replacement so Leaf management kept mum on the subject and considered their cards.

It was a wild weekend of confusion around the Gardens as players appealed to Ballard not to fire (or to reinstate, whatever the case may have been) their mentor, Roger Neilson. With Ballard not wanting to confirm anything prior to the start of the next home game, Toronto fans were uncertain who would be calling the next line changes against the tough Philadelphia Flyers (led by Bobby Clarke and Bill Barber) come Saturday night. To complete the circus, the game would be shown to a national television audience on *Hockey Night in Canada*. Just after the national anthem was completed, and with suspense building, Neilson calmly walked out toward his familiar spot to a large standing roar from the Toronto crowd. Roger was back!

Joel Quenneville would go on to play in 803 career NHL games, appearing in more contests than sixteen of the other twenty players chosen ahead of him in the 1978 Entry Draft. He would also coach the Chicago Blackhawks to the Stanley Cup in 2010 and in 2013.

The Ballard-Neilson fiasco must have shocked every Leaf player, especially impressionable rookies and youngsters such as Quenneville, Ron Wilson, and John Anderson. Once the puck dropped, however, the Leafs were out to show they could play for the coach they did not want to see fired.

The Flyers had a 2–1 lead late in the second period when captain Darryl Sittler scored with just seven seconds left. That goal seemed to re-energize the Leafs and they scored early in the third to make it 3–2. Philadelphia was not going to quit easily but then Sittler made a pretty pass to a wide-open Quenneville who slid a shot through the pads of Flyer goalie Rick St. Croix. The young Leaf rearguard had improved steadily since his call-up and his first-ever NHL goal made it 4–2. He retrieved the puck as a souvenir and it turned out to be the game winner in a game that ended 4–3. In any other game more might have been made of Quenneville's first tally but in "Hollywood North," as the Flyers liked to call the Gardens, the rookie's goal was just another sidebar story. However, that goal was only one of two scored by Quenneville for the Leafs in 1978–79, but it was likely his most memorable.

The Leafs made the playoffs in 1979, but after sweeping Atlanta in 2 straight games, they once again were ousted by the powerful Montreal Canadiens who went on to win their fourth-consecutive Stanley Cup. Quenneville played in all 6 post-season games for the Leafs and recorded 1 assist. It now looked like the Leafs had found a good young defenseman who could play in the big league, and he was only twenty.

However, less than a year later he was traded by the Leafs with Lanny McDonald to Colorado. Considering that future Hall of Famer Lanny McDonald was involved in the transaction, it is not surprising that Quenneville's inclusion in the deal was largely ignored. It turned out he deserved much better.

WENDEL CLARK

PARKHURST™

Wendel Clark

Leaf Record:
260 Goals,
181 Assists,
441 Points

Maple Leaf Moment: February 25, 1986

Toronto has had a number of high draft picks over the years since the Entry Draft began in 1969, many in the top-ten and even the top-five positions. But the Leafs have only made the first overall selection just once—in 1985 after a horrendous 20-win season in 1984–85 gave them that honor.

Five players stood out as the consensus best players available (including Craig Wolanin, Jim Sandlak, and Dana Murzyn), but the Leafs were focused on only two players in this group. Craig Simpson of Michigan State was a natural goal scorer but he had initial reservations about coming to Toronto. Simpson later said he would be fine with being a Leaf, but it did not matter because the club knew all along that truculent winger Wendel Clark from the Saskatoon Blades was their man. This time Toronto management made no mistake.

The Maple Leafs had not had an impact rookie (especially at the forward position) on their team for many seasons by the time eighteen-year old Clark joined the club in 1985–86. It was certainly one reason the Leafs were often surpassed by other teams who had youngsters join their clubs and make an immediate impact.

Clark's rookie campaign was shortened to 66 games because he broke a bone in his foot early in the season, but the left-winger had made his presence known and on certain nights, he was the Leafs best player. One of those nights came on February 25, 1986, when the Leafs hosted the New York Rangers.

By the time the evening was over Clark had registered his first career hat trick and talk about a Calder Trophy (not given to a Leaf since Brit Selby in 1966) win was in the air. Clark's first of the night turned out to be the winning goal in a 7–3 triumph over the Broadway Blueshirts.

> Wendel Clark recorded eight career hat-tricks as a Maple Leaf (2 of those games were 4-goal efforts) and he also holds the team record for most career playoff goals with 34. Clark's sweater number 17 was honored by the Leafs on November 22, 2008.

Russ Courtnall fed a cross-ice pass to Clark to start the sequence that led to the winning goal. Clark took the feed, and hesitated for a second, before letting a howitzer of a drive go that Ranger netminder John Vanbiesbrouck could only wave at as it sailed high into the net. Clark explained that he was thinking about cutting back inside before deciding to shoot. "I saw an opening and went for it," Clark recounted. Courtnall also assisted on Clark's two other tallies as the young line mates showed some good chemistry.

Clark's 3-goal outburst may have been spurred on by a scuffle with New York veteran defenseman Ron Greschner. Both were given 5-minute majors even though it really was not much of a fight. Nevertheless, Clark stormed out of the penalty box ready to inflict some real damage on the visitors. "That probably got me going," Clark said of his tussle with Greschner. "Sometimes it works that way. I had a touch of the flu." Later in the third period Clark rocked Ranger forward Bob Brooke with a resounding bodycheck that had the Gardens crowd applauding Clark's every effort. In typical Clark fashion, he tried very hard to deflect attention away from himself as praise was heaped on him after the game. "As the team improves, the profiles of the individuals will improve. But right now, I feel the best thing to do is work hard and keep a low profile," he said. It was suggested that Clark might be captain material since the

Leafs had just taken the coveted "C" away from Rick Vaive (who had also scored and added one assist versus New York). But Clark would not be drawn into such a discussion and suggested the captaincy should go to a veteran player.

Clark was in no way effusive about his play, but others were not so shy when talking about the tough Leaf rookie. Rangers coach Ted Sator said, "Clark is a complete hockey player and he will get better." Added Greschner, "He's a good young player."

Toronto coach Dan Maloney did not hold back any praise when he said,. "I'm biased but in my mind there is no one around like him. I can't say enough about the kid; he's a great player. He gives our team a burst. He's a hard worker. Even in practice he bears down all the time. And when he gets the puck around the net, he always tries to bury it."

Clark would go onto set a team record for most goals by a rookie with 34 while finishing second to Gary Suter of the Calgary Flames in the Calder Trophy race for top rookie in 1985–86. Clark would go on to score 37 times in his second year with the Leafs.

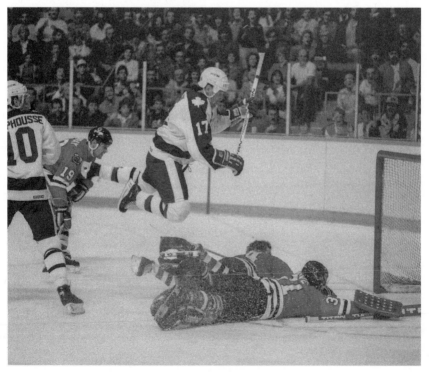

Vincent Damphousse
Left Wing

Vincent Damphousse

Leaf Record:
118 Goals,
211 Assists,
329 Points

Maple Leaf Moment: 1991 All-Star Game

The Maple Leafs were not quite sure if center/left-winger Vincent Damphousse was going to be available to them when they were scheduled to select sixth overall at the 1986 Entry Draft. However, the New Jersey Devils threw a bit of a twist into the selection process when they selected Neil Brady (who would go on to play just 86 NHL games) with the third pick. It was something of an unexpected choice, but that meant Quebec junior star Damphousse was likely going to be there when it was Toronto's time to choose. And sure enough, the Maple Leafs nabbed the six-foot-one, 200-pound Montreal native who had recorded 323 points (including 214 assists) in 203 junior games.

The slick playmaker was very mature for his age and he made the Toronto team in his first attempt even though he was just nineteen-years old. Damphousse quickly proved he belonged in the NHL. He had a 46-point (21-goal) rookie season followed by a 48-point year in 1987–88. His next two seasons saw him record 68 and 94 points respectively and by the 1990–91 season, he had become a legitimate NHL star. Damphousse was never an overly aggressive player, but he was never afraid to go where he needed to be to set up a goal or score one himself.

He and winger Daniel Marois (another Montreal native drafted by the Leafs) proved to be a top French-Canadian duo, something more readily expected in Montreal than Toronto!

Damphousse was the Maple Leafs lone representative at the NHL All-Star Game that was held at an emotionally charged Chicago Stadium on January 19, 1991. The Gulf War was on the minds of most people that Saturday afternoon and the American national anthem (sung by Wayne Messmer) had everyone in the building letting out a tremendous roar in support of the troops. The entire scene made Damphousse nervous, in fact he was shaking in awe he was so moved by it all.

So it is not surprising it took the Leaf left-winger a while to get going along with line mates Steve Yzerman and Adam Oates, although he did score his first goal of the game to give the Campbell Conference a 2–1 lead to end the first period. Damphousse was rather quiet in the second, but in the third he let loose with a tremendous 3-goal effort. The score was 8–4 for the Campbell team but the Wales Conference was not out

Vincent Damphousse is one of only four Leafs to ever win the All-Star Game MVP. The others include Bruce Gamble, Eddie Shack, and Frank Mahovlich. Damphousse's four-goal performance in the All-Star Game was matched by Mario Lemieux, Wayne Gretzky, Mike Gartner, and Dany Heatley.

the game yet. Then Damphousse went to work and scored 2 more goals (in less than three minutes) to put the game out of reach. With less than three minutes to play, he added his fourth with a wicked drive right from the slot area that sailed over goaltender Andy Moog's shoulder. It put a finishing touch on an 11–5 Campbell Conference victory. The Leafs leading scorer on the season (73 points in 1990–91) had just finished the game of his life.

Damphousse's great effort earned him game MVP honors (beating out Oates who had a 5-point game). And the Leaf player said it was a game he would never forget. "It's a day I'll remember the rest of my life. I didn't think I'd make it through my first shift my hands were shaking so bad," Damphousse recounted." "My legs felt like they weighed 200 pounds." The fact that he was playing on a great team was not lost on the Leaf player who would not see post-season action after the 1990–91 regular campaign was over. "I just feel on top of the world right now. Just to make this team and play with all these superstars was a thrill, but to win this [the MVP award] as well…"

Campbell Conference coach John Muckler was also impressed, saying Damphousse "played a heck of a game."

Just when it looked like Damphousse had made a major breakthrough, the Leafs sent him to Edmonton in a multi-player deal prior to the 1991–92 campaign. One year later he won a Stanley Cup with the Montreal Canadiens. He would finish his career with 1,205 points (432 were goals) in 1,378 games played. All said, Damphousse certainly proved himself one of the best first-round draft choices in Leafs history.

Rob Pearson

Leaf Record:
49 Goals,
42 Assists,
91 Points

Maple Leaf Moment: 1992–93 Season

The Maple Leafs have not had a first-round pick in far too many NHL Entry Drafts. But in 1989 the Toronto club had three first-round choices and they selected a trio of players all from the same junior team! The Leafs liked the Belleville Bulls roster so much they chose Scott Thornton (third overall), Rob Pearson (twelfth), and Steve Bancroft (twenty-first), but only one of these three first-round choices played a significant amount of hockey as a Maple Leaf. Thornton was traded away in 1991 while Bancroft never played in a single game for Toronto. Pearson, on the other hand, would appear in 192 career games in a Maple Leaf uniform.

As the 1992–93 season began under new Leafs coach Pat Burns, Pearson looked to establish himself as a regular NHL player who was going to build on his 14-goal (in 47 games) performance the previous year. His defensive skills needed a lot of work, but the Leafs badly needed his scoring touch (and his aggressive play) on the wing. They would give Pearson every chance to prove himself a first-round draft selection that should not be sent back to the minors.

One of his first big games of the new campaign came on the night that the Toronto Blue Jays won their first World Series title. It was

October 24, 1992, and the San Jose Sharks came into Toronto to play the Leafs. Most Toronto sports fans (and many across Canada) were glued to their TVs watching the Blue Jays defeat the Atlanta Braves. No doubt there were more than a few empty seats at the Gardens that night, but the Leafs put on a pretty good show for those in attendance.

Toronto opened the scoring after just 1:20 of play when Peter Zezel knocked home a rebound after getting help from Pearson and defenseman Todd Gill. After the Leafs went up 2–0 the Sharks got one back, but Pearson quickly doused any hopes of the Sharks biting back by scoring his third goal of the year on a wrist shot in the slot. Pearson was feisty all night long and seemed to combine well with Zezel at center. The Leafs added another before the period ended and then cruised to a 5–1 win, their fifth of the new season, putting them in first place in their division.

In one of his last games as a Maple Leaf, Rob Pearson took on Tim Hunter of the Vancouver Canucks in a fight during a 1994 Western Conference final game after Hunter tried to take liberties with Toronto star Doug Gilmour. It was the kind of play the Leafs expected from the robust winger, but did not see often enough during the 1993–94 season and playoffs.

Pearson's next real highlight came on a road trip to Boston on November 14. The Leafs had not won in Beantown since 1987 but when Pearson opened the scoring in the first period, things were going to be different this time around. After taking a nice feed from Doug Gilmour in the face-off circle, Pearson seemed to lose control of the puck for just an instant but recovered quickly enough to whip home a wrist shot past Andy Moog in the Bruins net. The goal proved important as it gave the Leafs the lead and although Boston scored to tie the game before the end of the first, the Leafs never looked back, posting a very significant 4–1 win in a very unfriendly building.

The play of youngsters like Pearson caused Bruins superstar defenseman Ray Bourque to comment, "The Leafs have had some talented players over the years but it seems now that Pat Burns is getting the most out of them. They played just a good, sound hockey game."

The Toronto coach was pleased that he was getting scoring

from other sources. "We needed to have some guys come forward on offense with a few goals and they did tonight [twenty-one-year old Kent Manderville also scored in the contest]... I won't be carrying any passengers," Burns added. The win was the Leafs ninth of the year and kept them at the top of the Norris Division.

Pearson went on to score a career-best 23 times in 1992–93 (while recording 211 penalty minutes) and added two more in the post-season when the Leafs nearly made it to the Stanley Cup finals. A disappointing 12-goal season (which included injuries and a lack of on-ice discipline) the following year caused a rift between the twenty-two-year-old and Leafs management. He was dealt to the Washington Capitals during the off-season with the Leafs getting center Mike Ridley in return. Pearson also played with St. Louis before his 269-game NHL career was over. While Pearson did not live up to the goal-scoring expectations placed on him when he was drafted, Leaf fans will remember his robust play during a great year for the Toronto club.

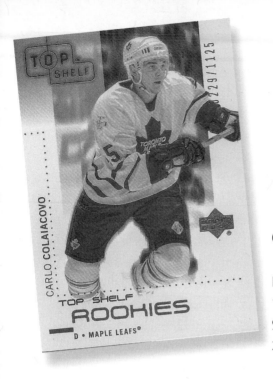

CARLO COLAIACOVO

TOP SHELF
ROOKIES
D • MAPLE LEAFS®

Carlo Colaiacovo

Leaf Record:
12 Goals,
21 Assists,
33 Points

Maple Leaf Moment: April 7, 2007

As often happens during the NHL Entry Draft, teams taking a player express surprise that their man was still available when it came to chose. The Maple Leafs had the seventeenth pick overall in 2001 and were pleased to see defenseman Carlo Colaiacovo was still on the board when they were called up to the podium. For some time the Maple Leafs had their eye on the Toronto native because of his solid performance for the Erie Otters of the OHL.

After the draft, Colaiacovo was sent back to junior for more development time. When the blueliner was done playing for Erie, he had recorded 136 points in 209 career games. Colaiacovo then went on to play for the Leafs American Hockey League farm teams in St. John's, Nova Scotia, and Toronto but he would, on occasion (when he was not injured), get in a few games with the big club. Such was the case in 2006–07 when he got into 48 Leaf games.

The match on April 7, 2007, provided one of the most unusual settings in the long and storied history between ancient rivals Toronto Maple Leafs and the Montreal Canadiens. It was the final night of the regular season and both teams needed the victory. A win for the Habs would assure them of a spot, but a victory for the Leafs would still mean they had to wait one more day in hopes that the New York Islanders would lose their final contest of the regular season. Adding to the drama was the fact that the game was played before a coast-to-coast television audience on *Hockey Night in Canada* on a Saturday night!

The contest lived up to the pre-game hype with an unexpected brand of entertainment that featured a night of mistakes, bad goaltending, and 11 goals by the time the game was done. The Leafs had a 2–1 lead after one and made it 3–1 early in the second with a goal by Alex Steen. But then Montreal's Michael Ryder scored 3 straight times and Chris Higgins added another to give the Habs a 5–3 lead. By this point the Leafs had removed starting goalie Andrew Raycroft and brought in back-up J.S. Aubin. Although Aubin gave up a goal on a Montreal power-play, the move would ultimately pay off.

Carlo Colaiacovo's career as a Maple Leaf lasted 111 games (12 goal, 21 assist), but he made the playoffs twice (in 2008–09 and 2011–12) as a member of the St. Louis Blues. He signed as a free agent with the Detroit Red Wings in 2012, signing a two-year deal; however, Colaiacovo's contract was bought after the 2012–13 season, making him a free agent in the summer of 2013.

With less than three minutes to play in the second period, Colaiacovo managed to glove a puck down at the Montreal blue line and let a shot go that took a crazy hop past Montreal netminder Cristobol Huet. It was the young defenseman's eighth goal of the year and the most important since it put the Leafs right back in the do-or-die contest. Two power-play goals early in the third (by Bryan McCabe and Kyle Wellwood) gave the Leafs a 6–5 lead they nursed the rest of the way. Montreal was now eliminated from playoff contention. Unfortunately for the Leafs, however, the Islanders beat the New Jersey Devils the next day which also began the Leafs golf season.

Colaiacovo indicated after the game that he had been bothered by a bad knee for over a month but had played through the pain. He was the Leafs nominee for the Masterton Trophy (given to the player who best exemplifies perseverance, dedication, and sportsmanship) and it was believed Colaiacovo's strong finish secured him a top-four defense position on the team. "I'm definitely pleased with my progress. I've come a long way." Leafs mentor Paul Maurice agreed with the blueliner's year-end assessment, but both coach and player would soon be gone.

Ron Wilson's appointment as Leafs coach sealed Colaiacovo's fate with the Toronto club. He and Steen (also a first-round draft choice) were both dealt away in a trade that saw the Leafs acquire Lee Stempniak. A little while later Toronto had nothing to show for the trade while Colaiacovo and Steen found more playing time while prospering in St. Louis.

For a brief moment it looked like Colaiacovo had scored a significant goal for the Leafs to close out the 2006–07 campaign, but it turned out to be his only moment in the Leaf spotlight.

NAZEM KADRI
MAPLE LEAFS · C

Nazem Kadri

Leaf Record:
46 Goals,
67 Assists,
113 Points

Maple Leaf Moment: January 20, 2013

When the Maple Leafs went to Montreal for the 2009 NHL Entry Draft, they were hoping to make a deal to move up from the seventh position in the first round; however, they were unable to make such a move that might have landed them such high-ranking prospects as John Tavares, Matt Duchene, Evander Kane, or even Braydon Schenn, all considered high-quality forwards. Ottawa approached the Leafs hoping to snag Toronto's seventh choice before the Leafs went up to the podium, but the problem was both teams wanted the same player. So the Leafs rejected Ottawa's overture and selected center Nazem Kadri from the OHL's London Knights.

Kadri had the reputation of being a feisty, creative player who could score. He was also not shy about being physical. Kadri produced 78 points (25 goals, 53 assists) in just 56 games in his last season prior to the draft. The six-foot, 188-pound pivot was on skates by the time he was four years old and his father, Sam, made sure his son had the opportunity to play the game he loved. Sam Kadri came to Canada when he was three years old, but his family could not afford to let him play hockey, even though he very much wanted to do what interested all the other kids in Canada. Sam worked hard to make sure Nazem had the opportunities that had eluded him as a child. At one point Sam worked at two jobs to help feed his family and then he became a successful used car dealer in London. His success in the car business helped him find the time to get Nazem to the hockey rink and he was able to see the youngster make the London Junior Knights by the time Nazem was six years old.

The Kadri family is of Lebanese decent and Nazem immediately became the highest drafted Muslim player in NHL history. The Montreal crowd booed the Leafs selection but in a fine twist of irony, Kadri and his father appeared in a Toronto newspaper photo the day after the draft each wearing a Montreal Canadiens sweater!

A native of London, Ontario, Nazem Kadri played for Team Canada at the World Junior Championship during the 2009–10 season and recorded 8 points (3G, 5A) in 6 games to help Canada earn a silver medal.

Kadri hoped he could be a role model for other Muslim kids who might want to play hockey and he really wanted to get off to a good start as a Maple Leaf. He put in a strong effort when he attended the Leafs first training camp in the fall of 2009, but was sent back to junior for one more season. It was believed Kadri needed to work on strengthening his body and improve his defensive game. Kadri went back to London and recorded 93 points (35 goals, 58 assists) in 2009–10 for the Knights and also got into 1 NHL game with the Leafs as emergency call-up due to injuries.

The next two seasons saw Kadri refining his game with the Toronto Marlies of the American Hockey League (AHL) but he also saw some more action with the Leafs. Coach Ron Wilson did not seem too impressed with the youngster and played him on the left wing, a position that did not really suit his skill set at the NHL level. He recorded 12 points in 29 games for the Leafs in 2010–11, but he was eventually sent back to the Marlies for more refinement. Marlies coach Dallas Eakins kept working with Kadri on his overall game and the slick center racked up 81 points in 92 games over a couple of seasons.

Since the NHL was in lock-out to start the 2012–13 campaign,

Kadri was back in a Marlies uniform producing at just under a point per game pace (26 points in 27 games played). When the NHL camps finally opened in January 2013, the Leafs gave the youngster another shot. Randy Carlyle was now the bench boss and he was much more willing to give Kadri a start at center. It would prove to be a wise move since playing in the middle meant Kadri could display more of his natural skills.

Despite the promotion to the big team, there were still questions about Kadri when the Leafs opened their season on Saturday, January 19 in Montreal. The game was broadcast in front of a national audience on *Hockey Night in Canada*.

After 4:51 minutes of play, Kadri scored the first goal of the game on a power-play opportunity. Kadri swatted a loose puck past Montreal netminder Carey Price to get Toronto on the scoreboard and silence the raucous Montreal crowd (for a few minutes at least). The Leafs made it 2–0 on a goal by Tyler Bozak and then checked well enough to win the contest 2–1. Kadri took a boarding penalty in the third and did not get a great deal of ice time, but his work was well received by Carlyle who said Kadri deserved to play more.

When the game was over Kadri noted that all the players who had come up from the Marlies made a contribution. "I know what these guys can do. It didn't surprise me [goalie Ben] Scrivens stood on his head and made some great saves. He battles."

Defenseman Mike Kostka also up from the Marlies (and playing in his first-ever NHL game) assisted on Kadri's goal while winger Leo Komarov also played his first game in the big league after some time in the AHL.

Kadri leveraged his solid performance in Montreal to become the Leafs' second-best point producer (44 points in 48 games, including 18 goals) during the 2012–13 season when the Maple Leafs finally returned to the playoffs. In 2013-14 Kadri upped his point total to 50 (20G, 30A). Even though they may have wanted to select others first at the 2009 Entry Draft, it may turn out that the Toronto Maple Leafs made one of their best-ever first-round picks when they look back on the career of Nazem Kadri!

Morgan Rielly

Leaf Record:
2 Goals,
25 Assists,
27 Points

Maple Leaf Moment: January 15, 2013

When the Toronto drafted defenseman Morgan Rielly fifth overall during the 2012 NHL Entry Draft Maple Leafs general manager crowed about how in his view they had taken the best player available. He went as far to say he would have selected Rielly first overall if he had that choice (even though players like Nail Yakupov and Alex Galchenyuk were selected ahead of Rielly). The 6',1", 205-pound blueliner built his game around his great skating ability and for being able to take the puck out of his own end. He also had an offensive flair by setting up teammates with great passes. Still, many dismissed Burke's comments as the typical bluster he would propagate about whatever he was doing at the time but on this occasion Burke's categorization of the youngster may yet prove to be correct.

One of the reasons Rielly may have 'slipped' to fifth was a serious knee injury suffered while playing junior for the Moose Jaw Warriors of the WHL. Although he had recovered from the ligament surgery, there was always the chance the injury could derail or hamper his chance at a stellar NHL career. The Leafs wisely returned him to Moose Jaw for the 2012-13 season where he recorded 54 points (including 12 goals) in

64 games played. When his junior season was over he joined the Leafs farm team for 14 regular season games (three points) plus another eight in the playoffs. The professional experience received with the Toronto Marlies of the AHL gave the youngster a taste of playing against older men and the 19-year old did not look out of place.

As the 2013-14 Maple Leafs training camp unfolded, Rielly was making a strong case to stay with the team and not be sent back to junior for one more season. Toronto coach Randy Carlyle, once a very talented NHL defenseman in his own right, decided to keep the youngster to start the year. By the 10-game mark of the season when an initial decision had to be made, Rielly was told to find a more permanent place to live because he was staying. "We're not guaranteeing that the player's going to be here for the rest of the year, because the 10-game barrier is gone," said Carlyle. "The option of him going to the American Hockey League is not available to us, so he's either going to play with us or go to junior … We see his game developing and we think he can play in the National Hockey League right now. But he is 19 years old. The games are going to get tougher, they're going to get bigger and he's going to be exposed to more of the higher skill level of the league."

Between 2011 and 2014, Morgan Rielly has represented Team Canada as a junior and as a professional (at the '14 World Hockey Championships). In 32 total appearances for Team Canada to date, Rielly has recorded 18 points (7G, 11A).

There was no doubt Rielly struggled at times but that was only natural for such a young defenseman playing in the NHL for the first time. But Rielly showed no fear about playing his style of game and his puck moving skills were very impressive. One opposing team who got to see Rielly's slick talent level was the Buffalo Sabres when they paid a visit to the Air Canada Centre on the night of January 15, 2013. The Sabres were in the mist of one of their worst seasons ever but the Maple Leafs needed the two points to stay in the playoff race. The Leafs opened the scoring on a marker by Phil Kessel but Buffalo replied with two goals to take the lead. Toronto winger Nik Kulemin tied the score in the second period.

Before the middle frame was over, Rielly scored his second goal of the season after being set up by teammates Nazem Kadri and Mason Raymond to give the Leafs a 3-2 lead. Rielly calmly jumped into the attack and his shot beat Sabres goalie Ryan Millar for his first ever goal at home as a Maple Leaf. Teammate and fellow defenseman Tim Gleason noted how easily Rielly handled the faster pace of the NHL game. "I wish I was like him when I was that age," said the veteran blueliner. "I was a nervous wreck." Rielly's goal did not stand up as the game winner because the game went to a shootout. The Maple Leafs scored three times in the shootout to win the contest 4-3. After the game Rielly reflected on the evening by saying, "If our team had a choice, we'd try to end the game a bit earlier. But it turns out we're pretty good at (shootouts). So we have to keep working at them. After you win one you can't get too high. After you lose one you can't get too low. That's just how it goes." Rielly post-game comments clearly indicate he is very mature young man.

Rielly must improve his play in his own end of the ice (he was a minus 14 as a rookie) but so does the entire Maple Leaf team. It is expected that Rielly will soon be the Leafs top defenseman and will be the blueliner they build around. It is too bad Burke is not around Toronto to see the youngster fully develop but he can watch the talented Rielly from afar in Calgary.

MOLSON
CANADIAN.
PROUD SEASON SPONSOR

SEC	ROW	SEAT	PRICE
103	**20**	**11**	**$165.00**
Enter Through Gate 3			INCL $18.98 TAX

★ REVISED SCHEDULE ★

★ 2013 REGULAR SEASON ★

HOME ★ GAME

11

2013 REGULAR SEASON HOME GAME 11

— WEDNESDAY, MARCH 6 ★ 7:30PM —

THE PASSION
THAT UNITES US ALL

692956150924

Brian Spencer joined the Maple Leafs during the 1970-71 season.

THREE-STAR SELECTION

Don Simmons • Eddie Litzenberger • Billy MacMillan
Brian "Spinner" Spencer • Rocky Saganiuk • Daniel Marois
Mike Gartner • Lonny Bohonos • Gary Valk • Eric Lindros
Cody Franson

MANY YEARS AGO, DURING the 1936–37 hockey season, it was decided to introduce a new feature at the end of games played at Maple Leaf Gardens. One of the main sponsors of Leaf radio telecasts (no television yet) was Imperial Oil, a gasoline company with agents and distributors right across Canada. The company introduced "Three Star" gasoline that year at all their Esso stations and decided a good way to promote their new product was to pick the best three performers of the Saturday night hockey game (which was broadcast coast-to-coast) and call them the three stars of the contest. The idea became quite a popular feature for hockey fans at the arena and those listening at home and the three star selection soon spread from city to city.

Even though title sponsorship no longer exists, the tradition still continues to this day and fans still wait at the end of each game to see who was selected so they can give them a warm round of applause. The following Maple Leaf players waited to hear the Toronto crowd give out one last appreciative roar as they stepped out to take a "three-star" bow after a particularly great evening of hockey:

Don Simmons

Leaf Record:
28 Wins,
21 Losses,
7 Ties,
5 Shutouts

Maple Leaf Moment: April 20 and 22, 1962

Boston Bruins goalie Don Simmons played in the Stanley Cup final two years in a row (1957 and 1958). Montreal, however, defeated Boston both times on their way to five-straight championships. Despite the fact that it was Simmons's first two post-season appearances, he showed he could compete against the best team in hockey.

The Bruins eventually tried others in net, forcing Simmons back to the minors. Leafs coach and general manager Punch Imlach knew Simmons had something to offer so he traded goalie Ed Chadwick for his rights. It would work out well for both the Leafs and Simmons.

During the Original Six era, backup goalies were not often heard or seen. Each team had one netminder and all other goalies played elsewhere else in the system (teams were not required to dress a second goalie until the 1965–66 regular season). A replacement was only brought up when the starter was hurt.

During the playoffs, teams were more inclined to have another goalie standing by, but they rarely saw action unless there was an injury. Such was the case with Simmons in the 1962 playoffs.

Simmons had spent most of the 1961–62 season in the minors

with Rochester where he won 24 games. He was also 5–3–1 with Toronto that year (when he filled in for Bower) and then again with the Leafs for the post-season. He saw no action against the New York Rangers in the semi-finals and was expecting to be a spectator when the Leafs met Chicago in the Stanley Cup finals. However, an injury to Bower in the fourth game in Chicago forced Simmons out of his suit and tie. After a quick change in the dressing room, he was out on the ice guarding the Leafs net. It was a tough spot to be in but Simmons had experience playing in important games when he was with the Bruins.

Chicago tied the series at two games each with a 4–1 win in the fourth game, which made the fifth contest at Maple Leaf Gardens on April 20, 1962, all the more important. Luckily, the Leafs got off to a great start when Bob Pulford scored just 17 seconds into the game to give them a very quick lead. He added another late in the first, but Chicago got one past Simmons with less than two minutes to play in the period to make it 2–1. Simmons had stopped 12 of 13 Chicago drives to start the game, but the Black Hawks potent offense was in full gear in the second stanza. Ab McDonald scored twice in the first four minutes to give Chicago a 3–2 lead. McDonald was assisted on both goals by Bobby Hull and Stan Mikita.

Don Simmons was with the Maple Leafs for all three of their consecutive Stanley Cup wins from 1962 to 1964, but only saw playoff action in the '62 finals. In his three appearances (2 wins, 1 loss) in the finals, he wore sweater number 1 (normally Bower's number) instead of his usual number 24. He also wore a white "popsicle-style" face mask.

Simmons was showing some rust, having not played in some time, but the Leafs were determined not to go back to Chicago down a game. Toronto scored the next 5 goals (including two by Frank Mahovlich) before cruising to an 8–4 win. It was not the tidy type of hockey the Leafs normally played, but they were happy to be within one game of the championship. The Leaf goalie faced 30 shots (the Leafs pelted Chicago's Glenn Hall with 44 drives) and Simmons admitted he would have to be better next game.

"I didn't play as well as I wanted to," said Simmons. "You can't sit out a month and expect to be ready because no practice is like a game. But going in like this you're all keyed up. It isn't like starting the season and blowing a game knowing you've got 69 to go. I'm all right now." The entire team now looked ready to win the Leafs first championship since 1951. It would all come down to the night of April 22, a game played on Easter Sunday.

It was a close game all the way with no scoring until the third. The Leafs were all over the Black Hawks for most of the contest, but Hull scored the opener when Toronto's Dick Duff lost the puck to the Chicago superstar. Simmons had no chance on the play, but the wild celebration that followed gave the Leafs a chance to catch their breath. Less than two minutes later they tied the score on a goal by Bob Nevin and then Duff made up for his blunder by scoring the game-winning goal on a Toronto power play. The Leafs had to kill off a late penalty to Tim Horton, but Simmons would give the swarming Black Hawks nothing, stopping 20 of 21 shots on the night. At the final horn, Simmons made 1 last save before he charged out of his net into the arms of his jubilant teammates. He would share in the three-star selection along with Chicago netminder Glenn Hall. Simmons played the role of Bower's stand-in in a quiet and efficient manner and was now rewarded with a starring role and a Stanley Cup title.

Eddie Litzenberger

Leaf Record:
17 Goals,
23 Assists,
40 Points

Maple Leaf Moment: April 11, 1963

Right-winger Eddie Litzenberger was a twenty-nine-year-old veteran when the Maple Leafs picked him up on waivers in late December 1961. The six-foot-one, 174-pound winger had started out with the Montreal Canadiens in 1952–53, but was traded to Chicago where he enjoyed seven seasons with the Black Hawks. He scored more than 30 goals in three straight years with the Hawks and won a Stanley Cup title with the team in the spring of '61. The Chicago captain accepted the Cup from NHL president Clarence Campbell that year which marked Chicago's first championship since 1938.

After briefly appearing with the Detroit Red Wings, the Leafs snapped Litzenberger up for the rest of the 1961–62 season, giving them another veteran, winning presence on a team that had not won a Cup since 1951. The Leafs finished that year with a Cup victory making it two championships in a row for the lanky Litzenberger, who had 20 points (10 goals, 10 assists) in just 37 games for Toronto. The Leafs had obviously made a wise decision getting the right-winger because they would be back in the final once more in 1963.

The Maple Leafs began the '63 Stanley Cup finals on April 11, 1963, at home beating the Detroit Red Wings 4–2 to go up 1 game. Naturally, the Leafs wanted to make short work of the Red Wings (as they had with Montreal in the first series, which lasted just 5 games), and to do so, they would have to win their second straight at Maple Leaf Gardens. Unfortunately, they would also have to do it without star left-winger Frank Mahovlich who was out with an injury. Coach Punch Imlach decided to replace the "Big M" with Litzenberger who was experienced enough to play on his wrong wing and still contribute. Before the game was over, more than 14,000 Leaf fans on hand were glad they had a high-quality substitute on the bench for a vital game like this one.

Eddie Litzenberger would win the Stanley Cup once again with the Maple Leafs in 1964 (his last NHL contest was the seventh game of the finals against Detroit) making him the only player to win four straight championships between the years 1961 and 1964, one with Chicago and three with Toronto.

Litzenberger opened the scoring early in the first period when he beat Terry Sawchuk in the Detroit net. He was assisted on the play by Bob Pulford and Tim Horton. Litzenberger took a drive from about thirty-five feet out, but Sawchuk kicked out the rebound to the Leaf player who kept driving to the net and promptly rapped it home. The rangy Leaf then helped set up Ron Stewart for the second goal of the period to put Toronto up 2–0 before the opening frame was completed. Litzenberger spotted the speedy Stewart behind the Red Wing defense, sent the right-winger in all alone, and whipped a shot past a defenseless Sawchuk.

Detroit was down 3–0 before Gordie Howe, their only effective player of the night, finally got the Red Wings on the board. A penalty to Norm Ullman gave the Leafs a power play and Litzenberger picked up his third point of the night by getting the puck over to teammate Billy Harris. The puck was then relayed to Stewart who scored his second of the night to make it 4–1. Detroit got the only goal of the third (by Howe) to make it a 4–2 final, but the Leafs had the series well in hand as they made their way to Detroit for the next two games.

In the dressing room after the game, Leafs coach and general manager Punch Imlach crowed about the fact that the Leafs had so much depth. "I can reach down the bench and get someone who will do the job," he stated.

Litzenberger had played in only 58 of the 70-game regular season, but was ready when called upon to help out in the post-season. "You need skating in games to stay in the best shape," said the second star of the game. "When you don't play much you have to work that much harder in practice to stay even with the guys who play regular."

Imlach further commented that Litzenberger was not a great skater but he made up for it with determination and hard work which is why they kept him around to contribute off the bench during those historic Toronto hockey years.

The Leafs easily defeated Detroit in five games to end the '63 finals and prove that they were indeed the best team in hockey (the Leafs had also finished in first place during the regular season). And, even though he did not score again in the playoffs, everyone would remember the night Eddie Litzenberger was a star for the Maple Leafs with the Stanley Cup on the line.

Billy MacMillan

Leaf Record:
32 Goals,
26 Assists,
58 Points

Maple Leaf Moments: December 16, 1970 and December 25, 1971

Rugged right-winger Billy MacMillan was already twenty-seven when he made it to the NHL with the Maple Leafs for the 1970–71 season. The native of Charlottetown, Prince Edward Island, played junior hockey in the Toronto area with St. Michael's and Neil McNeil high schools. He then joined the Canadian National Team for the 1965–66 season after playing university hockey for two years. The Leafs signed him during the 1969–70 season and sent him to the Tulsa Oilers where he recorded seven points in three games that year.

The next season MacMillan was given an opportunity to start with the Leafs playing on a line with Gary Monahan and Dave Keon. After some initial trouble getting going, the trio, and the team, started to look good in that 1970–71 campaign. Even though the five-foot-ten, 185-pound MacMillan was a left-hand shot, he played right wing in Toronto and had to learn the position at the big-league level. By December, the Leafs had overcome their bad start to become a difficult team to play against. A young defense led by veteran Bobby Baun and a spunky group of forwards (such as MacMillan, Brian Spencer, Jim Harrison, and a rookie named Darryl Sittler) made the Leafs a respectable club after having missed the playoffs the year before with a dismal 29–34–13 record. On December 16, 1970, the Leafs rolled into Pittsburgh looking to avenge a poor 4–0 loss to the Penguins just eight days earlier.

The Maple Leafs inserted all-star netminder Jacques Plante into the net for one of his few road appearances. He made 37 saves and the Leafs came away with a satisfying 4–2 victory. MacMillan scored two key goals in this, the Leafs fourth straight triumph. Both goals (the first of which gave the Leafs a 2–1 lead) came when MacMillan took the puck from behind the net and came out in front to beat Les Binkley with a backhand. The goals were MacMillan's ninth and tenth of the season.

"I'll tell you something," Leafs vice-president King Clancy said after the game, "he's the surprise of the league. He's the best rookie in the National Hockey League without question." Flattering praise indeed, especially from someone who had been around the NHL for so long. Binkley was also very impressed with the tough winger. "That MacMillan has beaten me three times [this season] all on the same move. He is murder with that puck on the backboards and comes out like an eel in a barrel of grease," the veteran netminder marveled.

Billy MacMillan was picked up by the Atlanta Flames in the 1973 Expansion Draft and he also played for the New York Islanders before leaving the NHL. He coached and managed the Colorado Rockies and New Jersey Devils between 1980 and 1984. During his first year with the Leafs, MacMillan was named Prince Edward Island's "Citizen of the Year" no doubt for his NHL rookie performance.

As for MacMillan, he was pleased because it was an important win. "That has to be our biggest win of the year... We've got hot at the right time," he said about the Leafs current run of success. He was named the first star of the game.

MacMillan went on to score 23 goals to complete his first year as a Leaf, finishing second only to Gilbert Perrault (the Sabres young star had 38) in goals scored by first-year players. Perreault won the Calder Trophy as the league's top rookie that year while Jude Drouin of Minnesota finished second in the Calder race with 68 points. However, the Leafs were more than happy to see their somewhat older freshman excel in his first year and MacMillan's good play gave Keon a solid winger to work with that year.

The 1970–71 Leafs finished in fourth place in the tough East Division and had a good chance to upset the second-place New York Rangers in the first round of the playoffs. However, they lost a 2–1 series lead and eventually bowed out in six games.

The 1971–72 campaign was not nearly so good for MacMillan who only scored 10 goals, 3 of them coming on Christmas night against the Detroit Red Wings. It was MacMillan's lone hat trick as a Leaf and it came during a 5–3 win over the visiting team. He scored 2 goals on the power play, 1 of which was the game-winning tally. This was the final time the Maple Leafs played on Christmas and it marked the last time MacMillan had a star performance for the team over his 137-game career in Toronto.

MAPLE LEAFS

BRIAN
SPENCER

RIGHT WING

Brian "Spinner" Spencer

Leafs Record:
10 Goals,
20 Assists,
30 Points

Maple Leaf Moment: January 9, 1971

Brian Spencer was born in Fort St. James, a small town located in north-central British Columbia. The left-winger grew up dreaming about playing in the National Hockey League. A photo dated 1961 even shows a twelve-year-old Spencer and his twin brother each wearing Leaf sweaters. However, it was not easy for Spencer playing in such a remote part of Canada and being driven to succeed by his demanding father, Roy.

Never an overly talented or skilled player, Spencer made up for it with great heart and desire and a pugilistic style of play. The five-foot-eleven, 185-pound Spencer was good enough to play for four different junior teams in western Canada (over two seasons) where he recorded 74 points in 110 games. So the Toronto Maple Leafs took a chance on this raw talent and drafted Spencer in the fifth round (fifty-fifth overall) of the 1969 Amateur Draft.

Spencer cherished the letter the Leafs sent to him. It was signed by chief scout Bob Davidson advising him that he was now property of the Toronto club (Spencer kept the letter in an envelope for many years afterward). His father was very proud of his son and now felt that all the time he had put into Brian's development was finally going to pay off.

Leaf management sensed the youngster might have the potential to be a grinding winger who could play a tough game, so they assigned him to play the 1969–70 season with the Tulsa Oilers of the Central Hockey League (CHL). His first year as a professional saw him score 13 goals and total 32 points in 66 games while recording an eye-catching 186 penalty minutes. He earned a promotion to the Leafs for nine games in the 1969–70 campaign, but did not register a point.

Brian Spencer was restless and generally out of control after his NHL career ended. He ended up moving to Florida and was at one point acquitted of murder charges while facing a potential death penalty if he had been found guilty. He called on former teammates to help him out and find some sort of regular work after his acquittal but eventually found himself back in Florida. He was killed by a gun shot in June 1988 when he refused to hand over money or possessions (he really had neither) during a robbery. Spencer had suffered the same fate as his father – death from a bullet shot. He was 38 years of age when he died.

Spencer hurt his knee just before training camp in the fall of 1970 and soon found himself back in the minors. He had 14 points and 98 penalty minutes in just 22 games with Tulsa before Toronto brought him back up to the NHL. The Leafs were faltering badly (with a 6–18–1 record to start the 1970–71 campaign) and decided to give Spencer another look after winger Guy Trottier was injured on December 9. The Leafs had lost 4–0 the night before in Pittsburgh and were now facing the Montreal Canadiens at the Gardens.

The truculent winger was now wearing number 15 (he previously wore number 22) and helped the Leafs to a 4–0 win over Montreal in a game that featured a bench-clearing brawl. Spencer came off the bench to join in the melee and then took on and beat Habs defenseman Terry Harper in a second-period fight. The Leaf player was also given a 5-minute major for high sticking (on Harper), but the game film showed Spencer was wrongly accused. Nevertheless, the Leafs were more than pleased to see the scrappy Spencer flex his muscle with Leaf coach Johnny McLellan saying afterward, "We knew Spencer could play like this. He would have been with the club from the start except for the knee injury, so we had to send him down to Tulsa for a while."

Spencer did not change his style one bit and began to get more ice time. He fought everyone who was willing to drop the gloves (including notorious tough guys Keith Magnuson of Chicago, Tracy Pratt of Buffalo, and Gary Dornhoeffer of Philadelphia). He also lived through a terrible family tragedy when his father was killed by the Royal Canadian Mounted Police (RCMP). On the night of December 12, 1970, the senior Spencer drove to a Prince George television station to demand, at gun point, that the Leafs–Black Hawks game be shown in British Columbia instead of the Canucks-Seals contest (This occurred while Brian was being interviewed by Ward Cornell during a *Hockey Night in Canada* intermission.) Terrified employees at the station called police. Soon afterward, Spencer shot at the RCMP before he was hit four times with return fire. Despite his father's death, the incredibly tough-minded Spencer played the next night in Buffalo and recorded 2 assists in a 4–0 win over the Sabres. The youngster believed his father would have wanted him to play.

Spencer's best night as an NHL rookie came on January 9, 1971, when he scored 3 goals in a 5–2 Toronto win over Pittsburgh and was named the first star of the game. He scored twice in the first period and another late in the second to account for his hat trick. Spencer slapped a puck past Penguins goalie Al Smith after taking a pass from Paul Henderson for his opening tally and scored his second off a scramble in front of the Pittsburgh goal. He wacked a drive home for his final marker on a Leaf power play after taking a pass from defenseman Rick Ley.

The game represented a third of Spencer's goals for the 1970–71 season (he had 9 in 50 games played), but his infectious physical play helped the Leafs post a winning record (37–33–8) and earn a playoff spot. To be sure, making the post-season seemed like a very remote possibility in the early days of December before Spencer was called up to the big team. However, his stay in Toronto turned out to be brief -- but "Spinner" (a play on his last name and a recognition of his constant churning style on ice) Spencer's feisty approach to the game made him a very popular Maple Leaf during his two years with the club.

Spencer went on to play for the New York Islanders, Buffalo Sabres (where he recorded a career-high 41 points in 1974–75 and played in the '75 Stanley Cup final), and Pittsburgh Penguins before ending his 553-game career with 223 points.

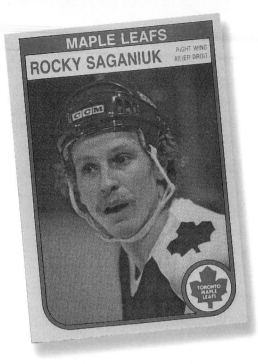

MAPLE LEAFS
ROCKY SAGANIUK
RIGHT WING
AILIER DROIT

Rocky Saganiuk

Leaf Record:
56 Goals,
62 Assists,
118 Points

Maple Leaf Moment: February 23, 1980

When Rocky Saganiuk played his first-ever game for the Toronto Maple Leafs on March 11, 1979, he was named first star of the contest. That night he had 1 goal and 2 assists in a 4–0 win over the Pittsburgh Penguins at Maple Leaf Gardens. The crowd loved the energy the small but stocky (five-foot-eight, 185-pound) right-winger brought to the game. The Alberta native was a second-round draft choice (twenty-ninth overall) of the Maple Leafs in 1977 after a good year with the 1976–77 Lethbridge Broncos (60 goals and 108 points) of the Western Hockey League (WHL). Saganiuk later led the American Hockey League in goals scored with 47 tallies in 62 games for the New Brunswick Hawks. His good play earned him a promotion to the Leafs for 16 games (registering 8 points) to close out the 1978–79 campaign. Saganiuk was now ready for a full-time job with the Leafs for the next season.

To say that the 1979–80 Maple Leafs were a team in transition would be a severe understatement. Bodies were flying all over North America as general manager Punch Imlach made all sorts of deals almost as soon as the season began. Included in the purge was all-star winger

Lanny McDonald (sent to Colorado) plus the heart-and-soul player, Dave "Tiger" Williams (traded to Vancouver), as Imlach was determined to make the Leafs faster and more offensive (and also, to play out his downright vindictiveness toward those he disliked). Too many changes over a short period rarely work, and this Leaf team was no exception, but they did make the playoffs as some new Leaf players began to emerge. Saganiuk was one of those fresh faces (players such as Laurie Boschman, John Anderson, Bill Derlago, and Rick Vaive were others) and on February 23, 1980, it looked like the new additions were going to be key contributors to Imlach's rebuilding process.

The Leafs were visiting the repurposed Winnipeg Jets on a Saturday night and the hometown team wanted to do well in front of a national television audience. (The Jets, along with the Edmonton Oilers, Hartford Whalers, and Quebec Nordiques, were absorbed into the long-established league that season as the NHL and the four surviving WHA franchises merged to form a twenty-one-team circuit). The trouble was, the first-year Jets had virtually no defense or

Rocky Saganiuk never lacked for confidence. When Lanny McDonald was dealt away, he asked the former Leaf star if he would give his blessing so he could take over sweater number 7. The gracious McDonald said it was alright with him but Saganiuk -- though not from a lack of effort -- could never fill that jersey.

goaltending of any caliber. The Leafs came into the game having won 2 out 3 road games and were looking for a third victory on their 5-game road trip. Toronto quickly dashed any home-team hopes with a strong effort in the first two periods.

Saganiuk opened the scoring at the 7:26 mark of the first period with the Leafs adding goals by Derlago and Wilf Paiement to take a 3–2 lead into the second. Winnipeg tied the score in the second, but then Saganiuk scored 2 straight goals to give the Leafs a lead they would not relinquish. Boschman sprung Saganiuk free with a pass that he wristed past Jets netminder Markus Mattsson on the glove side. He scored his next goal also on a wrist shot when Leaf defenseman Richard Mulhearn noticed Saganiuk was in the clear on a power play. The goal gave

Saganiuk his first career hat trick. The Leafs went up by three before the end of the second and then coasted home for a 9–3 victory.

"It appears my luck has turned for me and I actually could have had a couple of more had I played them properly," Saganiuk said of the game that featured virtually no defensive play. "I hit one post and I had an open side on a perfect pass. I let it go all in one motion and it went wide. But it's a great win for the team. Everybody in this room is flying high right now." It was the Leafs fourth win in the last five contests.

Leaf owner Harold Ballard shared Saganiuk's enthusiasm by telling reporters, "A lot of people criticized some of the trades we made but they're looking pretty good." As usual, Ballard's lack of hockey acumen was exposed as the Leafs limped into the playoffs with a 35–40–5 record for the 1979–80 regular season. They exited the post-season early after a first-round loss to the Minnesota North Stars in 3 straight games. It would be the first of many terrible seasons for the Leafs in the 1980s.

As for Saganiuk, he would only play three full seasons in Toronto, his promise quickly evaporating before going to Pittsburgh for 29 games during the 1983–84 campaign. That cold night in Winnipeg was where Saganiuk's star would shine brightest as a Maple Leaf.

Daniel Marois · Right Wing

TORONTO MAPLE LEAFS

Daniel Marois

Leaf Record:
106 Goals,
80 Assists,
186 Points

Maple Leaf Moments: February 17 and March 7, 1989

Quebec Major Junior Hockey has produced many high-scoring players and right-winger Daniel Marois was no exception, notching 116 goals in 165 games played. The six-foot, 190-pound Montreal native was drafted twenty-eighth overall in 1987 by the Maple Leafs who hoped Marois could keep scoring and improve his defensive play little by little. He played in 8 games for the Leafs farm team in 1987–88, recording 8 points for the Newmarket Saints. After playing for the Leafs in the 1988 playoffs (scoring 1 goal), Marois appeared ready for a steady spot on the club for the following year.

The 1988–89 Maple Leafs were a terrible team on defense (tied for third-worst by allowing 342 goals against), but they did have a few players who could score. Center Ed Olczyk had 38 goals and 90 points, while winger Gary Leeman scored 32 times. Tom Fergus and Vincent Damphousse were very reliable point producers, but the surprise of the Leafs attack was rookie winger Daniel Marois. Having spent only a very brief time in the American Hockey League the previous year, the Toronto club was not sure he was ready for the rigors of the big league. However, Marois made the team and put together a good rookie season.

A natural goal scorer, Marois's first career hat trick happened on February 17, 1989, in New York. The Leafs were in for a game against the Rangers and went on to stun the usually noisy patrons at Madison Square Gardens with a 10–6 win. Ten goals in one contest has always been a rarity in the NHL and the 17,242 in attendance did not appreciate the visiting team thrashing their hometown heroes. Remarkably, it was only 2–1 for the Leafs at the end of the first period with the Rangers tying it immediately at the start of the second. Then the Leafs let loose with 6 goals over the remainder of the middle frame taking an 8–4 lead in the process. Marois scored the last goal of the second stanza and then added 2 more in the third to seal the win for the Leafs. All the goals were needed since the Leafs gave the Rangers 51 shots on goal. Had it not been for goalie Allan Bester, it might have been a 10–10 tie!

Daniel Marois scored his first goal as a Maple Leaf during a playoff game against the Detroit Red Wings on April 12, 1988. The Leafs won it 6–5 in overtime. It was a pretty effort with Marois making Red Wing defenseman Mike O'Connell look silly at the Detroit blue line before he beat goalie Glen Hanlon with a high snap shot.

Marois now had 20 goals on the season and renewed confidence from the game since his three goals came against veteran NHL netminders John Vanbiesbrouck, who gave up 2, and Bob Froese, who gave up the other.

"That's my first hat trick and I'm very happy. Other rookies have hat tricks, so I needed that. Those three goals give me punch for the rest of the season." While not the most elegant statement, Marois's prediction was accurate: about three weeks later in his home province of Quebec, he recorded his second hat trick of the year.

The Leafs had an outside shot at the playoffs when they arrived to play the Quebec Nordiques on March 7. Marois's parents and brother and sister were all in attendance and saw him open the scoring at the 3:08 mark of the first. He added a goal in each of the next two periods (including the game winner) in the Leafs 6–4 win. Ironically, Marois nearly missed this game because the Leaf coaches planned to sit him out. Only an injury to Leeman opened up a spot for Marois this night.

"It was good for me," Marios said after the game. "It [the potential benching] shook me up a bit. But Wendel talked to me and told me 'Don't let your head down and keep working hard.'" Marois took Clarke's advice and produced another 3-goal effort. The win also kept the Leafs in the playoff hunt, which was not decided until the final game of the season. (An overtime loss to Chicago eliminated Toronto from the post-season.)

The future looked bright for the sharp-shooting Marois. He finished with 31 goals in his first year, second among rookies to Tony Granato of the Rangers who had 36. Marois then upped his total to 39 the next season. But a coaching change early in the 1990–91 season (he did not see eye-to-eye with Tom Watt), together with injuries, helped derail a once-promising career. However, for a couple of seasons there was no better goal-scoring star (he was named one of the three stars of each of the two games highlighted here) for the Maple Leafs than the young man from Quebec.

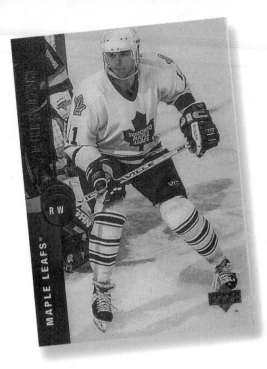

Mike Gartner

Leaf Record:
53 Goals,
33 Assists,
86 Points

Maple Leaf Moment: May 12, 1994

Maple Leafs general manager Cliff Fletcher was looking everywhere to upgrade his Toronto club prior to the start of the 1994 post-season. The Leafs were having a good year during the regular season (they would finish 43–29–12, good for 98 points), but Fletcher felt the team needed a boost going into the grueling playoffs marathon. Turned down by many teams for what he really wanted (likely an impact forward or depth on the blue line), Fletcher made a deal to get Ottawa native Mike Gartner from the New York Rangers. Unfortunately, the Leafs had to give up Glenn Anderson in return, one of the best playoff performers in the history of the game. Gartner was not happy to leave the Rangers (who went on to win the Stanley Cup that year), but it was clear New York coach Mike Keenan was anxious to make the switch. At least the former 50-goal scorer was going to a team with a good chance to go all the way.

The San Jose Sharks were the upstart team of the 1994 post-season. First, they upset the mighty Detroit Red Wings in 7 games and now they had the Toronto Maple Leafs on the verge of elimination in the second round of the playoffs. The Sharks won the opening game of the best-of-seven series right in Maple Leaf Gardens. They then took two out of three in San Jose to put the Leafs on the brink of ouster. However, the 1993–94 Maple Leafs were still a gritty team who had learned much from their journey deep into the 1993 post-season. With the final 2 games slated for the Gardens, the Leafs felt they still had a good chance to advance to the Western Conference for the second consecutive season. The sixth game was played on May 12, 1994, before a very nervous Toronto crowd of more than 16,000.

If Leaf fans were anxious before the game, one can only imagine the angst felt throughout the Gardens as the teams headed for overtime with the score tied 2–2. Their worst fears were nearly confirmed when the Sharks rang a shot off the goal post behind netminder Felix Potvin less than two minutes into the extra session. The Sharks then messed up two great chances to score. As one big sigh of relief followed another, an unexpected goal from Gartner at the 8:53 mark of the first overtime period ended the game. It was a surprising goal because Gartner's shot seemed harmless enough yet it found its way past Sharks netminder Arturs Irbe after it struck his foot and then trickled underneath him.

Mike Gartner scored 708 career goals (with five NHL teams) and was inducted into the Hockey Hall of Fame in 2001.

Even Gartner was caught off guard. "It couldn't be called a pretty goal but it looked pretty good from my angle," Gartner said after the game. "I just shot it along the goal line [after taking a pass from Doug Gilmour] and as he [Irbe] was coming across, it hit his skate. We just gave ourselves a one game reprieve. We played a gutsy game but we feel we can play better." Gartner was lucky to be in the game because his errant stick cut a Shark earlier in the game but the infraction was ruled accidental (another Shark player was ruled to have moved Gartner's stick) by the officials. But no matter, Gartner's important goal silenced critics who said he was not a clutch playoff performer. (And it should also be noted that Gartner scored the only goal when the Leafs defeated Chicago 1–0 in the sixth game of the series to eliminate the Blackhawks. Afterward, Gartner would have none of the talk about his personal performance but remained focused on team instead.)

Gartner set up Wendel Clark for a key goal in the Leafs 4–2 win over the Sharks in the seventh game of the series, but that proved to be the last great triumph for that Leaf team. After an opening game win over Vancouver in the next round, the tired Maple Leafs lost the next four.

As disappointing as the loss was, it did not take away from Gartner's stellar post-season performance. Later on, Gartner called his overtime winner versus the Sharks one the highlights of his career and it earned him a selection as one of the game's three stars. Truthfully, Gartner was never an exceptional playoff performer, but in the '94 playoffs he was certainly a top performer for the Maple Leafs.

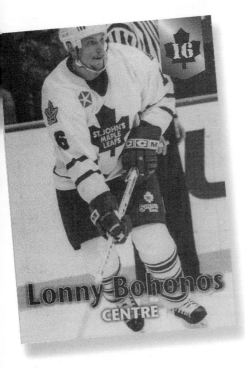

Lonny Bohonos

Leaf Record:
6 Goals,
3 Assists,
9 Points

Maple Leaf Moment: May 9, 1999

The Maple Leafs acquired Lonny Bohonos from the Vancouver Canucks in exchange for former first-round draft choice Brandon Convery in March 1998. Bohonos had 6 points in 6 games to close out the 1997–98 season, but spent most of 1998–99 in the American Hockey League (AHL) with the St. John's Maple Leafs where he had a pretty good year, recording 34 goals and 82 points in 70 games. The Leafs brought him up to the big team after St. John's fell out of the playoffs -- and it was not expected that Bohonos would be anything but an extra player used only in case of injury.

The Leafs had already defeated the Philadelphia Flyers in the first round of the '99 post-season and were pleased with their lineup as they got ready to meet the Pittsburgh Penguins in the next round. However, a poor effort on home ice resulting in a 2–0 defeat in the series opener had coach Pat Quinn rethinking his roster. First-line winger Freddie Modin was having an especially hard time and was pointless in the playoffs. The Leafs really needed to boost their top line so Bohonos replaced Modin on the line with Steve Thomas and captain Mats Sundin. It was a tall order for the youngster who had yet to play a full NHL season, but

Bohonos was poised to contribute and quickly gave the Leafs the spark they needed.

The second game of the series was played on May 9, 1999, at the Air Canada Centre. The Penguins were hoping to get out of Toronto with 2 wins before heading home. However, just 6:06 into the first period, Bohonos scored the opener when he put in a rebound past Tom Barrasso in net. Leaf defenseman Danny Markov took the shot and Bohonos was in the right spot to shovel it in. Before the first was over, Leaf rearguard Dmitri Yushkevich took a shot that was tipped by Bohonos and then re-directed by Sundin to put the Leafs up 2–0. Two points in his first playoff period to ignite the Leafs attack— very impressive, especially from a player nobody had counted on to be dressed for this game!

Lonny Bohonos had 9 points in 9 playoff games for the Leafs in the '99 post-season and then never played for the team again. He would play in Europe and in the minor leagues of North American until 2006.

The Penguins were never really in this game, but crept back to within 3–2 in the third when Bohonos helped Sundin set up Thomas for the insurance goal with less than four minutes to play. The final 4–2 score flattered the Penguins somewhat (although Toronto netminder Curtis Joseph had to be sharp in stopping 25 of 27 shots), but it was a big relief to the Leafs. Although Sundin was considered the first star of the game with two goals and a pair of assists, it was just as clear that Bohonos had played a big role in the Leafs victory with a 3-point night. His efforts also earned him a place among one the best three Toronto players for this playoff match (with Joseph being the other). In the dressing room after the game, the twenty-six-year-old Bohonos was surprised to see so many reporters and cameras gathered around his stall.

He answered the question of why he fit in so well alongside Sundin by saying, "Speed, I think. I got back of their 'D' and created some scoring chances. I'm not afraid to shoot the puck and go to the net. I don't go looking for fancy plays."

Quinn also commented on Bohonos's game. "Lonny's skills fit

better with Mats than some of the other guys you might think were options," the happy coach said. "Lonny's had to overcome a few things," Quinn continued. "One is size—he's not a real big guy. He's got some NHL skills but when he doesn't have the puck, he needed to work on that area [of his game]."

Bohonos's solid play did not stop after his first big night. When the Leafs clinched the series in Pittsburgh four games later, he scored an important goal (his third of the series) and got the Leafs on the board after they were down 2–0. He was an offensive force all night and took five of Toronto's 30 shots on goal.

Like the rest of the Maple Leafs, Bohonos faded against the Buffalo Sabres as the team lost the next playoff round, dashing any hopes of getting back to the Stanley Cup finals. Bohonos, however, will always be remembered for his surprisingly good play that made him a playoff star for the Maple Leafs in 1999, if only for a short while. Perhaps Bohonos summed it best when he said to one reporter, "It's the highlight of my career just playing a playoff game in Toronto."

Gary Valk

Leaf Record:
31 Goals,
63 Assists,
94 Points

Maple Leaf Moment: May 17, 1999

Left-winger Garry Valk was thirty-years old and without an NHL job after playing in the league with Vancouver, Anaheim, and Pittsburgh for eight seasons starting in 1990–91. Then came a phone call from the Maple Leafs offering the 6'1", 200-pound defensively oriented Valk a tryout with the team. The Leafs were looking to remake their roster and offered Valk a chance to make their club. The native of Edmonton signed his Leaf contract on October 8, 1998 and along with it the opportunity to revive his NHL career.

When Pat Quinn took over as coach of the Maple Leafs for the 1998–99 season, a number of players from the previous year were given different roles while new players were added to the roster. Some of the fresh faces were youngsters on defense such as Tomas Kaberle, Danny Markov, and, later on, Bryan Berard. Veteran players such as goalie Curtis Joseph, and winger Steve Thomas were also brought in to balance out the club, which led to a good season for the team with a surprising 45–30–7 record. Valk was one of the veteran players added to give the team a checking presence among a group that emphasized attack. Valk scored eight goals during the season and totaled 29 points—very respectable totals given his ice time. However the left-winger saved his best moment for the playoffs, in an overtime game no less.

The Leafs were able to sneak past the Philadelphia Flyers in the first round of the playoffs winning the series in six games. It was expected that Toronto would be able to get by their second-round opponent in easier fashion, but the Pittsburgh Penguins had other ideas. Their lineup featured superstar Jaromir Jagr and goalie Tom Barrasso, both experienced stars who were also two-time Stanley Cup champions. It did not look good for the Leafs after the first game, a 2–0 Penguins win right in the Air Canada Centre. Quinn made some lineup changes, however, and the Leafs bounced back to even the series at 2–2 by the end of the fourth contest. The Leafs won the fifth game at home 4–1, but had to return to Pittsburgh for the sixth contest on May 17, 1999.

Garry Valk played in 770 career games for five NHL teams (Vancouver, Anaheim, Pittsburgh, Toronto, and Chicago) and finished with 100 goals and 256 points.

The Leafs found themselves down 2-0 but came back to take a 3-2 lead (on goals by Lonny Bohonos, Valk and Sergei Berezin) before allowing the Pens to tie it up in the second period by Jagr. The third period was scoreless, forcing the game into overtime with the Penguins facing elimination on home ice. Yanic Perreault of the Leafs won a face-off in the Penguins end   and Berezin fired a shot at Barrasso that was stopped but the rebound lay tantalizing in the crease. Valk quickly moved in and swept the puck past the Penguins goalie just 1:57 into extra time, diving on his stomach to get his shot off. The Leafs had just earned a spot in the conference final.

"Just to be a big part of a big game is every kid's dream,"Valk said afterward. "When playing street hockey you want to score a big goal in the Stanley Cup playoffs. All those years of hard work paid off... didn't know right away that it went in. I saw the red light go on and I was on my stomach." He also commented on the Leafs' ability to bounce back after a bad start. "We were down 2–0 and we could have packed it in and said let's wait for game 7. But we battled back. We fought the crowd [the loud Penguins fans at the Civic Arena)]. We fought adversity and we came out on top." It was especially sweet for Valk because he was with the Pittsburgh club in 1997–98 and at one point it looked like his career might be over since no NHL team was looking to sign him until the Leafs gave him a chance.

The Leafs looked poised to make it to the Stanley Cup finals for the first time since 1967, but the Buffalo Sabres ended those hopes when they won the conference final in 5 games. Valk finished the '99 playoffs with 7 points in 17 games, marking it the best post-season of his career. There is no doubt his game in Pittsburgh was the one time his performance in the playoffs made him the star of the night.

ERIC LINDROS
MAPLE LEAFS® • C

Eric Lindros

Leaf Record:
11 Goals,
11 Assists,
22 Points

Maple Leaf Moments: October 5, 15, and 24 2005

It was inevitable that one day Eric Lindros would play for the Maple Leafs, his hometown team. It might have happened in 1991 when the junior star was available and went number one in the draft, but the Leafs had foolishly traded away their first-round choice for that year and then had to do everything possible (including making more dubious trades) not to finish last overall. If the Leafs had finished in the basement, they would have handed over the first pick to New Jersey (who still ended up with a great player when they took defenseman and future Hall of Famer Scott Neidermayer with the third pick from Toronto). Years passed, but Lindros never wavered from wanting to be a Maple Leaf one day. And that day finally arrived in the summer of 2005 when Toronto signed the six-foot-four, 240-pound center as a free agent.

The much-anticipated start of Lindros's Maple Leaf career came in the opening game of the 2005–06 season, the first NHL game after the lockout year. The Ottawa Senators came into the Air Canada Centre as the favorites on October 5, 2005. The Leafs lost captain Mats Sundin early in the game (he took a puck in the eye area) thrusting Lindros into the spotlight as the Toronto club tried to make up for the loss of their most talented player. The score was tied late in the game when Lindros snapped a wrist shot past Dominik Hasek in the Ottawa net to give the Leafs a brief 2–1 lead with just 1:31 to play. The fans at the ACC gave Lindros (who was born in London, Ontario, but grew up in Toronto) a great ovation, but Ottawa tied the game with a late goal. The game went to a shoot-out—the first in NHL history—and the Senators took it on a goal by Dany Heatley. Lindros missed on his chance in the shoot-out but still secured a point for Toronto with his first goal as a Maple Leaf.

Ten days later on October 15, the Leafs traveled to Montreal for a Saturday-night contest that was televised on *Hockey Night in Canada*.

Eric Lindros scored 8 goals in his first 10 games as a Maple Leaf. He finished his NHL career with 865 points in 760 games.

It was a close game throughout, but it was decided by Lindros' consistent efforts. With the score tied 1–1 and the Leafs on a powerplay, Lindros picked up the puck deep in the Leafs end and made a long pass to Alex Steen. Steen passed puck to Kyle Wellwood who spotted a hard-charging Lindros on the wing. Lindros rifled a hard wrist shot over the shoulder of Montreal netminder Jose Theodore to give the Leafs the lead.

The Habs came back to tie the score, but in the third Lindros struck again. The Leafs managed to keep the puck in at the Montreal blue line and eventually Steen drove a puck at the Habs net. Theodore made the save, but Lindros had gone straight to the front of the goal and promptly swept home the rebound to give his team a 3–2 lead. Montreal tried hard to tie it again, but the Leafs held them off for an important victory.

After the game, Leafs coach Pat Quinn commented on the play of the game's first star. "He's showing responsibility and accountability that we were hoping to get [when the Leafs signed Lindros]... and he's showing it right now."

Montreal captain Saku Koivu also took the time to praise Lindros' fine play in the game. "He's a strong man, tough to maintain down low." Those are the exact characteristics that were always evident when Lindros was playing at his best.

Lindros also helped the Leafs record their first-ever shoot-out win (October 24) when he beat Andrew Raycroft of the Boston Bruins to secure a 5-4 Toronto victory. The goal capped a great month for one of the new Leafs recruited to the team after some veteran players had been let go.

When he signed ($1.55 million for one year) with the Leafs, Lindros commented on how it was a dream come true for him. "Looking back to the conversation I had with my brother many years ago, we always discussed coming back to Toronto. Unfortunately, Brett can't do it, but I have an opportunity to fulfill that. This is the hotbed of hockey. This is going to be a lot of fun."

Just when it looked like the Leafs had made a steal of a deal in bringing Lindros to the city he so much wanted to play in, a hand injury derailed his year and limited it to just 33 games played in the 2005–06 season. Lindros' impactful NHL career would only last one more season (with Dallas) before he was forced to retire due to reoccurring injuries. His greatest achievements came with the Philadelphia Flyers, but for one month Lindros was a star in the city where hockey matters most.

Cody Franson

Leafs Record:
14 Goals,
69 Assists,
83 Points

Maple Leafs Moment: May 13, 2013

When the Toronto Maple Leafs agreed to take Matthew Lombardi's contract off the hands of the Nashville Predators, they had to extract something more to make the deal worthwhile. Defenseman Cody Franson fit the bill perfectly since it gave the Leafs a twenty-five-year-old developing blueliner to add to their young roster. Franson not only had good size (six foot five, 213 pounds) but also showed some offensive flair (8 goals for Nashville in 2010–11). The Leafs heavily promoted their new blueliner and the Toronto fans were quite excited to have the British Columbia native on the team.

However, Franson's efforts at training camp were less than inspiring and coach Ron Wilson never seemed to connect with the former 2005 third-round pick (seventy-ninth overall). Franson started the season in the press box and only managed to get into 57 games for the Leafs in 2011–12, although he did register 21 points. Franson showed flashes of what the Leafs wanted so much, but his lack of playing time made it very difficult for him to show any consistency. The Leafs eventually replaced a faltering Wilson behind the bench with Randy Carlyle to complete the 2011–12 campaign, but there was too little time left for Franson to salvage his year.

The lockout-shortened 2012–13 season gave Franson a fresh start and Carlyle seemed to get the message across to Franson that he wanted to see the large defender play his position. He was soon teamed with rugged minor-league veteran Mark Fraser who made the team out of training camp and the two made for a very effective blueline tandem. Franson started to play with much more purpose and direction while scoring 5 goals and totaling 29 points while playing in 45 of the 48-game regular season schedule, recording his one hundredth career point in the process. His shot from the point always seemed to find a way of getting through to the net and his work in his own end was quite effective, evidenced by his plus-4 record. The Leafs were also much better in the 2012–13 regular season and made the playoffs with the fifth-best record in the Eastern Conference.

The Leafs were matched up against the Boston Bruins in the first round of the playoffs and few gave the blue and white much of a chance against the 2011 Stanley Cup champions. Nevertheless, the Leafs hung tough and despite falling behind 3–1 in the series, they came back to force a seventh and deciding game in Boston on May 13, 2013. Once again the experts thought there was no way the Leafs could win 3 games in Boston (a very inhospitable place for Toronto over the previous two seasons) in one series, but the visitors had other ideas.

Cody Franson had 6 points (3 goals, 3 assists) in the 7-game series versus Boston. The last Leaf defenseman to score 2 goals in one playoff game was Tomas Kaberle against Philadelphia on April 14, 2003. Leaf defenseman and hockey legend King Clancy scored twice in a Stanley Cup final game on April 7, 1932, against the New York Rangers. Ironically, that game was also played in Boston. The Leafs swept the Rangers in 3 straight games that year to capture the Stanley Cup.

A Franson giveaway cost the Leafs the opening goal of the contest before the six-minute mark of the first, but he more than made up for it when he tied the score, snapping home a shot while the Leafs were on a power play. Then, in the second, Franson swept in a rebound near the Boston net to give the Leafs a 2–1 advantage going into the third period. Toronto added 2 more goals to make it 4–1 at the 5:29 mark of the final stanza. It was 4–2 for the Leafs with less than two minutes to play when the roof caved in and the Bruins tied it with a pair of late goals. In overtime, the Bruins scored the winner at the 6:05 mark. The Leafs' season was over.

Like all other players in the Toronto dressing room after the game, Franson found it hard to explain why the Leafs let their guard down and allowed the Bruins back in the contest. "They got a few quick ones on us to tie the game... it is tough to stay composed in that situation," Franson said of his team, the youngest club in the NHL post-season. "Any type of playoff experience is going to help you. Unfortunately, this is an experience were going to have to carry over the summer," added that "We gave ourselves a chance to win and going into the third we wanted to keep our foot on the gas." For his great effort in this game (one of the best playoff performances by a Leaf defenseman ever), Franson was named the second star of the contest, but he likely would have been the first star if the Leafs had hung on to the lead.

Franson could well become a major star on the Leafs blue line if he can build on his 2012–13 performance. Carlyle said he told Franson he must work on his quickness to get to pucks faster—good advice for the young veteran from a former Norris Trophy winner.

Franson did play so effectively in 2013-14 (although he did record 33 points), however it should be remembered that he is still developing and a new one-year contract for the 2014-15 season should give him plenty of incentive to improve.

Mike Gartner (#11) scored an overtime goal for the Maple Leafs against the San Jose Sharks in the 1994 playoffs.

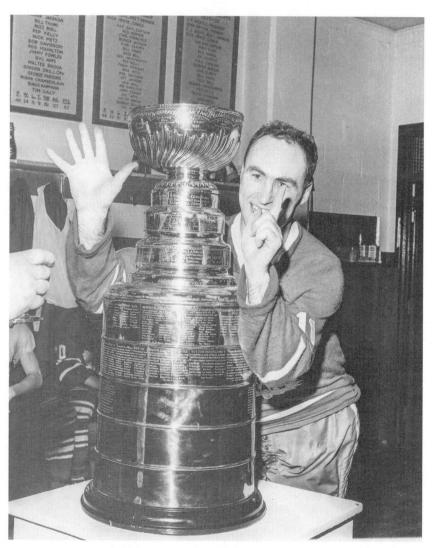

Red Kelly won four Stanley Cups with the Maple Leafs after being acquired
from the Red Wings.

TRADED FOR BY THE MAPLE LEAFS

Gerry Ehman • Red Kelly • Don McKenney • Paul Henderson
Jim Harrison • Bernie Parent • Dan Daoust • Eddie Olczyk
Bryan Berard • Phil Kessel • Jonathan Bernier

TRADES HAVE A WAY of rejuvenating a team and the Maple Leafs have made their share of spectacular deals in efforts to shake up the team or find a missing piece of the puzzle. Sometimes they have worked out very well. Other times, fans have wondered (even for decades) why such transactions were even contemplated. All said, good or bad, most followers of the Maple Leafs love to talk about deals!

Trading players is a big part of the business of hockey and when they work well (such as the acquisition of Red Kelly from Detroit), every Leaf fan thinks they "stole" the player coming to Toronto. When deals go bad, everyone cannot wait to get the acquired player out of town as fast as possible—even if that means making another questionable trade. The following players were acquired by the Leafs in trades and had left very positive marks playing for their new team in Toronto:

Gerry Ehman

Leaf Record:
26 Goals,
31 Assists,
57 Points

Maple Leaf Mome ıts: 1958–59 Season and Playoffs

Gerry"Tex"Ehmar was a member of the Detroit Red Wings organization but was going no vhere with that team at the big-league level. The solid six-foot, 180-p/ ınd right-winger got another chance when Boston grabbed his r´ ,hts, but he was still largely remained a minor-league player ˮ..ıcn Imlach was a manager in the Boston organization for a peri/,d before he took over in Toronto as coach and general manager. He recalled that Ehman was a very useful player (who would score 31ı career goals in the American Hockey League). On December 23, 1958, the Leafs acquired Ehman and sent cash to Detroit (who had now reacquired the rights to the twenty-six-year-old) to complete a deal for the winger. It was some of the best money the Leafs ever spent in a trade.

Few but Imlach could have dreamed up the idea that a veteran minor-leaguer like Ehman could contribute much to a bottom place team like the 1958–59 Maple Leafs. Not only that but the Leafs coach even predicted that Ehman would score big goals for the Toronto club. He was right. In the final 38 games of the season, Ehman put up 25 points (12 goals, 13 assists) and helped lead the charge of an improbable Leafs drive to a playoff spot.

The Leafs were in fifth place with 5 games remaining but 7 points behind fourth-place NewYork. The Leafs won their last 5 games (including a 2-game sweep of the Rangers over a weekend), and edged the Broadway Blueshirts by one point (65 to 64). Ehman's impressive play made him a standout over the second half of the season, but he saved his best for the playoffs, especially against his former team the Boston Bruins.

The Leafs flew right to Boston after securing their spot in the post-season on the last night of the regular season in Detroit. The Bruins were strong favorites to oust the upstart Maple Leafs, but Imlach would not even let his team think about losing now. The Boston club was more than ready, and took the first 2 games by scores of 5–1 and 4–2. The Leafs looked like they might be running out of gas at the most inopportune moment. Their only hope now lay in returning home to Maple Leaf Gardens and their hometown fans starting on March 28, 1958.

It was a tight contest all the way through, but Ehman played the role of Leaf hero on this night with 2 important goals. His first came in the third period when he tied the game 2–2, sending the contest into overtime. Billy Harris dug the puck out in the Boston zone and set up Ehman with a pass. Ehman let go a low drive that got past two Bruin defenders and behind netminder Harry Lumley. That set the stage for Ehman early in the overtime session. After Leaf goalie Johnny Bower made three good stops on Bruin scoring attempts, Harris once again made all the right moves to set up Ehman for a shot. Recalling that Lumley was susceptible on the far side, Ehman drove the puck to the long side of the net past the goalie's reach. "I just let it go in the general direction of the far corner and it hit the target,"

When Gerry Ehman was traded to Toronto he said he was glad to get another opportunity to make the NHL. "I was a bit discouraged when Detroit sent me down [to the AHL]. I worked like a dog in the American league to earn a chance." Ehman was not on the Leafs roster when they won the Stanley Cup in 1962 and 1963, but he was part of the team when they won the championship in 1964 scoring 1 goal in 9 playoff games. He finished his NHL career with 214 points (96 goals, 118 assists) in 429 games.

Ehman said after the game. The goal got the Leafs back in the series but Ehman was not finished yet.

The Leafs evened the series then earned the lead in the best-of-seven with a 4-1 win in Boston. The Bruins, however, rallied to win the sixth contest in Toronto, which forced a deciding game back in Boston on April 7, 1959.

The Leafs were down 2–1 in the third before center Bob Pulford tied the game with his third goal of the series. The robust Leafs center let a shot go from the Bruins blue line which goalie Harry Lumley stopped but Pulford followed up to knock in the rebound. It looked like the game was headed for overtime when Ehman whipped home a pass from Frank Mahovlich to give Toronto the go-head goal with less than three minutes to play. The Leafs then checked until the clock ran out on the hometown Bruins. It was Ehman's sixth goal of the series and it assured each Leaf player of an extra $2,000 for advancing in the playoffs.

The Leafs faced the powerful Montreal Canadiens in the finals, but were only able to take one game, a 3–2 overtime win on home ice. Ehman was unable to score against the Habs, but he did notch four assists to bring his playoff point total to 13—the most of any Toronto player in the post-season.

Ehman made what seemed like an insignificant minor-league deal into one of the best moves in team history. It also made Imlach something of a prophet. The Leafs miracle finish to garner a playoff spot and their fine performance in the '59 playoffs provided the start to the Toronto Maple Leafs dynasty of the 1960s.

Red Kelly

Leaf Record:
119 Goals,
232 Assists,
351 Points

Maple Leaf Moments: 1961–62 Season and Playoffs

It was Red Kelly's refusal to go to the New York Rangers that kept the very skilled defenseman/center available to the Maple Leafs. The Detroit Red Wings had traded Kelly to the Rangers, but the classy thirty-two-year old veteran refused to report and announced he was retiring. Maple Leafs management sensed they could pry Kelly out of the Red Wings and received permission to speak to the Simcoe, Ontario, native and former St. Michael's Majors star. The meeting with Kelly was held in secret and the slick playmaker agreed to come to the Maple Leafs. General manager Punch Imlach offered defenseman Marc Reaume to Detroit and the Red Wings accepted, making Kelly a Maple Leaf on February 10, 1960. Imlach moved Kelly to the center position and gave him sweater number 4. It could be argued that this was the greatest deal in Leafs history as Kelly helped the team to four Stanley Cups starting with the 1961–62 championship.

When the 1961–62 NHL season began there were only four active players who had recorded 200 or more goals over the course of their careers: Gordie Howe (469 goals) of the Red Wings was one while the other three – Bernie Geoffrion (304), Jean Beliveau (274), and Dickie

Moore (211) – all played for the most dominating team of the 1950s, the Montreal Canadiens. Only thirty-two players had scored 200 or more goals to this point in NHL history, and Kelly was knocking on the door of the exclusive club with 188 tallies by the end of the 1960–61 campaign. Former Leaf players who had hit the 200-goal mark included Ted Kennedy, Harvey Jackson, Max Bentley, Harry Watson, Charlie Conacher, Syl Apps, and Tod Sloan. Kelly was determined to join this illustrious group during the 1961–62 campaign and had 199 goals going into the Christmas Day contest scheduled for Chicago. While it was not unusual for NHL teams to play on December 25, this one was set for a Monday evening, a night when NHL arenas were rarely open during the Original Six era. However, history was going to be made in the "Windy City" on this special holiday occasion.

Leonard "Red" Kelly would coach the Los Angeles Kings when the league expanded to twelve teams in 1967–68. He would go on to coach the Pittsburgh Penguins (1970 to 1972) and the Maple Leafs (1973 to 1977). Kelly coached the Leafs to above .500 records in three of his four seasons in Toronto while taking the team to the playoffs every year.

The Leafs had won 4 of their last 5 games, but a 7–4 loss to the rather lowly Boston Bruins on home ice the night of December 23 had left a bad taste in the mouths of the players and coach Imlach. The Leafs were looking for their nineteenth win (they would go on to record 37 victories that year) of the season when they arrived in Chicago but the Black Hawks, led by Bobby Hull, Stan Mikita, Pierre Pilote, and goaltender Glenn Hall, were extremely tough on home ice.

More than four minutes into the contest and with the Leafs on a power play, Kelly followed up on a shot by teammate Dave Keon and knocked home the rebound from about five feet out to hit the coveted 200-career-goal plateau. In all that game, the Leafs had the lead three different times (on goals by Dick Duff and Tim Horton), but Chicago fought back each time to make the final score 3–3. Despite the fact that the Leafs had given up the lead three times, Imlach was pleased with his team's effort. And rightly so, as the Leafs went 6–2–2 over their next 10 games on route to a second-place showing and then a Stanley Cup win in the spring of 1962.

Kelly's other best-remembered goal that season came in the playoffs when he scored in the second overtime against the New York Rangers in the fifth game of the semi-finals. The series was even at two games each when the Leafs hosted the Rangers on April 5. Whoever won this game would likely take the momentum needed to go on and win the series. Not surprisingly, Kelly came through again for the Leafs. "Gump [Worsley] had the puck under his arm above his elbow with about one-third of it showing. He moved a little and it squirted loose... and I shoved it in. He thought he had it smothered," Kelly explained after the game about his winning goal. The Leafs beat New York 7–1 in the next game to take the series.

In the '62 finals versus Chicago, Kelly added 3 points in 6 games to help assure Toronto of its first Stanley Cup since 1951.

There is little doubt that the Leafs trade for Red Kelly was the key acquisition that made the Toronto club a dynasty from the second he arrived until the moment he left in 1967 to become an NHL coach.

Don McKenney

Leaf Record:
15 Goals,
30 Assists,
45 Points

Maple Leaf Moments: February 22 and 23, 1964

Don McKenney was a pretty good player during the Original Six era, but was not always on the best teams. The native of Smith Falls, Ontario, was in the Boston system for a few seasons and made two trips to the Stanley Cup final (in 1957 and 1958) with the Bruins. He was a consistent 20-plus goal scorer and won the Lady Byng Trophy in 1959–60 when he had a career-high 69 points. Despite his good performance, McKenney was dealt to the New York Rangers in 1962. Unfortunately, the Broadway team was just as bad as the Bruins, leaving the left-winger to languish on another stagnant team. Luckily, the Leafs wanted him included in a deal meant to shake up the defending Stanley Cup champions. He went to Toronto along with veteran Andy Bathgate, and both players helped breathe new life into the Leafs to close out the 1963–64 season.

Getting traded at any time can be a traumatic event, but when you have to play against the team that dealt you on the same day that the deal was completed, the emotions can run high. Such was the case for McKenney and Bathgate who found themselves in the Maple Leafs dressing room on Saturday, February 22, 1964. McKenney posed for photos in sweater number 17 before the game and was then interviewed on *Hockey Night in Canada* with Bathgate during one of the intermissions. The two were certainly drawing the attention of Leaf fans everywhere that were anxious to hear from the two newest members of the Toronto team. More importantly everyone was waiting to see how the pair would fit in with their new teammates on the ice. If there was any nervousness on the part of the new Leafs it must have quickly dissipated when Toronto started the game in fine fashion.

McKenney was placed on a line with Toronto captain George Armstrong and Dave Keon and the trio was very effective playing a two-way game while producing some offense. Early in the first period, McKenney sprung Armstrong with a long pass who then beat Jacques Plante with a blistering drive off the post to make it 1-0. The teams were tied 2-2 after one period but the Leafs went up by one on a goal by Ron Stewart in the second stanza. Then McKenney scored his first as a Leaf and tenth of the season when he took Armstrong's pass and put a low, backhand drive past Plante. The Toronto crowd of 14,220 went home happy having witnessed a 5–2 Leafs victory and a team rejuvenated by the trade. (Bathgate had 1 assist on the night playing alongside Frank Mahovlich and Red Kelly.) McKenney was selected as one of the three stars of the game and later said, "It was a great way to get started. I hope I can keep it up."

> *Don McKenney was elated to be traded to the Maple Leafs, stating, "I just couldn't play hockey here [in New York]. I was always hearing stories that I was going to Toronto and there's just no hockey atmosphere in New York. It's just too big." McKenney also played with Detroit and St. Louis before retiring after 798 career NHL games and recording 582 points.*

If all the excitement of Saturday was not enough, the two teams traveled to New York for a rematch the very next night. The McKenney, Keon, and Armstrong line was pretty much responsible for the Leafs 4–3 victory at Madison Square Garden that night as well. Keon had 2 goals (including the game winner with just twenty-eight seconds to play), Armstrong had 3 assists, and McKenney scored his second goal in as many nights when he rapped home a rebound from a Bathgate drive from the point on a Leafs power play. When the Leafs made the trade they were 24–21–10. After the trade and at the end of the season, they had 33 wins and 78 points; good enough for third place in the NHL standings. McKenney recorded 15 points (including 9 goals) in 15 regular season games as a Maple Leaf and then added 12 points in 12 playoff games to help secure Toronto's third straight championship. He scored a total of 4 post-season markers and his most important tally came in the sixth game of the semi-finals against Montreal when he notched the all-important opening goal of the contest. The Leafs were facing elimination that night, but McKenney backhanded a drive past Montreal netminder Charlie Hodge in the second period. The Leafs won the contest 3–0 and then beat the Habs 3–1 in Montreal in the seventh game. A leg injury in the finals against Detroit cut his playoff participation by a couple of games, but he still managed 1 goal and 5 assists in the finals versus Detroit.

Despite his great performance to close out the 1963–64 season and playoffs, McKenney was only a Leaf for one more season (19 points in 52 games in 1964–65) part of which was played in the minors. Although he was seen as a secondary acquisition compared to Bathgate, McKenney turned out to be one of the most valuable players in the Leafs drive for their third consecutive Stanley Cup. The Leafs gave up a great deal to make the trade, but it was worth it to pick up such a reliable veteran like McKenney.

PAUL HENDERSON   L. WING
TORONTO MAPLE LEAFS

Paul Henderson

Leaf Record:
162 Goals,
156 Assists,
318 Points

Maple Leaf Moment: January 31, 1971 and February 26, 1972

When Paul Henderson was traded to Toronto he was shocked and disappointed. Having been in the Detroit Red Wing organization since he was a junior star (49 goals in 1962–63 for the Hamilton Red Wings), Henderson felt betrayed by Detroit. Maple Leafs coach and general manager Punch Imlach had always liked the speedy five-foot-eleven, 180-pound left-winger with a hard shot. In fact, Imlach once told Henderson he was going to acquire him in a trade someday. When that day finally arrived on March 3, 1968, the two teams completed a blockbuster seven-player deal. Despite his initial reservations, Henderson soon found the atmosphere in Toronto to be quite acceptable.

"Even though I'd had no favourite team as a kid, Maple Leaf Gardens was a special place. You could feel the tradition as you walked the halls and corridors," Henderson wrote years later. "The thought of being on *Hockey Night in Canada* every Saturday was a dream come true. I knew there would be pressure but that's when I played my best hockey."

The trade was too late to save the Leafs 1967–68 season (just one year removed from winning the Stanley Cup), but the following campaign saw Henderson score 27 times (his best showing to that point) and the Leafs were back in the playoffs. The 1969–70 season was not a great one for Henderson (20 goals) who played despite a bad groin, nor was it a good year for the Leafs who missed the playoffs for the second time in three years. But the 1970–71 season was a bounce-back year for all concerned with Henderson scoring 30 goals and the team getting back to the post-season after recovering from a very bad start.

On January 31, 1971, the Leafs were in Montreal for a Saturday-night meeting. Henderson had one of his best games as a Maple Leaf when he scored once (he had another marker disallowed) and added 3 assists in the 5–4 victory. The Leafs scored 5 times on just 20 shots directed at Rogie Vachon and Phil Myre. The win was important because it put the Leafs only 6 points back of the Habs in the East. It also gave the Toronto side a much needed boost and, although they finished in fourth place, their effort to close out the 1970–71 season was a strong one for a team that had such an up-and-down campaign.

When Paul Henderson returned from the '72 series, phone operators at the Leafs office answered calls with the phrase "Maple Leaf Gardens, home of Paul Henderson." After a somewhat acrimonious contract battle with Leafs owner Harold Ballard, Henderson signed with the Toronto Toros of the World Hockey Association in 1974. He stayed in the WHA until he returned briefly to the NHL with the Atlanta Flames in 1970–80.

In the '71 playoffs, Henderson scored 5 goals against the New York Rangers and nearly helped the Leafs get off to a 3–0 series lead. Instead, they had to settle for a 2–1 advantage because of some poor goaltending by veteran Jacques Plante. In the end, the Rangers overpowered the Leafs to take the series in 6 games while Montreal switched to goalie Ken Dryden and won the Stanley Cup!

Not surprisingly, hopes for the rejuvenated 1971–72 Leafs were higher than before but few players met the new expectation level. Henderson was one of those who played better than the previous year scoring an NHL career-high 38 goals. Three of these goals came on February 26 when the Leafs hosted the second-year Vancouver Canucks. The Canucks scored first on a goal by Andre Boudrias but, powered by two Henderson goals, the Leafs went up 4–1 by the time the first period was over. A second-period assist and another goal (his thirty-second of the year) helped secure Henderson's status as the first star of the game that ended 7–1 for the Leafs. Toronto's new power play featuring forwards Dave Keon, Norm Ullman, Ron Ellis, with Jim McKenney and Henderson manning the points, was especially effective (connecting for 3 goals). The Canucks used two goalies, but neither Dunc Wilson nor rookie Ed Dyck (making his first appearance in the NHL) could stymie the Leafs on this occasion.

A relieved Henderson said after the game, "For the first time in two months we can really enjoy a couple of tall cool ones on the weekend." The Leafs got Sunday off as a result of their Saturday-night drubbing of the Canucks and that obviously made the win that much sweeter. In the seventy-eighth and final game of the 1971–72 season (at Boston), Henderson scored a pair of goals to bring his total to 38.

His superior performance during the season (he was the tenth-leading goal scorer in the NHL) earned him an invitation to Team Canada for the historic Canada-Russia Series in September 1972. Henderson's performance against the Russians was of heroic proportions; he had the game-winning goal in each of the final three contests, a feat that made him a Canadian icon for generations. The Leafs were certainly happy and proud that they had made the deal Imlach promised so many years ago!

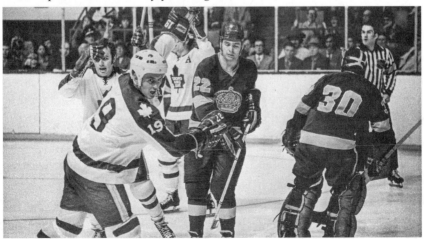

JIM HARRISON CENTER
TORONTO MAPLE LEAFS

Jim Harrison

Leaf Record:
39 Goals,
47 Assists,
86 Points

Maple Leaf Moment: April 6, 1972

When the Maple Leafs made a trade for center/winger Jim Harrison in 1969, he was something of an unknown quantity to Toronto fans since he had primarily played in western Canada as a junior. The Alberta native was a very good junior player for the Estevan Bruins where he scored more than 30 goals in three straight seasons. The husky (five-foot-eleven, 185-pound) and aggressive Harrison also helped the Edmonton Oil Kings win the Memorial Cup in 1966, but returned to Estevan for the national junior title in 1968. Once he finished junior, the Boston Bruins assigned Harrison to play minor-league hockey in Oklahoma City. By 1969, the Bruins were loaded at center with Phil Esposito, Fred Stanfield, and Derek Sanderson manning all available spots. The Leafs wanted a physical player behind centers Dave Keon and Norm Ullman, so they sent Wayne Carleton (a left-winger they once had high hopes for after a stellar career with the Marlboros) to the Bruins to complete the deal. Although Harrison was only with the Leafs for two and half years, he gave them exactly what they were looking for.

The 1971–72 edition of the Maple Leafs never met fans' expectations, but still managed to make the playoffs with a rather mediocre record of 33–31–14, good for fourth spot in the East Division. All this did was set up a first-round playoff series with the first-place Boston Bruins (54–11–13). For many years before this it had been a 1 vs. 3 and 2 vs. 4 playoff format). The change in the playoff system was not going to help the Leafs this year, but they gamely believed they could make it a series. The Bruins, however, were smarting from a first-round playoff defeat a year ago and were in no mood to let an inferior club beat them again. The Leafs had only won a single game against Boston all season long while the Bruins won four and tied another. The "Big Bad" Bruins," as they were known, may have been a tad over confident going in against the scrappy Maple Leafs but that was understandable.

The first game of the series was a 5–0 whitewashing of the Leafs. But two nights later, on April 6, 1972, the Toronto was much more resilient. Boston scored twice in the first period on goals by Fred Stanfield and Phil Esposito, but in the second, Keon and Jim McKenny evened the score early in the period. Boston's Johnny Bucyk gave the Bruins a 3–2 lead going into the third, but a tally by little Guy Trottier tied the score with ten minutes left to play in the game. Then

Jim Harrison scored 39 goals and 86 points in his first season as an Oiler and recorded a 10-point night (3 goals, 7 assist) in the process. He also played for Cleveland (WHA), Chicago (NHL), and once again in Edmonton (NHL) for the 1979–80 season. Over his 556 professional hockey game career, Harrison recorded a combined grand total of 422 regular season points.

early in the overtime, Harrison took a pass from Pierre Jarry and fired a shot from about thirty-five feet out that rocketed past Bruins goalie Gerry Cheevers. The Leafs shocked the hockey world (and probably themselves) by winning a playoff game right in the Boston Garden!

The game-winning puck was retrieved for Harrison who then passed it on to Leafs owner Harold Ballard for mounting. The twenty-four-year- old Harrison admitted that he had not scored many goals in the NHL thus making his overtime tally the finest of his young career. He also said that coach King Clancy (filling in for a large part of the 1971–72 season for the ulcer-ridden Johnny McLellan) told the team they could win the game.

"He [Clancy] always has something to say before any period. After the first he said to get our shots on goal, we were wasting chances. Before the overtime he told us we could win," recounted Harrison.

In the Boston dressing room Cheevers told reporters that there was no way he could stop Harrison's drive. "He shot it about 100 miles an hour off the drop [pass]. I wasn't about to get that one."

The Leafs would never have come close in this game if it was not for the stellar work of goalie Bernie Parent who faced 40 shots on the night. Parent had predicted a win for his team before the game, but it took Harrison's goal and a brilliant stop by Parent on Bobby Orr in the last minute of regulation, to make the goalie's bold prediction come true. The Leafs hoped Parent would continue his good play back in Toronto, but despite some valiant efforts, the Leafs lost 2–0 and 5–4 in Maple Leaf Gardens. A 3–2 loss back in Boston closed out the Leafs season, but the Bruins were effusive in their praise about how well the Leafs had played throughout the five-game series.

The overtime winner by Harrison was his only goal and point of the 5-game series. It was also his final tally as a Maple Leaf. In the summer of 1972, Harrison signed to play in the World Hockey Association with the Alberta (later Edmonton) Oilers. For a brief moment the trading of a one-time potential superstar in Carleton had paid off for the Maple Leafs and gave the Toronto fans something to remember when they challenged the likes of Orr, Esposito, Sanderson, and the best team in hockey.

MAPLE LEAFS

BERNIE
PARENT

GOALIE

Bernie Parent

Leaf Record:
24 Wins,
25 Losses,
12 Ties,
3 Shutouts

Maple Leaf Moment: October 27, 1971

After the aging Maple Leafs unexpectedly won the Stanley Cup in 1967, there were many questions about what to do going forward. One of the key issues was goaltending. The remarkable Johnny Bower would last only two more seasons while journeyman netminder Bruce Gamble would waver between playing great to being rather average. Veteran Jacques Plante was brought in in 1970 but he too was a stop-gap measure (although he was a league All-Star in 1971). It was clear the Leafs needed a rising star in net and found him when the Philadelphia Flyers decided to make Bernie Parent available. Parent was already a young veteran at this point and therefore highly desired by the Leafs. To get Parent, Leafs general manager Jim Gregory gave up Gamble and forward Mike Walton in a the three team-swap to land the 26-year-old goalie. It was by far the best deal of Gregory's career and it looked like the Leafs were set in goal for a long time.

When Parent became a Leaf during the 1970–71 season, he was credited with sharing a 6–0 shutout of the California Golden Seals on March 24 with veteran netminder Jacques Plante. However, early in the 1971–72 campaign, Parent got his first solo shutout as a Leaf on October

27, 1971. The lowly Vancouver Canucks provided the opposition during the mid-week contest at Maple Leaf Gardens and it turned out they would make a bit of history on their own.

The game featured absolutely no goal scoring at all – one of the very few NHL games that ended 0-0. The fans in attendance were alternately excited and bored but most felt it was a generally well-played game considering the lack of scoring. Interestingly, there were also no penalties called in the first or third periods but nine minors (five to Vancouver) were handed out by referee John Ashley in the second stanza.

When Bernie Parent wanted to come back to the NHL, the Leafs were practically forced to give his rights back to Philadelphia since that is the place where the netminder wanted to play. The return the Leafs got in the deal with the Flyers was highly questionable given that Parent went on to meet the great expectations Toronto once had for the young goalie. The Maple Leafs traded Parent back to the Flyers in the summer of 1973 and they received a 1973 first-round draft choice (which they used to select Bob Neely) and goaltender Doug Favell. The Leafs also had to send the Flyers a 1973 second-round draft choice, which they used to select former Toronto Marlboro defenseman Larry Goodenough.

Vancouver goalie Dunc Wilson recorded the first shutout in Canucks history that night (they were playing in only their second NHL season) and the Vancouver netminder earned plenty of praise for his efforts. Time and again he stopped Maple Leaf shots that should have been goals and his save on Toronto's Paul Henderson breakaway attempt late in the third saved the game for his team. In all, Wilson (who would go on to play for the Leafs in 1973–74) stopped 34 shots and earned his first career shutout.

Parent was not so busy in the Leafs end but still had to be excellent on chances by Orland Kurtenbach, Fred Speck, and Dale Tallon who nearly gave the Canucks the only goal they would have needed. "I don't think Kurtenbach had a chance," Parent said. "I moved out and cut down the angle and he couldn't do a thing but fire wide. Tallon's shot got by me but the puck hit the post. I remember Speck firing from the slot. I threw up my arm and it hit me just above the elbow." No matter how he made the saves, Parent's performance in this game was exactly how the Maple Leafs pictured him playing for the team on a nightly basis.

Parent would record two more shutouts during the 1971–72 season (a 2–0 win over Pittsburgh and a 4–0 blanking of the Los Angeles Kings) and would post a 17–18–9 record in 47 games played (with a 2.56 goals against average that was good for the eighth best mark in the league). While that might not seem like a great record for a promising goalie such as Parent, it was actually quite good considering the Leafs were not a highly talented team, especially on defense. The Leafs were not too concerned about the won-loss record and considered Parent not only their goalie of the present and future, but also one of the best in the NHL.

However Parent's then-wife Carol (who had grown up in New Jersey) did not like Toronto much at all and with the Leafs taking their usual hard stance in contract negotiations, Leafs owner Harold Ballard refused to give the talented netminder his just financial rewards. Parent promptly signed with the WHA in January 1972 not even giving the Leafs another thought. Club management fought hard to woo Parent back and even claimed his contract with the new league was not valid. Yet all their efforts were for nothing even when Parent left the WHA a year later. He went on to become one of the best goalies in all of hockey to the point where he eventually he became a Hall of Fame inductee.

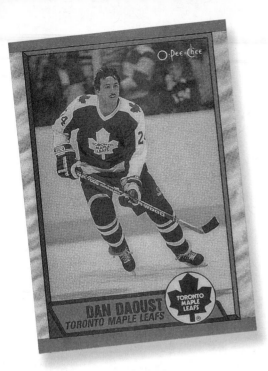

Dan Daoust

Leaf Record:
87 Goals,
166 Assists,
253 Points

Maple Leaf Moment: April 12, 1987

The Montreal Canadiens signed free-agent center Dan Daoust in the summer of 1984 and put the Montreal native in their farm system. Daoust had been a pretty good junior player with the Cornwall Royals (102 points in his final season there), but his small size (five foot ten, 160 pounds) scared NHL teams away to the point where he was not even drafted. Although he put up good numbers with Montreal's minor-league team in the AHL, the Nova Scotia Voyageurs, the Canadiens decided he could not beat out any of their other centers and made him available in a trade with the Leafs for a third-round draft choice in December 1982. Considering what they gave up, the Leafs came out on the positive side, landing a player who was with them for eight NHL seasons.

After arriving from Montreal, Daoust gave the Leafs some quality playmaking by notching 33 assists in his first 48 games to end the 1982–83 season. He then posted seasons with 56 and 37 assists as he helped with many goals scored by Leaf sniper Rick Vaive. By the 1985–86 season, however, Daoust recorded only 13 assists and 20 points as he started to assume more defensive responsibilities as young snipers such as center like Russ Courtnall, Vincent Damphousse, and Tom Fergus began to emerge on offense. In 1986–87, Daoust played in only 33 games due to a severe knee injury and his point total did not even reach double digits that year (3 goals and 4 assists). The Leafs missed the feisty center when he was not in the lineup and it showed: they finished a rather unimpressive 32–42–6, good for only 70 points but still earning them a playoff spot in the perennially weak Norris Division. If Daoust had not been able to contribute much in the regular season, he now had plenty of energy left for the playoffs.

The Leafs faced St. Louis in the first round of the '87 post-season. The teams spilt the first 2 games before the Blues came to Toronto for games three and four. A late rally in the third contest at Maple Leaf Gardens earned the Blues a 5–3 win and a 2–1 series lead making the next game, played on April 12, 1987, of paramount importance to the Leafs' cause. It was a long, vicious game that was tied 1–1 going into the third period when Daoust scored the game-winning goal. Greg Terrion had put a shot on Blues netminder Rick Wamsley before Daoust jumped on the rebound to give the Leafs the lead just 1:43 into the final frame. Toronto's Ken Wregget made the save of the game when he caught a blistering shot from Blues defenseman Gino Cavallini to preserve the 2–1 victory. The series was now even at 2 games each.

Dan Daoust scored 5 goals and added 2 assists in 13 post-season games in the '87 playoffs. He had the third best playoff point total on the team that year (tied with Russ Courtnall who also had 7), putting him just behind Wendel Clark (11) and Mike Allison (8).

While Daoust's goal was significant, it was his work watching Blues center Doug Gilmour that was noticeable. At times Daoust was glued to Gilmour's every move, but he also got help from line mates Terrion and Gary Leeman. "He [Gilmour] was more upset in the third period," Daoust said later. "I hooked him in a bad spot once and he told me to watch my stick. There was a lot of stick work out there on the part of both teams. And I think that is the way it's going to be."

Toronto coach John Brophy agreed. "Things were getting a little chippy out there," Brophy said of the game that featured sixteen minor penalties and a good deal of nastiness. "St. Louis likes to hook and grab and hold. And when you do it to them, they fall on the ice. Well, we can hook and grab and hold with anybody."

Daoust stayed on Gilmour the rest of the series and the Leafs won the next 2 games to defeat the Blues 4 games to 2. The last game was played at the Gardens and Gilmour dropped his gloves and went after Daoust as the final contest was drawing to a close. Tired of being shadowed, hooked, and hacked at all over the ice, the Blues star did his best to get at Daoust and he had to be restrained by the officials to prevent a fight, but it was all in vain as the Leafs had a commanding 4–0 lead in the game. It was not pretty but Daoust did the job required to shut down the other team's best player and drive Gilmour to distraction and ultimately, causing him to lose his composure.

"They got frustrated," Daoust said. "It was a checking series. It was always 1–1 or 1–0 going into the third period. The whole line played well. We just told each other get the puck out and pick up your man."

Beating the Blues was sweet revenge for the Leafs after having lost to them in the 1986 playoffs. This time the man they acquired from Montreal showed them the way.

Eddie Olczyk

Leaf Record:
116 Goals,
151 Assists,
267 Points

Maple Leaf Moment: December 9, 1989

The Maple Leafs had always been interested in center Eddie Olczyk and, in fact, nearly got his rights in an arbitration battle with the Chicago Blackhawks regarding the signing of defenseman Gary Nyland. The Leafs were not awarded Olczyk at that time, but when Chicago sought Rick Vaive, Steve Thomas, and Bob McGill in a trade in September 1987, the Blackhawks had no choice but to include the Chicago native in the trade (along with Al Secord).

Olczyk had played some junior hockey in Ontario so he looked forward to being a Maple Leaf. When he scored 42 goals in 1987–88, it seemed like Toronto had something to good to show for the deal that was clearly lopsided in favor of the Blackhawks. Olczyk thrived the following year, racking up a 90-point season playing on a line with Mark Osborne and Gary Leeman.

Sometimes the grueling NHL schedule works in favor of one team and not so much the other. Such was the case when the Montreal Canadiens paid a visit to Maple Leaf Gardens on December 9, 1989. The Habs were coming off a 6–6 Friday-night tie with the Winnipeg Jets while the Maple Leafs sat idle, waiting for them to arrive for their

Saturday night tilt which was to be televised on *Hockey Night in Canada*. Montreal had lost the Stanley Cup final the previous spring and were clearly the favourites to beat the Leafs just as they had done less than a month earlier at the Forum in overtime. However the Montreal club was tired from their game Friday and did not get into Toronto until the early hours of Saturday morning. Rather than start regular netminder Patrick Roy, Montreal coach Pat Burns decided to go with twenty-year-old Andre Racicot, who would be playing in his first NHL game. It would prove to be a costly mistake.

The Leafs were charged up, and even though no one in the crowd of 16,382 that night expected a win for the hometown club, the men in blue and white were ready for this one. Sensing they could get to Racicot, the Leafs stormed to the attack. Tom Fergus opened the scoring in the first minute (at the thirty-nine-second mark, to be exact) and then Olczyk scored his first of the night less than three minutes later. The big Leaf center was in behind the Montreal defense when he took a pass from Tom Kurvers before backhanding a shot over Racicot for his tenth of the year. Before the Habs knew what hit them, the Leafs had built up a 5–0 lead (which included Wendel Clark's one hundredth career goal) in the first period before Montreal got one back late in the opening frame. Racicot was out of the game by the time the Leafs were up by three, but that did not stop the hungry Leafs on this night.

Eddie Olczyk was eventually traded to the Winnipeg Jets on November 10, 1990, along with Mark Osborne. The Maple Leafs received defenseman Dave Ellett and winger Paul Fenton in return. Olczyk was the first-ever Leaf to score 30 goals in each of his first three seasons with the team.

Montreal scored to open the second period, but Olczyk quickly restored Toronto's 4-goal lead with his second of the game. This time Olczyk got a good bounce as the puck went off the skate of Montreal defenseman Eric Desjardins and shot past Roy. Montreal narrowed the game to 6–3 in the third to make the Gardens crowd uneasy once again, but Olczyk came to the rescue with his third goal of the night. This time he scored on a clear breakaway and put a backhand drive over Roy's shoulder. The game ended with some fighting, but the Leafs walked away 7–4 winners having outshot Montreal 38–36 in the wide-open contest.

Olczyk had not scored in the previous seven games and there were rumors swirling about that he was going to be dealt to the Jets for Dale Hawerchuk, but he put all that behind him to record his second career hat trick. "I thought we blitzed them pretty good," Olczyk said after the game. "All we wanted to do was not let them come at us, but to take it to them."

Toronto coach Doug Carpenter echoed what many Leaf fans were feeling. "I thought we owed them something [from their November loss]. We had to come out and jump on them and we did that."

This game was typical of the 1989–90 Leafs: a high-scoring affair with little or no defense. They would finish the season with an even 38–38–4 record, earning them a playoff spot.

This Leafs team featured seven players with 20 or more goals while two others had 19. Gary Leeman had 51 goals playing on the wing alongside Olczyk, which made the acquisition of the former Blackhawk look only that much better. In the end, "Eddie O" would have 267 points in 257 games with Toronto.

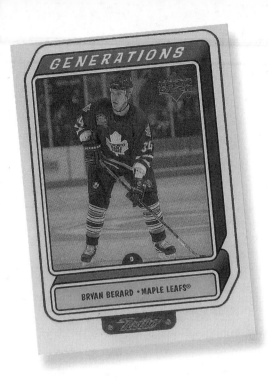

BRYAN BERARD • MAPLE LEAFS®

Bryan Berard

Leaf Record:
8 Goals,
41 Assists,
49 Points

Maple Leaf Moment: April 14, 1999

When the Maple Leafs signed goaltender Curtis Joseph it meant that incumbent netminder Felix Potvin was prime trade material. After a few rumored deals fell through, the Leafs finally arranged to trade Potvin to the NewYork Islanders. In return, the Leafs picked up defenseman Bryan Berard, a former number-one overall draft pick of the Ottawa Senators in 1995 (he had just come off a superb junior career with teams in the Detroit area). The smooth-skating blueliner was dealt to the Islanders before he ever played a game for the Senators and he enjoyed a good rookie year on Long Island with 48 points (including 40 assists) in 82 games. He scored 14 times (and totaled 46 points) the following year (1997–98), but Islanders management seemed displeased with their young star. His poor defensive record may have had a large influence on how the NewYork club viewed his future. When the opportunity to get a quality goalie such as Potvin came up, Mike Milbury, the Islanders general manager, decided Berard was expendable. The deal for Berard was completed in January 1999. The Leafs were thrilled to have a player such as Berard join their team since defenseman with potential are always a valued commodity in the NHL.

The 1998–99 Maple Leafs were a team that was surprisingly good during the regular season, considering especially that they were coming off a horrible year in 1997–98. Under new coach Pat Quinn the Leafs stressed a puck-moving offensive that relied on their goalie to make the big save. It seemed like a perfect fit for a player like Berard who had a flare for joining the attack. He did not score many goals for the Leafs that year (he had 5 in 38 games to finish the 1998–99 campaign), but his defensive game improved greatly and he earned a plus-7 rating, an improvement from his days with the Islanders where he was once a minus 32!

The Leafs were tuning up for the '99 playoffs (having already locked up fourth spot in the Eastern Conference) when the Islanders came to Toronto for the second-last game of the season. It was April 14, 1999. Potvin started in goal for New York and he had a very good game back in the city that once adored him. The game went into overtime tied *Bryan Berard recorded 329 career points in 619 games played for a rate slightly better than a point every other game—a very good record for a defenseman who did not have the full use of his right eye for a large part of his career.* 2–2 before Berard made his mark with the winner. The Leaf defenseman joined the rush just forty-two seconds into extra time and beat Potvin with a shot right along the ice. It was the Leafs thirty-eighth shot of the game and the crowd gave Potvin a loud cheer when he was named the first star of the game. But it was also time for a new Leaf hero and on this night it was the youngster Berard.

"Yeah, it felt good," Berard said of the game winner against his former team. "Was Milbury even there? I didn't see him. I know were getting ready for the playoffs but that goal was special." He also spoke about the former Leafs netminder. "Felix played great. I know he's had a tough time with injuries [Potvin had recently missed 22 games]. I hope it works out for him."

The Berard-Potvin trade may have been the focus of this contest, but it should be noted that the Leafs won their forty-fifth game of the season that night (establishing a team record that would be equaled twice more). And they also recorded their ninety-seventh point of the season.

Berard had a pretty good playoff in '99 (with one goal and nine points in 17 games played), but a streaking Buffalo Sabre club did the Leafs in during the Eastern Conference final. While the future looked exceedingly bright for Berard, a serious eye injury suffered in a game against Ottawa on March 11, 2000 pretty much ended any hope of a stellar career. He had a long period of recuperation and then decided he was better off not returning to the Maple Leafs. "I think the pressure would have been on Toronto to take me back and I just didn't think it was fair to Toronto," Berard said years later. "Then, I thought at the time for myself I really wanted to get away from the injury. I really wanted to start over. I knew in Toronto the pressure would have been on me a lot more."

Berard went on to play for the New York Rangers, Boston Bruins, Chicago Blackhawks, Columbus Blue Jackets, and once more for the New York Islanders before calling it a career. He reflected on his time with the Maple Leafs by saying, "I loved Toronto. I loved being a Leaf. A few things happened and there's nothing you can do about an eye injury. I wish things could have worked out differently and I could have been a Leaf for a long time. It was great to have just been there."

Most Leaf fans would agree that they would have wanted to see Berard play his entire career in a blue-and-white uniform; that is how excited they felt when the team made a deal to acquire a player who had once been judged to be the best junior player available.

Phil Kessel

Leaf Record:
156 Goals,
177 Assists,
333 Points

Maple Leaf Moment: October 8, 2011

The Maple Leafs have completed many controversial trades over their long history in the National Hockey League and none more so than the acquisition of right-winger Phil Kessel. It was fairly obvious to most that Kessel would not go back to the Boston Bruins after the 2008-09 season was over – a year that saw the sharp-shooter score 36 goals for Beantown. However, coach Claude Julien did not quite see eye-to-eye with the player the Bruins selected fifth overall in the 2006 Entry Draft. Julien wanted to see his wingers work along the boards and play a strong two-way game, and that wasn't Kessel's approach to the game.

Kessel nearly signed a deal with the Nashville Predators, but Toronto general manager Brian Burke wanted to make a splash in his new role with the team. The Bruins extracted a large price for Kessel and got Toronto's first-round pick in 2010 (Tyler Seguin) and 2011 (Dougie Hamilton), plus a second-round choice in 2010 (Jared Knight). Suddenly the pressure was on Kessel to not only play well for the Maple Leafs but to be a superstar on a team that was rebuilding after the 2004–05 lockout.

Kessel did not play a complete season in 2010–11 because of a shoulder injury, but he still scored 30 times and registered 55 points in 70 games. Those were good numbers for most but Kessel was expected to produce more and the team floundered with the second-worst record (30–38–14) in the entire NHL. Boston received the second overall pick of the draft and selected the highly regarded Seguin. Leaf fans were angry with Burke who had not protected his team during the Entry Draft (by allowing the Leafs a choice, either to take or pass on a selection, if their draft position was in the top five in one of the years when the first-round draft picks were owed to the Bruins). In fact, Burke claimed he never even asked his Boston counterpart if he could get such a consideration!

In 2012–13, Toronto coach Randy Carlyle had Phil Kessel playing a two-way game in the belief that offense can come from good defense. He had a team leading 52 points (20 goals, 32 assists) in the 48-game schedule that ended with the Maple Leafs back in the playoffs. Kessel added 6 points (including 4 goals) in 7 playoff games during the 2013 post-season. Kessel has totaled 333 points in 364 regular season games with Toronto to date.

Kessel's second season in Toronto saw his numbers improve to 32 goals and 64 points And he played in all 82 games. However, the Leafs still missed the playoffs after the 2010–11 season.

The Leafs were hoping for a much better year in 2011-12 and wanted to get off to a strong start. They opened the season with a 2-0 win over the Montreal Canadiens on home ice and then hosted the Ottawa Senators on October 8, 2011, a Saturday night contest featuring the "Battle of Ontario." The Leafs opened the scoring in the first frame with Mikhail Grabovski and Kessel getting the markers. Kessel's goal was a wrist shot that flew over the shoulder of Ottawa netminder Craig Anderson.

The second period was more Leafs as Kessel assisted on a goal by Joffrey Lupul and then scored his second with a backhand that beat Anderson to give the Leafs a 4–0 lead. The teams exchanged goals early in the third to make it 5–1, but the Senators then staged a furious comeback to narrow the gap to 5–4. As Leaf fans feared that their team was going to suffer a huge collapse, Kessel rode in to the rescue with his third of the night—a hard snap-shot past Alex Auld who had taken over in the Ottawa net to start the final frame.

The Leafs hung on for a 6–5 win, but after the game, talk shifted to Kessel's first career hat trick as a Maple Leaf."I got good passes and was fortunate to bury them,"Kessel said in the dressing room."I'm happy for sure but the main thing is we got two points. I'm excited."Kessel was not exactly comfortable with the media demands of playing in Toronto, but he clearly wanted to emphasize that the team was doing well and that the focus should not be on his own performance so much.

Toronto coach Ron Wilson was no doubt pleased to see his star winger breakout with a good game."He worked hard all night and it was great for Phil, great for his confidence."

Kessel would go on to score 37 goals in 2011–12 and finished fifth in league scoring (not a position many Leafs have enjoyed over the last number of years) with 82 points in 82 games played. He should have been named to one of the NHL's end-of-season All-Star teams, but having the Leafs miss the post-season once again hurt his chances for that accolade. However, the trade the Leafs made with Boston was looking much better after Kessel's performance over the last five seasons with the Maple Leafs!

Jonathan Bernier

Leaf Record:
26 Wins,
19 Losses,
7 Ties,
1 Shutout

Maple Leaf Moment: October 2, 2013

When the Maple Leafs lost the seventh game of their first round 2013 playoff series against Boston, it caused team management to seriously consider adding new players to the roster for next season. One of the first areas of consideration was to bolster the netminding position since incumbent James Reimer played a large role in the Leafs losing the deciding game to the Bruins by letting a 4-1 third period lead slip away. There was no doubt Reimer had played well to get the Leafs to that point (coming back from being down 3-1 in games) but there was still a strong doubt when he and the rest team could not complete the expected triumph. Toronto had nearly landed Roberto Luongo from Vancouver at the trade deadline just before the '13 post-season began but that deal fell through at the last minute. Now general manager Dave Nonis had to find the Leafs someone else to compete with Reimer for the start of the 2013-14 regular season.

Goaltender Jonathan Bernier had been a first round draft choice (11th overall) of the Los Angeles Kings in 2006 but was languishing on the bench behind Jonathan Quick who had taken the team to a Stanley Cup championship in 2011. Kings' management told the 6', 180-pound

Bernier that they would trade him since they believed he deserved to be a starter somewhere else. Nonis had made previous inquiries about Bernier immediately after he was named the Leafs general manager but a deal could not be worked out at that time. Once the '13 playoffs were completed Nonis called once more and this time a deal was finalized that sent promising forward Matt Frattin and goalie Ben Scrivens to the Kings along with a second round draft choice. Toronto was very pleased to land a young goalie with so much promise but would not say any more than Bernier and Reimer would battle for the number one position at training camp and throughout the season.

When the regular season began it was Reimer in goal for the first game (on the road versus the Montreal Canadiens) and that choice left Bernier a little miffed since the native of Montreal wanted to start in his hometown. The Leafs edged the Habs 4-3 but their two-game road trip continued the next night, October 2, 2013, in Philadelphia against the Flyers. The Leafs hardly ever play well in the 'City of Brotherly Love' but Bernier turned in a stellar effort to get the Leafs a 3-1 win and a 2-0 start on the season. Bernier looked terrific while making 31 saves, 14 of which came in the first period alone. One of his saves came on a penalty shot awarded to Flyer winger Wayne Simmonds but Bernier was ready and made the stop against his former Los Angeles teammate. "He's a great player, and I know he has a great backhand as well. But I was hoping he'd shoot it," said a confident Bernier about Simmonds attempt after the game. Bernier's performance gave his team a chance to steal two points and they did so when another new Leaf, centre Dave Bolland, scored twice in the contest which also saw winger Phil Kessel get the other Toronto marker. The two road wins to open the season marked the first time the Leafs ever accomplished such a feat despite their long (and sometimes illustrious) history.

"Wins at the beginning of the season are just as important as ones at the end," head coach Randy Carlyle stated quite rightly when the

Jonathan Bernier had a record of 29-20-6 in 62 career appearances with Los Angeles and was with the Kings when they won the Stanley Cup in 2011.

game was over while leaving the question of which goalie would get the first start at home unanswered. (Reiemr would start against Ottawa but Bernier would take over about halfway through the game and get the Leafs a 5-4 shootout win). Carlyle was soon to face a dilemma about which goalie was going to be designated the main starter but the issue did not get really resolved until December when it was clear that Reimer was falling behind Bernier in on ice performance. When Bernier was named the starter for the Winter Classic to be played on January 1, 2014 in Detroit (a 3-2 shootout win for Toronto), it pretty much ended the debate about who the Leafs saw as their best goalie.

While Bernier was still learning how to be a number one netminder the Leafs were in good position for a playoff spot but then disaster struck when the new Leaf goalie was injured in a game against the Los Angeles Kings in early March. The Leafs then lost eight in row and recorded just two wins in their last 14 games. If Bernier (who sported a nifty record of 26-19-7 with a .922 save percentage before his injury) had been able to play some of those games (he only played once more after the Kings game), the Leafs would have had a much better chance to hold their playoff spot. Reimer faltered badly down the stretch and as the Leafs contemplated making major changes for the 2014-15 season, there was no doubt who the number one goalie is now. It looks like the investment made in Jonathan Bernier will be a good one for the team now and in the long term future.

TEEN RANCH ICE CORRAL

TUE NOV 16, 2010

PUCK DROP 7PM

 VERSUS

SECTION	ROW	SEAT	PRICE
103	20	11	$150.00
			INCL $15.42 TAX

Enter Through Nearest Gate

966283949992

MOLSON CANADIAN.
PROUD SEASON SPONSOR

SEC	ROW	SEAT	PRICE
324	11	7	$82.00

Enter Through Nearest Gate

TUESDAY MARCH 7, 2006
7:30 PM

VISIT MAPLELEAFS.COM TO CONFIRM GAME TIMES

 VS MONTREAL CANADIENS

TUNE IN TO LEAFS TV FOR EXCLUSIVE COVERAGE

GO LEAFS GO

899163273115

899163273115

SEC	324
ROW	11
SEAT	7

BIBLIOGRAPHY

BOOKS

Angus, Charlie. *Les Costello: Canada's Flying Father.* Novalis Publishing, Toronto, 2005.

Batten, Jack. *Hockey Dynasty.* Pagurian Press, Toronto, 1969.

———. *The Leafs in Autumn.* MacMillan of Canada, Toronto, 1975.

———. *An Anecdotal History of the Toronto Maple Leafs.* Key Porter Books, Toronto, 1994.

Baun, Bob. *Lowering the Boom: The Bobby Baun Story.* Stoddart Publishing, Toronto, 2000.

Berger, Howard. *Maple Leaf Moments.* Warwick Publishing, Toronto, 1994.

Bower, Johnny and Duff, Bob. *The China Wall: The Timeless Legend of Johnny Bower.* Fenn Publishing, Toronto, 2008.

Brewitt, Ross. *Clear the Track: The Eddie Shack Story.* Stoddart Publishing, Toronto, 1998.

Conacher, Brian. *As the Puck Turns.* John Wiley and Sons, Mississauga, 2007.

Ellis Ron and Shea Kevin. *Over the Boards: The Ron Ellis Story.* Fenn Publshing, Bolton, 2002.

Fitkin, Ed. *Come On Teeder!: The Story of Ted Kennedy*. Baxter Publishing Company, Toronto, 1950.

———. *Turk Broda of the Leafs*. Baxter Publishing Company, Toronto, 1950.

Henderson, Paul and Leonetti, Mike. *Shooting for Glory: The Paul Henderson Story*. Stoddart Publishing, 1992.

Harris, Billy. *The Glory Years: Memories of a Decade 1955-1965*. Prentice Hall, Toronto, 1989.

Hewitt, Foster. *Hockey Night in Canada: The Story of the Toronto Maple Leafs*. Ryerson Press, Toronto, 1962.

Hunt, Jim. *The Men in the Nets*. Ryerson Press, Toronto, 1967.

Hunter, Douglas. *Open Ice: The Tim Horton Story*. Viking Press, Toronto, 1994.

Imlach, Punch and Young, Scott. *Hockey is a Battle*. MacMillan of Canada, Toronto, 1969.

Leonetti, Mike. *Defining Moments*. Red Deer Press, Markham, 2011.

———. *Hockey Now!* (4th, 5th, 6th and 7th Editions) Firefly Books, Richmond Hill, 2010.

Leonetti, Mike and Iaboni, John. *Maple Leafs Top 100: Toronto's Greatest Players of All Time*. Raincoast Books, Vancouver, 2007.

Mahovlich, Ted. *The Big M: The Frank Mahovlich Story*. HarperCollins Canada, Toronto, 2000.

McDonald, Lanny and Simmons, Steve. *Lanny*. McGraw-Hill Ryerson, Toronto, 1987.

Obodiac, Stan. *The Leafs: The First Fifty Years*. McClelland and Stewart, Toronto, 1976.

———. *Red Kelly*. Clarke, Irwin and Co., Toronto, 1971.

Parent, Bernie. *Bernie! Bernie! Bernie!* Prentice Hall, Englewood Cliffs, 1975.

Salming, Borje and Karlsson, Gerhard. *Blood, Sweat and Hockey*. HarperCollins, Toronto, 1991.

Shea, Kevin. *Without a Trace: The Bill Barilko Story*. Fenn Publishing, Bolton Ontario, 2004.

Shea, Kevin and Patskou, Paul. *Diary of a Dynasty: Toronto Maple Leafs 1957-1967*. Firefly Books, Richmond Hill, 2010.

Sittler, Darryl and Goyens, Chrys. *Sittler*. MacMillan of Canada, Toronto, 1991.

Stellick, Gord. *Hockey, Heartaches and Hal*. Prentice Hall, Toronto, 1990.

Ulmer, Michael. *Captains: Nine Great Toronto Maple Leaf*. MacMillan of Canada, Toronto, 1995.

Williams, David and Lawton, James. *Tiger: A Hockey Story*. HarperCollins, Toronto, 1986.

NEWSPAPERS
The Globe and Mail
National Post
Montreal Gazette
The Toronto Star
The Toronto Sun

WEBSITES
cbcsports.ca
faceoff.com
globeandmail.com
hockey Hall of Fame.com
mapleleafs.com
NHL.com
the Hockey News
SI.com
SlamSports.ca
Wikipedia
website of each NHL team
youtube.com

MEDIA GUIDES
All Toronto Maple Leaf media guides issued since 1962

GAME PROGRAMS
Toronto Maple Leaf game programs from the 1960s to 2012–13

MAGAZINES
GOAL! Magazine
Hockey Scene
Hockey Digest (various issues)
Hockey Illustrated (various issues)
Hockey Night in Toronto (various issues)
Hockey Pictorial (various issues)

Hockey World (various issues)
Inside Hockey Magazine (various issues)
Inside Sports
The Hockey News (various issues)
Sports Illustrated (various issues)

GUIDES AND RECORD BOOKS
NHL Guide & Record Book (various issues)
Total Hockey (2nd edition)
Total NHL
Total Stanley Cup (Playoff Guide)

RADIO
AM640 (in Toronto)
FAN590 (in Toronto)
TSN 1050 (in Toronto)

TELEVISION
Hockey Night in Canada on CBC
That's Hockey on TSN
The NHL on TSN
Leafs TV

The publisher gratefully acknowledges the following:

PHOTOGRAPHS BY

Harold Barkley

John Maiola

Dennis Miles   .

Robert Shaver

Jim Wiley

York University Archives/Toronto Telegram Collection

Mike Leonetti (season tickets)

CARDS BY

O-PEE-CHEE/TOPPS

UPPER DECK

PARKHURST

PRO SET